Reasonable Accommodation in the Modern Workplace

Bulletin of Comparative Labour Relations

VOLUME 93

Editor

The series started in 1970 under the dynamic editorship of Professor Roger Blanpain (Belgium), former President of the International Industrial Relations Association. Professor Blanpain, currently Professor Emeritus of Labour Law, Universities of Leuven and Tilburg, is also General Editor of the International Encyclopedia of Laws (with more than 1,600 collaborators worldwide) and President of the Association of Educative and Scientific Authors.

In 2015 Frank Hendrickx, Professor of labour law at the Faculty of Law of the University of Leuven (Belgium) joined as a co-Editor. Frank Hendrickx has published numerous articles and books and regularly advises governments, international institutions and private organisations in the area of labour law as well as in sports law. He is the Editor-in-Chief of the European Labour Law Journal and General Editor of the International Encyclopaedia of Laws together with Professor Roger Blanpain.

Introduction

The Bulletins constitute a unique source of information and thought-provoking discussion, laying the groundwork for studies of employment relations in the 21st century, involving among much else the effects of globalization, new technologies, migration, and the greying of the population.

Contents/Subjects

Amongst other subjects the Bulletins frequently include the proceedings of international or regional conferences; reports from comparative projects devoted to salient issues in industrial relations, human resources management, and/or labour law; and specific issues underlying the multicultural aspects of our industrial societies.

Objective

The Bulletins offer a platform of expression and discussion on labour relations to scholars and practitioners worldwide, often featuring special guest editors.

The titles published in this series are listed at the end of this volume.

BULLETIN OF COMPARATIVE LABOUR RELATIONS – 93

Reasonable Accommodation in the Modern Workplace

Potential and Limits of the Integrative Logics of Labour Law

Editors

Roger Blanpain

Frank Hendrickx

Guest Editor

Frank Hendrickx

Contributors

Katayoun Alidadi

Kevin Banks

Karin Calitz

Anna Chapman

Guy Davidov

Nelly Diveeva

Frank Hendrickx

Mikhail Kharitonov

Guy Mundlak

Alan C. Neal

Fatima Nogajlieva

Sophie Robin-Olivier

Mia Rönnmar

Andrzej Marian Świątkowski

Steven L. Willborn

Wolters Kluwer

Published by:
Kluwer Law International B.V.
PO Box 316
2400 AH Alphen aan den Rijn
The Netherlands
Website: www.wklawbusiness.com

Sold and distributed in North, Central and South America by:
Wolters Kluwer Legal & Regulatory U.S.
7201 McKinney Circle
Frederick, MD 21704
United States of America
Email: customer.service@wolterskluwer.com

Sold and distributed in all other countries by:
Turpin Distribution Services Ltd
Stratton Business Park
Pegasus Drive, Biggleswade
Bedfordshire SG18 8TQ
United Kingdom
Email: kluwerlaw@turpin-distribution.com

ISBN 978-90-411-6258-8

Notes on Contributors

Katayoun Alidadi is a Research Fellow at the Max Planck Institute for Social Anthropology, Halle/Saale (Germany) and an Affiliate Scholar at Rice University in Houston (USA).

Kevin Banks is Associate Professor of Law and Director of the Centre for Law in the Contemporary Workplace at Queen's University (Canada).

Karin Calitz is Professor of Law at the University of Stellenbosch (South Africa).

Anna Chapman is Associate Professor in the Law School of the University of Melbourne (Australia). She is one of the Directors of the Centre for Employment and Labour Relations Law.

Guy Davidov is Professor of Law at the Faculty of Law of the Hebrew University of Jerusalem (Israel).

Nelly Diveeva is Professor in the Department of Labour Law and Occupational Safety at St. Petersburg State University (Russia).

Frank Hendrickx is Professor of Labour Law at the University of Leuven (Belgium). He holds a part-time Chair in European Labour Law at the ReflecT Institute of Tilburg University (The Netherlands).

Mikhail Kharitonov is Associate Professor of the Department of Labour Law and Occupational Safety at St. Petersburg State University (Russia).

Guy Mundlak is a full professor in the Faculty of Law and the Department of Labor Studies at Tel Aviv University (Israel).

Alan C. Neal is Professor of Law in the University of Warwick and an Employment Judge sitting in the London Central Region of the Employment Tribunals of England and Wales.

Fatima Nogajlieva is postgraduate student of the Department of Labour Law and Occupational Safety at St. Petersburg State University (Russia).

Sophie Robin-Olivier is Professor of Law at La Sorbonne School of Law, University of Paris I (France).

Mia Rönnmar is Dean of the Faculty of Law at Lund University and a Professor of Private Law, specializing in labour law and industrial relations. She is the President-Elect of the International Labour and Employment Relations Association (ILERA).

Andrzej Marian Świątkowski is Jean Monnet Professor of European labour law and social security, retired Professor of the Jagiellonian University, currently employed at the Jesuit University in Cracow (Poland).

Steven L. Willborn is Professor of Law at the College of Law of the University of Nebraska-Lincoln (USA).

Summary of Contents

Table of Contents

Introduction

Frank Hendrickx

I GENERAL BACKGROUND

This volume provides the papers of a project coordinated by the Institute for Labour Law of the University of Leuven with support of the Fund for Scientific Research Flanders in Belgium. The University of Leuven hosted the 2015 meeting of the International Association of Labour Law Journals (IALLJ), which went together with a scientific seminar with invited papers focusing on the topic of the present work: 'Reasonable accommodation in the modern workplace: potential and limits of the integrative logics of labour law'.

The above-mentioned research project examines the issue of work incapacity and disabled workers and the need to give it an approach against the broader background of (re-) integration. It is, in light of this, considered relevant to examine whether our labour law is sufficiently 'integration minded'. Integration is potentially a richer concept than, for example, employability, as it seems to also call on efforts from the labour market, and from employers, for the benefit of workers' individual interests, instead of asking workers to take care of themselves, or reinforce themselves in a context of change and, perhaps, precariousness on the labour market. It may imply an accommodating approach from an integrative and inclusive workplace perspective. This is not only relevant for an issue like disability, but potentially goes far beyond this. The 'integrative function' of labour law has been proposed by the late Bob Hepple[1] and we have defended it after him.[2]

The focus on the role of employment discrimination law, at least as a starting point, seemed highly relevant. Employment discrimination law received new impetus in the European Union (EU) since the adoption of new legislative instruments. In light of extended competences at the EU Treaty level, the EU adopted Council Directive

1. Cf. B. Hepple, 'The Future of Labour Law', *Ind. L.J.* 1995, 322.
2. F. Hendrickx, 'Foundations and Functions of Contemporary Labour Law', *ELLJ* 2012, afl. 2, 108-129.

2000/78 EC establishing a general framework for equal treatment in employment and occupation.[3] The Directive widely influenced national anti-discrimination laws in European States. Inspired by the experience of North American legal systems, it launched a system of rules for a new generation of discriminatory criteria, such as age, disability and religion or belief.

This body of rules and principles is now developing in a time in which diversity and employability constitute growing challenges for the modern workplace. The need to match workforce diversity, or the workers' own characteristics and choices, with the employers' organizational or business needs becomes increasingly challenging. In this horizon of anti-discrimination provisions and the 'integrative function' of labour law, the notion of reasonable accommodation arises. Accommodation can be seen as referring to adapting the workplace to make it more accessible and inclusive for workers. It can be imagined that the concept of reasonable accommodation in anti-discrimination law is an emanation of a broader accommodation duty in labour law and ultimately a legal translation of a more abstract integration concept.

The central question of the 2015 IALLJ scientific seminar, referred to above, was to find out whether the idea of reasonable accommodation, under the influence of employment (anti-) discrimination law, is winning ground in labour law and whether it can be seen to be influencing labour law in a broader way in light of an integrative logics of labour law. Although the perspective of legal development in the EU has been taken as a starting point, the analysis is made with perspectives from major jurisdictions and labour law systems around the world, including Australia, Canada, Israel, Russia, South Africa and the United States.

In discussing the potential and limits of the legal concept of reasonable accommodation, the project aims to examine how employment discrimination law gives shape to an accommodated workplace in three main areas of interest: age, disability and religion or belief. Different sub-questions were raised such as: What does reasonable accommodation exactly mean in these contexts? How is it related to formal or substantial equality claims or other notions such as (in-)direct discrimination in employment discrimination law? What is the scope of 'accommodation'? How is 'reasonable' defined? Which recognized business requirements may override the duty to accommodate the workplace? Alternative concepts may be regarded depending on the national legal system from which the analysis is made. The legal analysis used legislation, case law and legal doctrine as main sources.

II OVERVIEW OF THE ANALYSIS

The different individual contributions provide an extensive analysis taking into account various perspectives, though all circling around the same problem setting and questions set. Hereafter, an attempt is made to point at findings that are seen to be relevant or essential in order to provide a broader understanding and picture of the

3. *OJ* 2 December 2000, no. L 303.

place and position of reasonable accommodation in employment discrimination law as well as in the broader labour law context.

As is shown in the contribution of *Steve Wilborn*, the concept of reasonable accommodation as a framework for discrimination law, was initially developed in the United States in the areas of religious and disability discrimination. While the U.S. could be seen as a leading example, certainly for Europe, the U.S. system has been rather reluctant in applying the reasonable accommodation model further beyond these areas, although there are examples. It is, for example, not applied to age discrimination. In areas in which reasonable accommodation can work, the U.S. case shows that the standard for it can still be vague. The duty to make reasonable accommodation seems stronger and more effective for disability as compared to religion.

Kevin Banks shows us in his contribution that in Canada reasonable accommodation stands central in anti-discrimination law. The duty to accommodate arose out of the efforts of Canadian courts, tribunals as well as legislatures. The Canadian example sheds some light on how reasonable accommodation is viewed. For example, it is accepted that the extent of the required accommodation will depend upon the wealth and the size of employer. Furthermore, reasonable accommodation does not require pay without productive work. Disability is reported to be the most frequently used ground of accommodation in the case law and the concept of disability seems to be quite broad, including injury, illness and some temporary conditions. The idea of 'accommodation' is found in measures on leave for family reasons, workers' compensation and in accessibility statutes. As Banks points out, the Canadian experience 'demonstrates the possibility and the implications of implementing reasonable accommodation of a wide range of intrinsic personal characteristics and choices fundamental to human dignity through employer obligation and duties.'

A thorough insight in the system of Australia is offered by *Anna Chapman*. She shows that a number of legal mechanisms have developed through which a worker can seek to have adjustments made to individual work arrangements. The most firmly established right to reasonable accommodation relates to the attribute of disability, but modifications might also include, for example, modifications in working time in light of family responsibilities. Nevertheless, the only anti-discrimination statute at the Commonwealth level that contains an explicit obligation of reasonable accommodation is the 1992 Disability Discrimination Act. Reasonable adjustments are defined in the act, but it ultimately requires a balancing process, weighing up various matters. Chapman shows that State and Territory anti-discrimination legislative initiatives have largely mirrored the Commonwealth Act. Beyond the anti-discrimination provisions, the more recent Fair Work Act (2009) is reported as an area in which employee requests for accommodation are facilited for reasons of care responsibilities. However, it is pointed out that this Act provides a procedural framework for the process of requesting an adjustment or change. It does not seem to envisage a process of balancing the employee's interest in being accommodated against the interests of the employer.

In my own paper (*Frank Hendrickx*), I discuss disability and reintegration in work, focusing on the interplay between EU non-discrimination law and labour law. Importance is attached to the case law of the Court of Justice of the European Union

(CJEU). In *Chacon Navas* this Court used a medical model of disability discrimination law. In order to determine the concept of disability, the Court focused on the impairment(s) of a person concerned. However, in *HK Danmark* the CJEU left this approach in favour of a social model. It added that 'the concept of "disability" must be understood as referring to a limitation which results in particular from physical, mental or psychological impairments which in interaction with various barriers may hinder the full and effective participation of the person concerned in professional life on an equal basis with other workers.' It is remarkable that the CJEU is strongly influenced by the United Nations Convention on the Rights of Persons with Disabilities (UN CRPD), adopted on 13 December 2006. The UN CRPD has a broad and integrated approach of disability, encompassing various areas and sectors of individual and societal life, including the aim to cover all persons with a disability. The step from the medical model to the social model of disability is argued to be an inevitable one. The social model is more proper to a labour law understanding of integration. It also seems more appropriate in terms of a labour market policy model searching for strategies of employability and inclusion.

Alan Neal critically discusses the Europe-wide framework of regulation concerning disability discrimination. He refers to his proposition that normative compliance was being placed above functional integrative outcomes for disabled persons seeking to participate in the labour market. He drew this from the suggestion that Anglo-American Common Law experience had given rise to a 'promotional' model regarding disabled persons at work while the EU approach would bring an essentially 'penal' regime for this issue. That may, indeed, lead to wrong 'mind-set' and limit the impact of regulatory initiatives. He is also critical for what he names the 'one size fits all' nature of the equal treatment principle in EU legislation. The concept of reasonable accommodation in the European Directive is seen to provide a variety of 'exit gateways' to enable employers to avoid liability in cases of disability discrimination. Building further on Neal's suggestion it appears that the concept of reasonable accommodation in case of disability loses its potential when it remains (too much) locked in the model of equal treatment.

The model of Sweden is presented in the analysis of *Mia Rönnmar*. The Swedish system knows the concept for reasonable accommodation for disability discrimination law. It involves an assessment on a case by case basis. It is apparent that the assessment of reasonableness allows for reference to various factors including the employer's economic situation and the form and duration of the employment relationship. The case law on the subject, however, remains rather limited. Interestingly, Rönnmar refers to a complaint made under the UN CRPD in relation to a judgment from the Swedish Labour Court. The UN Committee did not find a violation of the UN Convention. Nevertheless, Rönnmar sees the case as a sign of the increased attention paid to international law and human rights law instruments in Sweden. That may be promising in light of the UN Convention. Furthermore, it is worth noting that Sweden introduced a new legal provision in order to ban inadequate accessibility for people with disabilities. The new ban has a wider scope than the previous requirement for reasonable accommodation and applies to working life and beyond. The aim of the ban is to increase accessibility for people with disabilities in order to achieve equality and increase participation. It remains to be seen whether this is an effective strategy.

Andrzej Świątkowski focuses on Poland. He refers to recent initiatives to bring national legislation in line with the EU anti-discrimination instrument. For this reason, Polish legislation was amended in 2010, in particular with regard to disabilities. The mentioned act has been effective from 1 January 2011. A new concept of reasonable accommodation to persons with disabilities was adopted in Poland following the principles that there is a positive obligation of each employer to adapt the workplace to the requirements and needs of 'non-typical' employees or candidate employees. At the same time, a justification (exception) is introduced and the criterion of reasonableness for employer refusal is applied. However, in Polish labour law no examples were reported which would illustrate the types and scope of adaptation of workplaces to the needs and requirements of persons with disabilities. Świątkowski opens the issue by referring to financial incentives for employers employing disabled employees and measures supporting disabled workers seeking (new) employment. It is clear that Poland applies a broader framework than merely a non-discrimination concept, but nevertheless has adapted its system to the EU legal framework of equal treatment.

With the contribution of *Katayoun Alidadi* the issue of reasonable accommodation for religion or belief is being dealt with. Alidadi treats this subject as well as company 'neutrality policies' in a theoretical and European context, with particular attention to Belgium. She argues that despite the steady rise of EU non-discrimination law, its effectiveness in addressing religious or philosophical disadvantage, remains limited. Aspects of reasonable accommodation may concern dress codes, time demands, religious and workplace demands, job duties and conscientious objections, and workplace socializing expectations or demands. According to Alidadi, 'the judicial legitimating of private sector neutrality policies (clauses banning religious, philosophical (and often also political) is legally flawed and must be reversed, sending the right -integrative- message out.'

Sophie Robin-Olivier discusses reasonable accommodation for religion and other motives in French labour law. It is interesting to note that, in France, the notion of 'reasonable accommodation' does not provide the concept to solve conflicts concerning religion in the workplace. Reasonable accommodation remains reserved for the field of disability law. In this context, in recent case law, no duty to accommodate was imposed on employers with regard to wearing the Islamic headscarf. This would rather be discussed under the French notion of '*laïcité*'. Robin-Olivier demonstrates that 'negative accommodation' rather than 'positive accommodation' seems to prevail. Nevertheless, she argues that under French rules implementing EU anti-discrimination law, accommodation is already a requirement, even if the concept is not used. She refers to the case law of the CJEU in which employers are not allowed to invoke a business related justification for differentiation if clients demand not to be provided services by a woman wearing an Islamic headscarf.

Beyond this, the idea of accommodation is found present in other sections of French labour law and, perhaps, in a stronger way than under discrimination provisions. For example, case law has made it clear that employers have to take into account workers' family lives when applying mobility clauses or when organizing working time. Robin-Olivier also refers to the concept of 'good faith' under which employers have an obligation to adapt workers to the evolution of the company or the job in which they are employed, which may imply reassigning the worker to new positions and provide training. The case law has been incorporated in a statutory solution and 'reclassification' was confirmed by the French Constitutional court as a constitutional right stemming directly from the 'right to work' protected by the French Constitution. The concept of reclassification comes back in disability law, which obliges employers to look for another position for an employee who is ill or disabled. Robin-Olivier shows the difference with reasonable accommodation. Whereas 'reasonable accommodation' includes a margin of appreciation, this is not the case with regard to the obligation to reclassify a worker: tasks must be adapted or other available positions must be offered and only when this is deemed 'impossible', the employer may dismiss the worker.

The contribution of *Karin Calitz* brings us to the legal system of South Africa and in particular to the concept of reasonable accommodation developed by the Constitutional Court in the context of a diverse society. It focuses on accommodation for religion and culture. In this context, Calitz points at the same problem raised by Alidadi and Robin-Olivier with regard to 'neutrality' policies. Where a workplace may adopt a neutrality policy to avoid accusations of discrimination, the question remains what is neutral and who decides what constitutes neutrality. It seems that a prima facie neutral practice may constitute indirect discrimination if there is a disproportionate impact on the worker.

The South African Constitution provides that neither the State nor any other person may unfairly discriminate directly or indirectly against anyone on one or more prohibited grounds. Sixteen grounds are listed, including religion and culture. Furthermore, the Labour Relations Act (LRA) protects employees from dismissal based on discrimination. The Employment Equity Act (EEA) was enacted to give effect to the equality clause of the Constitution in the workplace, excluding discriminatory dismissals (which are dealt with in the LRA). Case law in South Africa on reasonable accommodation of religion and culture in the workplace concern issues of dress code and time off for religious or cultural purposes. It is interesting to note that religion and culture are equally protected. It is worth noting that the concept of '*ubuntu*' is often used in South African jurisprudence. It means that people are people through other people. This may influence a way of (legal) thinking, supported by the purpose of accommodating different cultures in society.

Nelly Diveeva, *Mikhail Kharitonov* and *Fatima Nogajlieva* give us an insight into the Russian legal system. They focus on reasonable accommodation in the workplace in different areas. Accommodation in the field of religion and belief is very interesting, as it is reported that there are more than 23,000 religious organizations of 60 different kinds in Russia. The authors show that current Russian legislation does not provide for obligations of the employer to adapt workplaces to the religious needs of employees. However, some employers make adaptations in the work organization, for example during Ramadan.

Finally, *Guy Davidov* and *Guy Mundlak* consider the expansion of the duty to accommodate in labour law, drawing on Israeli law and developments, and they bring it a step further to the challenging question, which is ultimately a concern for our research project: what about a general duty to accommodate in labour law? They propose that, to justify 'a truly universal duty to accommodate' (on the labour market), it has to be pulled away from the context of employment discrimination. As they suggest, it requires a discussion on the basic structures underlying the employment contract, as a duty to accommodate challenges the central idea of managerial prerogative. As they interestingly propose, 'the duty to accommodate mirrors the managerial prerogative'. In order to make the idea work, the authors refer to the importance of criteria and legal concepts to strike the balance between rights and interests, such as the principle of proportionality, or the principle of good faith.

III CONCLUSIONS

The question is what general conclusions can be drawn from the analysis and the different perspectives. As a starting point, it seems clear that anti-discrimination law has had a huge impact on labour law, increasingly also in European jurisdictions. In most, if not all, jurisdictions, anti-discrimination provisions have served as a catalyst for employment rights. Furthermore, the notion of reasonable accommodation offers a lot of potential.

The full realization of rights under the approach of reasonable accommodation is, however, still a matter for debate. Some legal systems remain rather reluctant to apply it in full, and in areas in which reasonable accommodation can work, the standard for it can still be vague. In its application, a balance between employers' and employee's interests will be struck. Business related reasons will play a role, allowing for the employer to make justification for not providing accommodation to the worker. Financial cost, wealth or size of the employer may play a role.

It could be that the concept of reasonable accommodation is so much interlocked with the anti-discrimination provisions that it limits its promotional potential. For this reason, the development of the case law of the CJEU is interesting, as in disability discrimination cases, reference is made to the UN CRPD. In this UN instrument, a strong social and integrative model is applied and substantial outcomes prevail. This approach may stand model for other specifically protected areas, such as religion, belief or age. Also in these areas, contributors have indicated the importance of an integrative and human rights oriented approach. From the analysis made in this volume, it would seem that reasonable accommodation should work in different areas, like religion and belief or age. Also for those aspects, it is clear that the approach for these issues cannot be narrowed down to a formal anti-discrimination perspective, but should have a more substantial outcome orientation. This is why the neutrality policy-issue may be such a difficult question. Likewise, specific measures to adapt the workplace and working conditions to age may strictly appear to be discriminatory, but could also be seen as reasonable accommodation measures. What could be said is that disability law takes the lead in the accommodation approach, which makes the legal progress in this field all the more important.

When moving beyond the analysis of employment discrimination law, the concept of reasonable accommodation does not really appear in these terms. But in other areas of labour law, there are different traces for an accommodation or integration approach. It is, however, clear that this area still requires a lot of development. It takes us to the question how strongly an accommodating and integrative logic can grow in a broader labour law context. Taking into account the various contributions, including Davidov and Mundlak's reflections, there is good ground to conclude that labour law is quite receptive for it, but at the same time it may have an influence on the basic idea, the 'deal', or perhaps the paradigm, underlying the employment relationship and on the labour market. Instead of expecting workers to adapt themselves in function of (business) requirements related to the work organization or the labour market, workplaces and markets may have to offer steps or stepping stones too and make adaptations or investments accordingly in order to accommodate particular or personal needs of workers.

CHAPTER 1

Reasonable Accommodation in the United States

Steven L. Willborn

§1.01 A SHORT HISTORY OF REASONABLE ACCOMMODATION IN THE UNITED STATES

The concept of reasonable accommodation as a framework for thinking about discrimination was initially developed in the United States to apply to religious and disability discrimination.[1] The process of development in the two areas occurred over different time periods, but was notably similar. The first step was a broad, legislative statement announcing a principle of non-discrimination based on religion or disability. Then an administrative agency considered the meaning of non-discrimination for religion and disability respectively and determined that, in those contexts, non-discrimination meant accommodation. Finally, the administrative interpretations were incorporated into statute.

---

1. Before the modern civil rights movement, the phrase "reasonable accommodation" was largely absent from American law. In a Westlaw search of all federal cases from 1790 to 1964, only fifty-three cases used the phrase. Most of those cases used it in the context of accommodation for people traveling on public transportation. *See, e.g., Texas & Pac. Ry. Co. v. Stewart*, 228 U.S. 357 (1913). Only one of the cases came close to using the phrase in its modern sense, but even there it appeared only in dissent. In *Minersville School Dist. v. Gobitis*, 310 U.S. 586 (1940), the majority held that children could be excluded from public school for refusing to salute the flag for religious reasons. In dissent, Justice Stone argued that the school should be required to reasonably accommodate religious objections to saluting the flag. *Ibid.* at 603. The case was later overturned to align more closely with Justice Stone's opinion (with Justice Stone joining the majority opinion), but that case did not use the reasonable-accommodation language. *West Virginia State Board of Education v. Barnette*, 319 U.S. 624 (1943). Because of its use in the modern civil rights movement, the phrase is now ubiquitous. Using the same Westlaw database of all federal cases, the term was used in 1,478 cases in 2014 alone.

[A] Reasonable Accommodation of Religion

The concept of reasonable accommodation in the United States was first developed to apply to religious discrimination. When initially enacted, Title VII of the Civil Rights Act of 1964 had a flat prohibition on discrimination on the basis of religion; religion was simply included in the list of prohibited considerations, along with race, color, sex, and national origin.[2] Soon after the Act's effective date in 1965, the question arose whether it would be impermissible religious discrimination for an employer to discharge or refuse to hire a person who refused for religious reasons to work during the employer's normal work week.[3] In 1966, the Equal Employment Opportunity Commission (EEOC), the federal enforcement agency, issued a guideline saying that, for religion, the non-discrimination language of Title VII meant that employers were required "to accommodate to the reasonable religious needs of employees ... where such accommodation can be made without serious inconvenience to the conduct of the business."[4] The next year, the EEOC revised the language of its guideline to state the accommodation requirement in almost its modern form: employers must "make reasonable accommodations to the religious needs of employees and prospective employees where such accommodations can be made without undue hardship on the conduct of the employer's business."[5]

In 1971, the United States Supreme Court considered *Dewey v. Reynolds Metals Co.*,[6] a case in which a lower court had relied on the EEOC's guidelines to hold that it was permissible for an employer to discharge an employee for refusing to work on Sundays for religious reasons when the employer had provided the employee with the option of finding his own replacement. Uncertainties about how to apply the EEOC's reasonable-accommodation standard were very apparent when the Supreme Court was equally divided (with one Justice recusing himself). Consequently, the Court affirmed the lower court decision without issuing an opinion.

Reasonable accommodation first entered American statutory law in 1972 when Congress tried to provide clarity after *Dewey*[7] by amending Title VII of the Civil Rights Act of 1964 to add a definition of "religion:"

> The term "religion" includes all aspects of religious observance and practice, as well as belief, unless an employer demonstrates that he is unable to reasonably accommodate to an employee's or prospective employee's religious observance or practice without undue hardship on the conduct of the employer's business.[8]

2. Civil Rights Act of 1964, § 703(a)(1), Pub. L. No. 88-352, 78 Stat. 241 (1964).
3. This history is recited in the seminal Supreme Court case on religious discrimination under Title VII, *Trans World Airlines, Inc. v. Hardison*, 432 U.S. 63 (1977).
4. 29 C.F.R. § 1605.1 (1967).
5. 29 C.F.R. § 1605.1 (1968).
6. 402 U.S. 689 (1971), *affirming*, 429 F.2d 324 (6th Cir. 1970).
7. "This amendment is intended ... to resolve by legislation ... that which the courts apparently have not resolved. I think it is needed ... because court decisions have clouded the matter with some uncertainty." 118 Cong. Rec. 705-706 (1972) (remarks of Sen. Randolph) (Sen. Randolph concluded his remarks by placing the Court of Appeals decision in *Dewey* into the Congressional Record).
8. Equal Employment Opportunity Act of 1972, § 2(7), Pub. L. No. 92-261, 86 Stat. 103 (1972).

While the amendment explicitly incorporated the concept of reasonable accommodation into the statute, it did little to provide additional guidance. That had to await future judicial interpretations, which I describe in section §1.03 below.

[B] Reasonable Accommodation of Disability

The development of reasonable accommodation for individuals with disabilities followed a very similar path to its development for religion. The history begins with enactment of the Rehabilitation Act of 1973[9] which prohibited discrimination on the basis of "handicap"[10] (as the phraseology was then):

> No otherwise qualified handicapped individual ... shall, solely by reason of his handicap, ... be subjected to discrimination under any program or activity receiving Federal financial assistance.[11]

While the Rehabilitation Act included this expansive language to prohibit discrimination, the Act's application was fairly narrow. It applied only to the federal government, federal contractors, and recipients of federal financial assistance.[12]

In 1977, after some delay, the Department of Health, Education and Welfare (later renamed the Department of Health and Human Services), the main federal enforcement agency for the Rehabilitation Act, issued regulations to provide guidance about what non-discrimination in this context meant and, as with religious discrimination, the conclusion was that non-discrimination meant primarily a duty to accommodate:

> [Under the Rehabilitation Act, covered entities must] make reasonable accommodation to the known physical or mental limitations of an otherwise qualified handicapped applicant or employee unless the [entity] can demonstrate that the accommodation would impose an undue hardship on the operation of its program or activity.[13]

Years later, this conception of non-discrimination for individuals with a disability was incorporated into the Americans with Disabilities Act (ADA), which had much

9. Pub. L. No. 93-112, 87 Stat. 355 (1972), *codified at*, 29 U.S.C. §§ 701 et seq.
10. The definition of "handicapped individual" in the Rehabilitation Act of 1973 was a precursor of the current definition: "The term 'handicapped individual' means any individual who ... has a physical or mental disability which for such individual constitutes or results in a substantial handicap to employment." *Ibid.* at § 7(6), 86 Stat. at 361. But the Congress passed an amendment in the very next year to amend the definition to a form that later became the model for the Americans with Disabilities Act: handicapped individual means "any person who (A) has a physical or mental impairment which substantially limits one or more of such person's major life activities, (B) has a record of such an impairment, or (C) is regarded as having such an impairment." Amendments to the Rehabilitation Act of 1973, Pub. L. No. 93-516, § 111(a), 88 Stat. 1617, 1619 (1974).
11. *Ibid.* at § 504, 86 Stat. at 394, *codified at*, 29 U.S.C. § 794.
12. *Ibid.* at §§ 501, 503, 504, 86 Stat. at 390-394, *codified at*, 29 U.S.C. §§ 791, 793, 794.
13. 42 Fed. Reg. 22,676, 22,680 (May 4, 1977), *codified at*, 45 C.F.R. § 84.12(a).

broader applicability.[14] The statutory language was very similar to the administrative regulation under the Rehabilitation Act:

> [T]he term "discriminate" includes ... not making reasonable accommodations to the known physical or mental limitations of an otherwise qualified individual with a disability who is an applicant or employee, unless such covered entity can demonstrate that the accommodation would impose an undue hardship on the operation of the business... .[15]

As a result, development of the concept of reasonable accommodation for disability in the United States closely mirrored development of the concept for religion. The process began with a broad statement that discrimination on that basis was illegal, which was interpreted by an administrative agency to impose an accommodation requirement, which was later incorporated into statutory language.

§1.02 DEFINITION AND SCOPE OF REASONABLE ACCOMMODATION

[A] The General Structure of a Reasonable Accommodation Claim

Reasonable accommodation claims have a common general structure in the United States.

The first step is that the claimant has to demonstrate that she is eligible to be considered for an accommodation. For religion, this means that the employer's decision must have been based on "religion;" for disability, it means that the person must be an "individual with a disability." I will discuss both of these later in sections §1.03 and §1.04.

The second step is that the claimant must demonstrate that she is "qualified," that is, that she can perform the essential functions of the job with accommodation.[16] This has not been a major issue in religious discrimination, but it has been under the ADA. For reasons I will discuss later in section §1.04, this factor has become more important since 2008.

The third step of the analysis is to determine whether the accommodations requested are "reasonable." The meaning of reasonable differs substantially for religious and disability discrimination, as I will discuss later.

Finally, an employer may still prevail if it can demonstrate that the requested accommodation would impose an undue hardship on the employer.[17]

---

14. The employment sections of the ADA apply, with some exceptions, to all employers with fifteen or more employees. 42 U.S.C. § 12111(5)(A).
15. 42 U.S.C. § 12112(b)(5)(A). The non-discrimination language of the Rehabilitation Act itself, however, remains substantively unchanged, as does the regulation implementing it.
16. It is important to note here that there is an interaction between this element and the reasonable-accommodation requirement. A claimant must be able to perform the job *with accommodation*. As a result, the analysis of this element is closely connected with the determination of what kind of accommodation is required.
17. The relationship between reasonable accommodation and undue hardship has been problematic: If an accommodation is "reasonable," can it ever impose an "undue hardship"? The Supreme Court has addressed the issue generally. To demonstrate that an accommodation is

For both religion and disability, the claimant has the burden of proof on the first three steps above, while the employer has the burden of proof on the "undue hardship" element. The accommodation duty also includes a procedural requirement. The claimant and employer must engage in an "interactive process" to explore possible accommodations. Either side can violate this procedural requirement by failing to cooperate sufficiently, although the obligation is eased for individuals with mental disabilities that interfere with the ability to cooperate.

[B] Reasonable Accommodation and Antidiscrimination

There has been debate in the United States about the relationship between reasonable accommodation and antidiscrimination law more generally. The debate is about whether reasonable accommodation is new and different, or whether it is on the same general continuum as the other discrimination models (what we call disparate treatment and disparate impact). My own view is that resolution of the issue depends on the level of generality with which one views the issue. Viewed close-up, the reasonable accommodation model looks quite distinct. Viewed with a wider lens, however, the model approximates the other models, especially disparate impact.[18]

[1] Reasonable Accommodation as a New and Different Prohibition on Discrimination

The application of reasonable accommodation in particular cases makes it look like a new and different type of prohibition on discrimination.

Consider a disparate-treatment claim first.[19] An employer entertains job applications and rejects two applicants, the first because she is a woman, the second because she is an individual with a disability. Do the rejected applicants have good disparate-treatment claims?

The woman has a good claim. This is explicit, intentional discrimination because of sex. The only defense under Title VII would be that sex was a Bona Fide Occupational Qualification (BFOQ)[20] and that defense is narrowly construed to prevent it from swamping Title VII's general command to ignore the gender of workers in

reasonable, the employee need only show that it "seems reasonable on its face, i.e., ordinarily or in the run of cases." *US Airways, Inc. v. Barnett*, 535 U.S. 391, 401 (2002). On the other hand, to prove that a proposed accommodation imposes an undue hardship, the employer "must show special (typically case-specific) circumstances that demonstrate undue hardship in the particular circumstances." *Ibid.* at 402. In practice, the two tend to be discussed without much attention to their relationship. *See, e.g., Trans World Airlines, Inc. v. Hardison*, 432 U.S. 63 (1977) (discussing reasonable accommodation and undue hardship without explaining their relationship).

18. As a participant in these debates, my opinion on this should be considered skeptically.
19. These examples are from Steven L. Willborn et al., *Employment Law: Cases and Materials*, 545-546 (5th ed. 2012).
20. Title VII § 703(e), 42 U.S.C. § 2000e-2(e) (relying on a religion, sex or national origin is not illegal if the criterion "is a bona fide occupational qualification reasonably necessary to the normal operation of that particular business...)".

making employment decisions.[21] Importantly, cost considerations are not a part of the BFOQ defense.

The individual with a disability may also have a good claim, but it is much more fragile than the woman's. The ADA prohibits employers from considering disability in an invidious or stereotypical way. But the ADA contemplates that employers will often consider disability in a legitimate way. Indeed, the procedural aspect of the accommodation duty (the "interactive process") *requires* employers to consider disability. The employer can avoid ADA liability for its reliance on disability if the worker cannot perform the essential requirements of the job, if an unreasonable accommodation would be required, or if the accommodation would impose an undue hardship on the employer. These inquiries are different in kind from the BFOQ inquiry. Most importantly, cost considerations are the heart of the matter under the ADA, while they are banned under Title VII. Mere consideration of gender exposes an employer to considerable risk of a Title VII disparate-treatment violation. Consideration of disability, on the other hand, merely opens the door to ADA analysis; essential-job-duty analysis, reasonable accommodation, and undue hardship often provide defenses to liability.

Next consider a standard-fare disparate-impact claim. Suppose a job requires frequent lifting of 80-pound sacks. The employer screens out job applicants by asking them to lift an 80-pound sack. Two applicants are rejected because they could not lift the sack: a woman and a person in a wheelchair. How do their claims fare?

The woman has only a weak claim because, even though the requirement may have a disparate impact on women, the employer is likely to be able to defend successfully by demonstrating that the test is job related and consistent with business necessity.[22] The woman cannot argue that the 80-pound sacks should be split into 40-pound sacks to make it easier for women to hold the jobs. Title VII's standard disparate-impact analysis examines the test, not the job. By contrast, the rejected applicant with a disability can challenge the job itself. The reasonable accommodation model requires the employer to consider dividing the 80-pound sacks as a method of accommodation. If the employer could do that without much trouble, then the employer must do so.

These up-close comparisons of reasonable accommodation with disparate treatment and disparate impact make accommodation look like a new and distinct model of discrimination. Instead of prohibiting consideration of a suspect criterion, accommodation requires consideration of disability. Instead of severely narrowing the justifications for reliance on the suspect criterion, accommodation permits a wide-ranging inquiry. Instead of a general acceptance of the job duties assigned by an employer, accommodation requires the employer to adjust duties to match employee capabilities.

These comparisons between reasonable accommodation, on the one hand, and the disparate treatment and impact models, on the other hand, have lead some

21. The leading case on the bona fide occupational qualification defense is *Western Air Lines, Inc. v. Criswell*, 472 U.S. 400 (1985).

22. A disparate impact is not improper if the employer can "demonstrate that the challenged practice is job related for the position in question and consistent with business necessity." Title VII § 793(k)(1)(A)(i), 42 U.S.C. § 2000-e(k)(1)(A)(i).

commentators to argue that the ADA is a distinct model of discrimination which, even though it may be justified, places heavier burdens on employers than do prior antidiscrimination statutes, such as Title VII.[23]

[2] Reasonable Accommodation as One Manifestation of the General Non-discrimination Mandate

The claim that accommodation is a new and different kind of non-discrimination mandate is basically that "standard" discrimination law requires only "equal" treatment, while accommodation requires "special" treatment. The response to this claim begins by asking just what it means to say that a non-discrimination obligation requires "special" treatment and then to examine "standard" discrimination law to see if it also requires such treatment.

"Special treatment" can be defined as follows:

> [A] legal rule that requires employers to incur special costs in response to the distinctive needs ... of particular, identifiable demographic groups of employees, such as individuals with ... disabilities, and imposes this requirement in circumstances where the employer has no intention of treating the group in question differently on the basis of group membership.[24]

Those who claim that accommodation is merely one manifestation of the general non-discrimination mandate admit that "special treatment" describes the standard application of the accommodation model to categories such as disability and religion. But they claim that it also describes several features of "standard" discrimination law. First, it describes many normal applications of disparate impact. Disparate impact may require employers to change practices that serve their business interests (and, thus, it imposes special costs on employers), even though employers may have no intention of discriminating on the basis of group membership. For example, it may require employers to change certain grooming standards[25] or abandon certain job requirements[26] to attend to the distinctive needs of particular, identifiable groups. Second,

23. *See* Stewart J. Schwab & Steven L. Willborn, *Reasonable Accommodation of Workplace Disabilities*, 44 Wm. & Mary L. Rev. 1197 (2003) (ADA imposes hard preferences on employers requiring direct expenditures to comply, while Title VII only imposes soft, nondiscrimination preferences); Samuel Issacharoff & Justin Nelson, *Discrimination With a Difference: Can Employment Discrimination Law Accommodate the Americans With Disabilities Act?*, 79 N.C. L. Rev. 307 (2001) (Title VII is primarily focused on nondiscrimination with redistribution as a byproduct; the ADA, in contrast, is primarily redistributive and is not constrained by the nondiscrimination obligation); Pamela S. Karlan & George Rutherglen, *Disabilities, Discrimination, and Reasonable Accommodation*, 46 Duke L.J. 1, 41 (1996) (differences between reasonable accommodation under the ADA and "preexisting doctrines of employment discrimination ... are profound.")
24. Christine Jolls, *Antidiscrimination and Accommodation*, 115 Harv. L. Rev. 642, 648 (2001).
25. For example, in *Bradley v. Pizzaco of Nebraska, Inc.*, 7 F.3d 795 (8th Cir. 1993), the 8th Circuit held that a pizza franchise could not maintain a no-beard rule for its employees even though its customers preferred waiters with no beards. The no-beard rule had a disparate impact on African-Americans who disproportionately have skin conditions that interfere with shaving.
26. For example, in *Lanning v. Southeastern Pennsylvania Transp. Auth.*, 181 F.3d 478 (3rd Cir. 1999), the Court held that an employer could not maintain a physical test for police officers even

when the "normal" discrimination rules are applied to prohibit employers from attending to customer or co-worker discrimination, they again impose costs on employers even though the employer itself may not exhibit any discriminatory intent.[27] Third, when the "normal" discrimination rules require or permit affirmative action, they satisfy this definition of special treatment and so are similar to accommodation requirements.[28]

Thus, viewed more abstractly in this way, reasonable accommodation is merely one manifestation of the general non-discrimination mandate.

§1.03 REASONABLE ACCOMMODATION FOR RELIGION OR BELIEF

Reasonable accommodation for religion or belief is only necessary, by definition, if the plaintiff can demonstrate a religious belief. On this element, the courts interpret the law very generously in favor of coverage. At the Supreme Court level, this generosity takes its cue from cases addressing the issue of conscientious objection from military service. In *United States v. Seeger*, the Supreme Court defined religious belief as a "sincere and meaningful belief which occupies in the life of its possessor a place parallel to that filled by the God of those admittedly qualifying for [conscientious objection]."[29] Later, the Court said the term would include moral and ethical beliefs, excluding only beliefs that "rest[] solely upon considerations of policy, pragmatism, or expediency...." .[30]

The EEOC and the courts have applied these generous interpretations to claims of religious discrimination in employment. The EEOC's Guidelines on Discrimination Because of Religion refer to the two Supreme Court cases cited above, but re-emphasize the liberal interpretation by adding that the "fact that no religious group espouses [the employee's] beliefs or the fact that the religious group to which the individual professes to belong may not accept such belief will not determine whether the belief is a religious belief of the employee...."[31] Following this lead, the courts have found religious beliefs even in fairly questionable circumstances such as the Church of Body Modification, which celebrates body piercings,[32] and the World Church of the Creator, which favors

---

though it presented evidence of a statistically significant relationship between physical condition and job performance. The test had a disparate impact on women who were disproportionately unable to satisfy the test.

27. For example, in *Fernandez v. Wynn Oil Co.*, 653 F.2d 1273 (9th Cir. 1981), the Court held that an employer could not refuse to hire a woman as a company executive because South American clients preferred not to deal with women in such positions.
28. These arguments are fully developed in Christine Jolls' article, *supra* note 24. *See also* Noah D. Zatz, *Special Treatment Everywhere, Special Treatment Nowhere*, 95 B.U. L. Rev. 1155 (2015).
29. 380 U.S. 163, 176 (1965).
30. *Welsh v. United States*, 398 U.S. 333, 342-343 (1970).
31. 29 C.F.R. § 1605.1. The inquiry about whether a belief qualifies as religious overlaps with the issue of whether the belief is sincerely held. The latter issue is also interpreted very generously by the courts. *See EEOC v. Unión Independiente de la Autoridad de Acuedoctos y Alcantarillados de Puerto Rico*, 279 F.3d 49 (1st Cir. 2002) (summary judgment denied for employer even though sincerity of belief of an alleged Seventh Day Adventist was challenged by evidence of conduct inconsistent with the tenets of that religious, including lying on an employment application, divorce, and agreeing to take an oath).
32. *Cloutier v. Costco Wholesale Corp.*, 390 F.3d 126 (1st Cir. 2004).

white supremacy.[33] Thus, establishing the existence of a religious belief that requires an accommodation is quite easy.

The accommodation duty itself, however, is very weak.[34] The leading case is *Trans World Airlines, Inc. v. Hardison*.[35] In *Hardison*, a Saturday Sabbatarian asked that the normal shift schedule be modified so that he would not have to work on Saturdays. The Supreme Court announced a remarkably narrow view of the accommodation duty in holding that the employer did not need to make such an accommodation: An employer need not make an accommodation if it would impose any more than a *de minimus* cost on the employer or if it would require any burden on other employees. The Court reached this result by adopting a strict formal equality approach:

> There were no volunteers to relieve Hardison on Saturdays, and to give Hardison Saturdays off, TWA would have had to deprive another employee of his shift preference at least in part because he did not adhere to a religion that observed the Saturday Sabbath.
>
> Title VII does not contemplate such unequal treatment. The repeated, unequivocal emphasis of ... Title VII is on eliminating discrimination in employment, and such discrimination is proscribed when it is directed against majorities as well has minorities.... [I]t would be anomalous to conclude that by "reasonable accommodation" Congress meant that an employer must deny the shift and job preference of some employees, as well as deprive them of their contractual [seniority] rights, in order to accommodate or prefer the religious needs of others, and we conclude that Title VII does not require an employer to go that far.
>
> [TWA could also have accommodated Hardison's religious belief by replacing him] on his Saturday shift with other available employees through the payment of premium wages....
>
> To require TWA to bear more than a de minimus cost in order to give Hardison Saturdays off is an undue hardship.... [T]o require TWA to bear additional costs when no such costs are incurred to give other employees the days off that they want would involve unequal treatment of employees on the basis of their religion. [To do so] would in effect require TWA to finance an additional Saturday off and then to choose the employee who will enjoy it on the basis of his religious beliefs....
>
> [We will not] construe the statute to require an employer to discriminate against some employees in order to enable others to observe their Sabbath.[36]

The Establishment Clause of the United States Constitution may be one reason for the stingy interpretation of the accommodation duty for religion.[37] In general, the

33. *Peterson v. Wilmur Communities, Inc.*, 205 F.Supp.2d 1014 (E.D. Wis. 2002).
34. While most states follow the federal lead on the scope of the accommodation requirement for religion, by statute, Oregon has made the duty much stronger. Oregon Workplace Religious Freedom Act, Or. Rev. Stat. § 659A.033. This stronger duty tracks state laws strengthening constitutional protections for religion and applies them to the private workplace. *See infra* section §1.06[B].
35. 432 U.S. 63 (1977).
36. *Ibid.* at 81-86.
37. U.S. Const. amend. I.

Establishment Clause prohibits the government from favoring one particular religion over others or, more generally, from favoring religion over non-religion. With respect to the accommodation duty, the Establishment Clause claim would be that an overly strong accommodation duty would favor religion too much. In a later case, the Supreme Court used this rationale to strike down a state statute that provided an absolute right not to work on one's Sabbath.[38] The dissent in *Hardison* hinted that avoiding the Establishment Clause issue may have been one reason for the majority's narrow interpretation of the accommodation duty.[39] This, of course, is not a limiting principle on the duty to accommodate for disability or for other reasons.[40]

Taking their lead from *Hardison*, the lower courts have been quite reluctant to require employers to provide much accommodation for religion. The courts have denied plaintiff requests for religious accommodations because of minor costs to the employer,[41] because of minimal burdens on fellow employees,[42] and because of tension with collective bargaining agreements.[43] Plaintiffs tend to succeed in religious accommodation cases, not by focusing on the limited burdens of accommodation (as indicated above, *any* burden tends to defeat their claim), but by identifying similarly-situated employees who received similar accommodations for non-religious reasons. For example, in a recent high-profile case, the plaintiff prevailed by showing that the employer's refusal to hire her because of her religiously-based headscarf was inconsistent with exceptions the employer had made to its no-headdress policy for other employees for non-religious reasons.[44] Ironically, then, the religious accommodation requirement has evolved away from a judicial balancing of the costs of and need for accommodation towards a species of straight-forward disparate treatment discrimination: Has the employer made a similar accommodation for others for non-religious reasons?[45]

38. *Estate of Thornton v. Caldor, Inc.*, 472 U.S. 703 (1985).
39. 432 U.S. at 89-91 (Marshall, J., dissenting).
40. Given the evolution of the Establishment Clause since *Hardison*, it may not even be a limiting principle for religious accommodation anymore. *See Nakashima v. Oregon State Bd. of Educ.*, 185 P.3d 429, 444-445 (Or. 2008) (stronger religious accommodation requirement in Oregon law does not violate the Establishment Clause).
41. *See, e.g., Brown v. Polk County, Iowa*, 61 F.3d 650 (8th Cir. 1995) (employer not required to bear costs of hiring or lesser productivity of a replacement worker).
42. *See, e.g., Harrell v. Donohue*, 638 F.3d 975 (8th Cir. 2011) (scheduling a religious day off for plaintiff would impose burdens on fellow employees).
43. *See, e.g., Virts v. Consolidated Freightways Corp. of Del.*, 285 F.3d 508 (6th Cir. 2002).
44. *EEOC v. Abercrombie & Fitch Stores, Inc.*, 798 F. Supp. 2d 1272, 1287 (N.D. Okla. 2011). The case was high profile because it was later considered by the United States Supreme Court on other issues. 135 S. Ct. 2028 (2015). *See also Kilpatrick v. Hyundai Motor Mfg., Alabama, LLC*, 911 F. Supp. 2d 1211 (M.D. Ala. 2012) (plaintiff's claim for accommodation to permit religious observance on Friday evenings denied because plaintiff could not identify another employee who was granted such a release for a secular reason).
45. This type of analysis is similar to the analysis applied to pregnancy discrimination in the United States. *See infra* section §1.06[C].

§1.04 REASONABLE ACCOMMODATION FOR DISABILITY

A substantial majority of reasonable accommodation cases in the United States involve claims by individuals with disabilities.[46] Part of the reason for this is that, in contrast to claims for accommodation on the basis of religion, claims for accommodation based on disability have real bite.

As a preliminary matter, individuals are entitled to accommodation based on disability only if they are (1) individuals with disabilities; and (2) qualified to perform the essential functions of the job.

An "individual with a disability" is a person who (1) has a physical or mental impairment that substantially limits a major life activity; (2) a record of such an impairment; or (3) is regarded as having such an impairment.[47] Until 2008, falling within this definition was often a challenge; courts granted a summary judgment to employers in about 75% of the cases presenting this issue prior to 2008.[48] A principal purpose of the 2008 amendments to the ADA was to make it easier to fall within the class of people protected by the Act, to "reinstate [the] broad scope of protection ... available under the ADA."[49] The amendments did this by making it clear that words in the definition such as "substantially" and "major" needed to be interpreted more liberally in favor of coverage[50] and by specifically overruling a number of restrictive interpretations.[51] The amendments seem to have been successful in this regard; after the amendments, courts granted a summary judgment in only about 45% of the cases presenting the issue.[52]

The other prerequisite to reaching the reasonable-accommodation question is that the individual must be qualified to perform the essential functions of the job.

---

46. In the United States, reasonable accommodation claims are largely restricted to religious and disability discrimination and almost all of the cases in those categories make accommodation claims. The number of charges of disability discrimination filed with the federal enforcement agency, the EEOC, far outnumber the number of charges of religious discrimination. *See* EEOC, Charge Statistics FY 1997 Through FY 2014, at http://eeoc.gov/eeoc/statistics/enforcement/charges.cfm (about 25,000 charges of disability discrimination were filed annually from 2010-2014; about 4,000 charges of religious discrimination were filed annually over same time period).
47. Americans with Disabilities Act, § 3(1), 42 U.S.C. § 12102(1) (hereinafter "ADA").
48. Stephen Befort, *An Empirical Examination of Outcomes Under the ADA Amendments Act*, 70 Wash. & Lee L. Rev. 2027, 2050-2051 (2013).
49. ADA Amendments Act of 2008, § 2(b)(1), Pub. L. No. 110-325, 122 Stat. 3553 (hereinafter "ADA Amendments").
50. ADA Amendments §§ 2(b)(4) & (5).
51. For example, in determining whether someone is an individual with a disability, the ADA Amendments require that impairments that are episodic or in remission be considered as if they are active and that impairments that can be ameliorated by drugs or other mitigating measures should generally be considered in their unmitigated state. ADA Amendments § 4(a) *codified at*, 42 U.S.C. 12102(4). These requirements reversed prior judicial interpretations of the ADA.
52. Befort, *supra* note 48. Professor Befort thinks that these statistics underestimate the actual expansion in coverage because the amendments also discouraged employers from presenting the non-coverage claim as often. *Ibid.* at 2051. For another good review of the ways in which the 2008 amendments have made it easier for plaintiffs to establish that they are individuals with disabilities, *see* Nicole Buonocore Porter, *The New ADA Backlash*, 82 Tenn. L. Rev. 1 (2014).

Essential functions are not defined in the statute,[53] but the regulations and case law make this analysis much more structured than the reasonable-accommodation analysis. For example, the regulations list several criteria to be considered in determining whether functions are essential, such as the time spent performing the function, how specialized it is, and the number of other employees who might be able to perform it.[54] Thus, while the question overlaps considerably with reasonable accommodation because one must be able to perform the essential functions "with accommodation,"[55] the courts sometimes rely on essential-functions to decide cases at this stage so that they can avoid continuing on to the more complex and uncertain analysis required by reasonable accommodation.[56]

But the focus here is on reasonable accommodation: what are the standards for assessing reasonable accommodation in a disability discrimination case? The reasonable accommodation standard for disability is very vague and poorly defined. The ADA itself does not have a proper definition of the term;[57] instead, it merely list examples of accommodations that "may" be reasonable.[58] The Supreme Court has considered reasonable accommodation in only one case.[59] The word "reasonable" itself has tort overtones that are inapposite to this new context.[60] The distinction between reasonable accommodation and undue hardship is poorly understood.[61] This lack of guidance has resulted in a reasonable accommodation jurisprudence that has been described as "hopelessly muddled,"[62] "a standardless grab bag,"[63] and "severely underdeveloped."[64]

53. ADA § 101(8), 42 U.S.C. § 12111(8). The statute does not define "qualified" or "essential functions," but it does say that "consideration" should be given to the employer's judgment and any written job descriptions. *Ibid.*
54. 29 C.F.R. § 1630.2(n).
55. "The term 'qualified individual' means an individual who, *with or without reasonable accommodation*, can perform the essential functions of the employment position that such individual holds or desires." ADA § 101(8), 42 U.S.C. § 12111(8)(emphasis added).
56. The 2008 amendments to the ADA made it easier for plaintiffs to prove that they are individuals with disabilities, but made no changes to analysis of essential functions, reasonable accommodation, or undue hardship. Because of this, employers are less able to get cases dismissed by proving that plaintiffs are not individuals with disabilities which, in turn, means more cases turn on the essential-functions stage of the analysis. PORTER, *supra* note 52, at 69-70.
57. ADA § 101(8), 42 U.S.C. § 12111(9). Similarly, the implementing regulations contain only a very vague definition and a list of examples. 29 C.F.R. § 1630.2(o).
58. Since the word "may" is used, employers need not always make the accommodations listed in the statute as presumptively reasonable.
59. *US Airways, Inc. v. Barnett*, 535 U.S. 391 (2002) (holding that reasonable accommodation normally does not require an employer to violate a seniority system).
60. *See* NICOLE BUONOCORE PORTER, *Martinizing Title I of the Americans with Disabilities Act*, 47 Ga. L. Rev. 527 543-544 n. 91 (2013).
61. *Compare* MARK C. WEBER, *Unreasonable Accommodation and Due Hardship*, 62 Fla. L. Rev. 1119, 1122 (2010) (undue hardship defines limits of reasonable accommodation) *with* PORTER, *supra* note 60 (undue hardship and reasonable accommodation are distinct issues). *See also US Airways, Inc. v. Barnett*, 535 U.S. 391, 401-402 (2002) (reasonable accommodation considers reasonableness "ordinarily or in the run of cases," while undue hardship requires a showing of special, case-specific circumstances).
62. PORTER, *supra* note 60, at 549.
63. *US Airways, Inc. v. Barnett*, 535 U.S. 391, 414 (2002) (Scalia, J., dissenting).
64. WEBER, *supra* note 61, at 1122.

Despite this vagueness, however, there is no doubt that the reasonable accommodation duty for disability is much stronger than the one for religion. Employers often have to incur considerable costs to provide an accommodation.[65] Accommodations which impose some burdens on fellow employees are common.[66] But while there are a few guidelines which define the outer limits of the duty,[67] the core of the analysis is an unstructured balancing of factors which include cost to the employer, burdens on other employees, pressure on normal company practices, and ability to do the job.[68] The reasonable-accommodation duty also includes a procedural component. Employers must explore accommodation possibilities with individuals with disabilities; a failure to engage in this type of "interactive process" may itself violate the duty of reasonable accommodation.[69]

§1.05 REASONABLE ACCOMMODATION FOR AGE

The reasonable accommodation model has not been applied to age discrimination in the United States.[70] The closest cases involve whether age restrictions for high school athletes (e.g., they cannot be over 19 years old to participate) discriminate against individuals with disabilities. A number of courts have held that easing the age restriction may be a required accommodation, but those cases are based on the duty to accommodate individuals with disabilities, not on any obligation to accommodate age.[71]

---

65. In an early case, an employer was required to provide half-time readers for blind social workers at an annual cost of more than USD 6,500 per worker. *Nelson v. Thornburgh*, 567 F. Supp. 369 (E.D. Pa. 1983), *aff'd*, 732 F.2d 146 (3d Cir. 1984) (decided under the Rehabilitation Act). However, even though the duty may occasionally require expensive accommodations, most tend to be inexpensive. Peter David Blanck, *Transcending Title I of the Americans with Disabilities Act: A Case Report on Sears, Roebuck and Co.*, 20 Mental & Physical Disability L. Rep. 278 (1996) (72% of the company's accommodations required no cost, 27% cost less than USD 500, and 1% cost more than USD 500; average cost was USD 45).
66. *See generally* Nicole B. Porter, *Reasonable Burdens: Resolving the Conflict Between Disabled Employees and Their Coworkers*, 34 Fla. St. L. Rev. 313 (2007).
67. For example, the duty never includes creating a new position, re-assigning a current employee to create a position, or providing items of a personal nature (such as normal eyeglasses or hearing aids). Porter, *supra* note 60, at 546.
68. *See generally* ADA, §§ 101(9) & (10); 29 C.F.R. §§ 1630.2(o) & (p).
69. *See, e.g., Canny v. Dr. Pepper/Seven-Up Bottling Group, Inc.*, 439 F.3d 894 (8th Cir. 2006); *Cutrera v. Bd. of Supervisors*, 429 F.3d 108 (5th Cir. 2005).
70. Indeed, instead of easing the burdens on plaintiffs in age discrimination cases by using an accommodation model, the movement has been in the opposite direction. The two standard models for proving employment discrimination – disparate treatment and disparate impact – are both applied in ways that make it harder for plaintiffs to establish an age discrimination case than one based on race or gender. *See Gross v. FBL Financial Serv., Inc.*, 557 U.S. 167 (2009) (in disparate treatment cases, plaintiffs must prove that age was a but-for cause of the adverse employment decision, rather than merely a motivating factor as in race and gender cases); *Meacham v. Knolls Atomic Power Lab.*, 554 U.S. 84 (2008) (to defend in cases where plaintiffs can show a disparate impact, defendants must only show that it was reasonable to use the factor causing the disparity, not that use of the factor was required by business necessity as in race and gender cases).
71. *See, e.g., Cruz v. Pennsylvania Interscholastic Athletic Ass'n*, 157 F. Supp.2d 485 (E.D. Pa. 2001).

§1.06 BEYOND REASONABLE ACCOMMODATION

Reasonable accommodation began in the United States as a way to address discrimination based on religion and disability. Its growth and evolution occurred mostly within disability law. But directly and indirectly, the concept has seeped into other areas of American law.

The problem in talking about this is in defining "reasonable accommodation" precisely. First, there are several areas in American law where the reasonable-accommodation model has been applied directly, using that precise phraseology. These are clearly examples of reasonable accommodation seeping into other areas. But in other circumstances, there is a strong resemblance to the reasonable-accommodation model but the lineage is less clear. The general idea of identifying a particular subset of people who are entitled to special consideration is present, but not the precise reasonable-accommodation phraseology and balancing process. Thus, although there seems to be a relation, it is not clear if they should be considered a part of the reasonable-accommodation family. Finally, two areas – federal pregnancy and family leave law – are sometimes thought of as being a part of the reasonable-accommodation family, but they are distinct. I discuss these three categories below.

[A] Direct Descendants

Several states have directly appropriated the reasonable-accommodation model and applied it to employment in areas other than religion and disability. State laws have been enacted that require reasonable accommodation of pregnancy,[72] medical use of marijuana,[73] gender identity,[74] and workplace injuries.[75] At least two states also require victims of domestic or sexual violence to be reasonably accommodated.[76]

At the federal level, the Fair Housing Act was amended in 1988 to add a reasonable accommodation requirement.[77] Housing providers must make reasonable accommodation to rules, policies, practices and services when necessary to make it possible for individuals with disabilities to use housing. The duty applies broadly to those involved in the sale and financing of housing (including property owners, housing managers, homeowner association, lenders and real estate agents), although private individuals selling their own homes are exempt. The accommodation duty itself is very similar to the one in employment law; it includes an interactive-process requirement and may require housing providers to incur compliance costs, but it does

72. *See, e.g.*, Del. Code Ann. tit. 19, § 711(a)(3); Minn. Stat. § 181-9414; Neb. Rev. Stat. § 48-1102(11), (18).
73. Nev. Rev. Stat. § 453A.800(3).
74. Utah Code Ann. §§ 34A-5-109, 34A-5-110.
75. Alaska Stat. § 39.25.158.
76. Ill. Comp. Stat. 180 § 30(b); Haw. Rev. Stat. §§ 378-381.
77. Fair Housing Amendments Act of 1988, Pub. L. No. 100-430 § 6(a), 102 Stat. 1636, *codified at*, 42 U.S.C. § 3604(f)(3)(B).

not require "fundamental alternations" to the housing providers' normal operations (which is analogous to the "undue hardship" limitation in employment law).[78]

[B] Relatives

In other areas of American law, doctrine bears a strong resemblance to the reasonable-accommodation model, but the lineage is less clear and the offspring look different. The same interests are being protected in these areas - religion and disability - but they arise in contexts other than employment. Ironically, the reasonable-accommodation model was re-shaped in these areas because the versions developed in employment law were too weak.

First, for religion, Congress and many states have enacted so-called religious freedom restoration acts ("RFRA laws"). The laws were in response to *Employment Division v. Smith*,[79] a 1990 Supreme Court decision which limited the protections provided for religious belief under the First Amendment. Prior to *Smith*, citizens were sometimes entitled to exemptions from facially neutral laws; governments had an obligation to accommodate their religious beliefs.[80] But *Smith* held that the First Amendment did not create any exception for religious belief from neutral, generally applicable laws.

The RFRA laws were a response to *Smith*.[81] They reinstate the obligation of state actors to accommodate religious belief. Thus, they are a type of reasonable accommodation in that they identify a protected group entitled to special consideration. The RFRA laws, however, impose a much stronger accommodation requirement than the employment discrimination laws. The government must accommodate religious belief unless the challenged law or practice furthers a compelling government interest and is the least restrictive means of furthering that interest.[82]

This standard is much stricter than the one under Title VII. For example, in a recent case, the Supreme Court held that a prison violated a RFRA law by refusing to

78. For a good review of the reasonable-accommodation duty by the agencies charged with its enforcement, *see* U.S. Dept. of Justice & U.S. Dept. of Housing and Urban Development, *Reasonable Accommodation Under the Fair Housing Act*, May, 2004, *available at*, http://www.hud.gov/offices/fheo/library/huddojstatement.pdf.
79. 494 U.S. 872 (1990).
80. The leading cases were *Wisconsin v. Yoder*, 406 U.S. 205 (1972) and *Sherbert v. Verner*, 374 U.S. 398 (1963). *See also Lynch v. Donnelly*, 465 U.S. 668, 673 (1983)(the Constitution "affirmatively mandates accommodation, not merely tolerance, of all religions...").
81. The original RFRA Act, enacted in 1993, applied to both state and federal governmental actors. Religious Freedom Restoration Act of 1993, Pub. L. No. 103-141, 107 Stat. 1488 (1993). In 1997, however, the Supreme Court held that the Act's application to states and their subdivisions exceeded Congress' powers under the Constitution. *City of Boerne v. Flores*, 521 U.S. 507 (1997). In response, Congress passed a more limited act applying the heightened accommodation standards in narrower circumstances and a number of states have enacted their own mini-RFRA statutes. Religious Land Use and Institutionalized Persons Act of 2000, Pub. L. No. 106-274, 114 Stat. 803 (1990). For a list of states with mini-RFRA laws, *see* http://civilrights.findlaw.com/discrimination/religious-freedom-acts-by-state.html.
82. *See* Religious Freedom Restoration Act of 1993, 42 U.S.C. § 2000bb-1(b). The other RFRA acts have virtually identical language.

permit a prisoner to grow a half-inch beard. The prison could not meet its burden of proving that its no-beard policy was the least restrictive means of furthering a compelling policy.[83] In contrast, employers are commonly able to prevail under Title VII when their no-beard policies are challenged under Title VII.[84]

Education is another area where a stronger form of accommodation has been developed, this time for individuals with disabilities. At about the same time the reasonable-accommodation concept was being developed under the Rehabilitation Act,[85] Congress enacted the Education for All Handicapped Children Act,[86] which was later amended and re-named the Individuals with Disabilities Education Act (IDEA).[87] While the Rehabilitation Act and the ADA require reasonable accommodation for individuals with disabilities, IDEA requires much more. It requires that children with disabilities who are aged 3 to 21 receive a free, appropriate, and individualized education in the least restrictive appropriate setting. It also provides a set of procedural protections. The obligations of IDEA can be much more expensive and burdensome than mere reasonable accommodations. While there is overlap in the coverage of the ADA, Rehabilitation Act and IDEA,[88] IDEA sets a high substantive standard that must be met.

Thus, the analyses required by RFRA laws and IDEA are relatives of reasonable-accommodation: they also identify persons with religious beliefs and individuals with disabilities as subsets of people who are entitled to special consideration. But both statutes are also distinct from American discrimination laws requiring reasonable accommodation; they provide much higher levels of protection than mere reasonable accommodation.

[C] Different Families

Pregnancy and family leave would seem to be especially well suited to accommodation analysis. But neither is treated that way under federal law.

Pregnancy discrimination has an interesting history in the United States. When Title VII was first enacted, it did not contain any special provision for pregnancy discrimination. In the first case to reach the Supreme Court, the Court oddly held that pregnancy discrimination was not sex discrimination at all:

> The program [of disability insurance in this case] divides potential recipients into two groups: pregnant women and non-pregnant persons. While the first group is

83. *Holt v. Hobbs*, 135 S. Ct. 853 (2015).
84. *See, e.g., Brown v. F.L. Roberts & Co.*, 419 F. Supp. 2d 7 (D. Mass. 2006); *Bhatia v. Chevron U.S.A., Inc.*, 734 F.2d 1382 (9th Cir. 1984); *EEOC v. Sambo's of Ga., Inc.*, 530 F. Supp. 86 (N.D. Ga. 1981).
85. *See supra* notes 9-13 and accompanying text.
86. Pub. L. No. 94-142, 89 Stat. 773 (1975).
87. Pub. L. No. 102-119, 105 Stat. 587 (1991).
88. For a good and concise comparison of the overlapping protections, *see* Disability Rights Education & Defense Fund, *A Comparison of ADA, IDEA, and Section 504*, http://dredf.org/advocacy/comparison.html.

> exclusively female, the second includes members of both sexes.... [Thus, treating pregnancy differently] is not gender-based discrimination at all.[89]

Congress acted quickly to reverse this decision by enacting the Pregnancy Discrimination Act of 1978 (PDA) which defined sex discrimination to include discrimination:

> because of or on the basis of pregnancy, childbirth, or related medical conditions; and women affected by pregnancy, childbirth, or related medical conditions shall be treated the same for all employment-related purposes ... as other persons not so affected but similar in their ability or inability to work.... .[90]

In a recent case, the Supreme Court interpreted this language to require a variant of standard disparate treatment discrimination for pregnancy discrimination claims. The PDA does not require any accommodations by employers. Instead, it requires that, *if the employer makes accommodations for other similar workers*, then the employer must provide those same accommodations to pregnant workers. Thus, instead of determining the employer's obligation through the unstructured balancing process of reasonable accommodation, the PDA permits employers to set their own rules about what types of leaves and accommodations might be reasonable, but then requires employers to apply those rules equally to pregnant workers. This is a variant of disparate treatment discrimination, not an application of the reasonable-accommodation model.[91]

Family and medical leave is another area that seems a natural fit for the reasonable-accommodation model. But it is not the model used in American law. Instead, the federal Family and Medical Leave Act[92] creates a flat right of up to twelve weeks of unpaid leave, if certain conditions are met. The leave must be provided regardless of its reasonableness and there is no undue-hardship defense for the employer. The law protects employers by applying the obligation only to relatively large employers, by making the leave unpaid (which discourages workers from taking it), and by making the leave quite stingy by international standards.

As a result, these two related areas - pregnancy and family leave - seem especially well-suited to accommodation analysis. But that is not the type of analysis applied. The analysis for these two areas comes from different legal families.

89. *General Electric Co. v. Gilbert*, 429 U.S. 125, 135-136 (1976).

90. Pregnancy Discrimination Act of 1978, Pub. L. No. 95-555, 92 Stat. 2076 (1978), *codified at*, 42 U.S.C. § 2000e(k). This definition, notably, did not include the accommodation language inserted into Title VII only a few years earlier to apply to religious discrimination. *See supra* notes 14-15 and accompanying text.

91. After the 2008 amendments to the ADA, many pregnancy-related impairments now qualify as disabilities. When they do, an employer must reasonably accommodate them. But this does not mean that pregnancy needs to be accommodated. The cause of an impairment - whether pregnancy or something else - is irrelevant to the determination whether it is a disability under the ADA and, hence, entitled to accommodation. Disabilities, whether pregnancy-related or not, need to be accommodated; pregnancies, as such, do not. *See* Joan C. Williams et al., *A Sip of Cool Water: Pregnancy Accommodation After the ADA Amendments Act*, 32 Yale L. & Pol'y Rev. 97 (2013).

92. 29 U.S.C. §§ 2601 et seq.

CHAPTER 2

Reasonable Accommodation as Equal Opportunity in Canadian Employment Law

Kevin Banks

In Canada the main obligations of employers to reasonably accommodate employees arise directly out of anti-discrimination law. Rather than supplementing it, as in the US and in EU law,[1] in Canada duties to accommodate enact anti-discrimination law's core purposes. Adjudication has defined those duties in myriad contexts. Their centrality to Canadian anti-discrimination law has thus allowed the Canadian legal system to pioneer the idea and practice of reasonable accommodation at work. It has also enabled Canadian anti-discrimination law to challenge not simply intentional discrimination but also systemic practices – even those with legitimate business purposes – that impose unnecessary burdens on equality of opportunity.

At the same time, because they arise out of anti-discrimination law, most duties to accommodate are implemented primarily through its institutions. Those institutions were designed to address complaints of discrimination by individuals. As a result, the stance of Canadian workplace law towards reasonable accommodation remains for the most part fundamentally reactive. Experience has shown that this stance leaves accommodation gaps.[2] Canadians might therefore learn from other approaches to reasonable accommodation discussed in this volume.

1. See Kevin Banks, Roberta Nunin & Adriana Topo 'The Lasting Influence of Legal Origins: Workplace Discrimination, Social Inclusion and the Law in Canada, the United States and the European Union' (hereinafter, 'Lasting Influence'), in M. Finkin & G. Mundlak (eds), *Handbook of Comparative Labour and Employment Law* (London: Edward Elgar, 2015). This paper's analysis of the origins of reasonable accommodation requirements in Canadian employment law draws extensively upon the longer and more detailed treatment offered in Lasting Influence.
2. Kevin Banks, Richard P. Chaykowski & George A. Slotsve, 'Disability Accommodation in Employment: How Does an Aging Population Matter and What Might It Mean for Workplace Law and Policy?' (2013) 17:2 Canadian Labour and Employment Law Journal.

This chapter will begin by outlining the legal source and the origins of the duty to accommodate in Canadian anti-discrimination law. It will then sketch the limits of the duty, and how the duty has required the accommodation of religious belief and expression, disability, age and family status in Canadian workplace. Next it will turn to the relatively few sources of reasonable accommodation obligations that lie outside of anti-discrimination law. The conclusion briefly reflects on the limits of Canadian legal institutions in implementing reasonable accommodation at work.

§2.01 EMPLOYMENT DISCRIMINATION LAW AS THE PRIMARY SOURCE OF DUTIES TO PROVIDE REASONABLE ACCOMMODATION

In Canada the duty of employers to reasonably accommodate employees arises out of the requirements of a legal defence – the bona fide occupational requirement (BFOR) defence – to a finding of prima facie discrimination. The requirement that an employer prove that it offered reasonable accommodation, the most demanding element of the defence, effectively defines the workplace equality of opportunity sought by anti-discrimination statutes. A brief exploration of the legal key doctrinal features of Canadian anti-discrimination law and their political and jurisprudential origins will make this clear.

I will begin with an outline of the relevant doctrine and then turn to its origins. In general terms, under Canadian law, an employee seeking to demonstrate discrimination on a prima facie *basis* is simply required to show that he or she has a characteristic protected from discrimination under the *Code*; that he or she experienced an adverse impact with respect to employment; and that the protected characteristic was a factor in the adverse impact.[3] To show that a protected characteristic was a factor in the adverse impact, a complainant need only demonstrate that it contributed to causing the impact, and not that it was the sole or primary cause.[4]

The onus then shifts to the employer to prove that its actions, practices or policies constitute a BFOR, if that defence is available under the statute. In general terms, to do so the employer must demonstrate that:

(1) the employer adopted the measure in question for a purpose rationally connected to the performance of the job;
(2) the employer adopted the particular measure in an honest and good faith belief that it was necessary to the fulfilment of that legitimate work- related purpose; and
(3) that the measure is reasonably necessary to the accomplishment of that legitimate work-related purpose.[5]

3. *Québec (Commission des droits de la personne et des droits de la jeunesse) c Bombardier Inc*, 2015 SCC 39 at para. 63, [2015] 2 SCR 789 [*Bombardier*].
4. *Ibid.* at para. 48.
5. *British Columbia (Public Service Employee Relations Commission) v. B.C.G.E.U.*, [1999] 3 SCR 3 at para. 54, 176 DLR (4th) 1 [*Meiorin*].

Where discrimination is not invidious, the first two branches of this test are often relatively easily met. The rational connection test allows employers wide discretion to define purposes and requirements related to the jobs that they create. It is under the third branch of the test that review of employer action becomes more searching. To show that the measure is reasonably necessary, the employer must demonstrate that it is impossible for it to accommodate individual employees sharing the characteristics of the claimant without undue hardship.[6] This definition of reasonable necessity has the effect of creating a duty to accommodate, and makes accommodation central to the definition of equal opportunity in Canada.

The duty to accommodate arose out of the efforts of Canadian courts, tribunals and legislatures to both define and place reasonable limits upon employer responsibility to address the adverse impacts of employer policies and practices on the opportunities of women and members of minority groups. These efforts were informed at early and critical junctures by the claims and experiences of members of religious minorities.

Between the early 1960s and the mid 1970s all Canadian jurisdictions enacted comprehensive anti-discrimination statutes, commonly referred to as 'human rights codes'.[7] One of the first to do so was Ontario, Canada's most populous province. Ontario's legislation and the debates surrounding it were influential elsewhere in Canada. The movement for legal protection against discrimination in Ontario was led by a loose coalition of religious, labour, and ethnic community organizations.[8] At the centre of this movement were Jewish organizations aiming to change the pervasive anti-semitic practices of Post World War II Canadian society.[9] Jewish leaders saw the protection of democracy and the elimination of discrimination against religious and racial minorities as inextricably linked. Many saw the pursuit of these aims as essential to ensuring that Canadian society would not again react with indifference to the persecution of Jews at home or abroad. They also saw that the project of eliminating anti-semitism entailed seeking greater acceptance of all religious, racial and ethnic minority rights. Labour leaders joined the cause in part because they viewed the elimination of racial, religious and ethnic prejudice as making for a more egalitarian society in which the aims of the labour movement would find a better reception in local and national politics.

During the 1970s Canada explicitly reimagined itself as a multicultural society.[10] Equality advocates argued before legislatures, courts and tribunals that genuine

6. *Ibid.*
7. Walter Tarnopolsky, in William Pentney & John D. Gardner (eds), *Discrimination and the Law*, (Toronto: Carswell, 1990) at 2-4, 2-13 [Tarnopolsky].
8. R. Brian Howe, 'The Evolution of Human Rights Policy in Ontario' (1991) 24:4 Canadian Journal of Political Science 783 [Howe]; Irving Abella, 'Presidential Address: Jews, Human Rights and the Making of the New Canada' (2000) 11 Journal of the Canadian Historical Association 3 [Abella]; Carmela Patrias & Ruth A Frager, '"This Is Our Country, These Are Our Rights": Minorities and the Origins of Ontario's Human Rights Campaigns' (2001) 82:1 Canadian Historical Review 1 [Patrias & Frager]; James St. G. Walker, 'The Jewish Phase in the Movement for Racial Equality in Canada' (2002) 34:1 Canadian Ethnic Studies 1 at 3 [Walker].
9. Abella, *supra* note 8; Walker, *supra* note 8.
10. See Joseph Garcea, 'Provincial Multiculturalism Policies in Canada, 1974-2004: A Content Analysis' (2006) 38:3 Canadian Ethnic Studies 1; Patricia Wood & Liette Gilbert, Patricia Wood

equality of opportunity required removal of unnecessary barriers to participation in social and economic life, regardless of whether such barriers were created intentionally or not.[11] Governments responded towards the end of that decade and into the next with initiatives to expand the scope of anti-discrimination protections. Just as importantly, early leading cases before courts and tribunals dealt with adverse impacts on the basis of religion and sex. In these cases employer rules clearly and directly caused disadvantage based on protected grounds: employees lost their jobs because attendance requirements conflicted with tenets of religious faith, as did women who failed physical strength and endurance tests. The relationship between rules, practices and adverse consequences was either evident on its face, or was easily demonstrated through a rudimentary statistical analysis. Moreover, it was fairly obvious that identical treatment would not produce meaningful equality of opportunity, given widely understood physiological differences between women and men, or the obvious constraints on the behaviour of people imposed by faithful observance of religious tenets. These cases forced into the open a consideration of the extent of employer obligations to treat differently people who are adversely affected on the basis of fundamental personal characteristics by employer standards and practices reflecting needs and characteristics of members of the workplace majority or mainstream.

In response, by the end of the 1970s a number of human rights tribunals and lower courts had adopted and applied adverse impact theories of discrimination.[12] This approach was not unanimously accepted however, and eventually the issue of whether human rights code prohibitions on discrimination extended to adverse impacts came before the Supreme Court of Canada. In *Ontario (Human Rights Commission) v. Simpsons-Sears Ltd* (hereafter '*Simpsons-Sears*') the Court upheld the adverse impact doctrine, defined a set of employer responsibilities and obligations flowing from the doctrine, and linked both to the purposes of anti-discrimination legislation.[13] It was this definition of employer responsibility to afford equal opportunity that embedded the duty to accommodate in Canadian anti-discrimination law.

In *Simpsons-Sears* a Seventh Day Adventist challenged an employer requirement that she work on Saturdays, something that her religious faith forbade her to do. The factual record made it clear that the employer requirement was for legitimate business reasons and not as a result of any intent to discriminate on the basis of religious faith. The Court accepted with relatively little discussion the proposition that the human rights code's aim of removing of discrimination requires addressing the differential effects of employment rules, even those made only for sound economic or business

and Liette Gilbert, 'Multiculturalism in Canada: Accidental Discourse, Alternative Vision, Urban Practice' (2005) 29:3 International Journal of Urban and Regional Research 679.

11. See Ontario Human Rights Commission, *Life Together: A Report on Human Rights in Ontario* (Toronto: OHRC, 1977) (where the OHRC argued for anti-discrimination laws providing a positive right to equal opportunity in order to promote acceptance of religious, ethnic, racial, gender and other forms of diversity).
12. Tarnopolsky, *supra* note 7 at 4-44, 4-52.
13. [1985] 2 SCR 536, 52 OR (2d) 799 [*Simpsons-Sears*].

reasons.[14] The Court then considered the implications of this proposition for employers, and in particular to what extent they may be required to accept employee religious practices and read the duty to accommodate into the operation of the human rights code. In a key passage, it derived the duty from the special role of employers in relation to employees, and the need to preserve a social structure in which rights are both protected and reconciled with each other:

> The Code accords the right to be free from discrimination in employment. While no right can be regarded as absolute, a natural corollary to the recognition of a right must be the social acceptance of a general duty to respect and to act within reason to protect it. In any society the rights of one will inevitably come into conflict with the rights of others. It is obvious then that all rights must be limited in the interest of preserving a social structure in which each right may receive protection without undue interference with others. This will be especially important where special relationships exist, in the case at bar the relationship of employer and employee. In this case, consistent with the provisions and intent of the Ontario Human Rights Code, the employee's right requires reasonable steps towards an accommodation by the employer.[15]

Having accepted the proposition that there is an employer duty to accommodate, the court found it necessary to 'put some realistic limit upon it'.[16] Consistent with the aim of creating a social structure in which 'each right may receive protection without undue interference with others,' the Court articulated those limits as follows:

> The duty in a case of adverse effect discrimination on the basis of religion or creed is to take reasonable steps to accommodate the complainant, short of undue hardship: in other words, to take such steps as may be reasonable to accommodate without undue interference in the operation of the employer's business and without undue expense to the employer.[17]

The court thus treated equality of opportunity as requiring positive steps to remove barriers by accommodating the protected differences of employees, even where those barriers arose for legitimate business reasons and the employer would have maintained them regardless of any discriminatory motivation. The limits of that responsibility are reached when an employer faces 'undue hardship'.

While based on an interpretation of the Ontario Human Rights Code, the *Simpsons-Sears* analysis was soon applied under all Canadian human rights statutes. In the years immediately following *Simpsons-Sears*, the Supreme Court of Canada clarified that the duty to accommodate always requires employers to take into account the individual circumstances of those to whom general rules apply unless doing so would cause undue hardship;[18] that the undue hardship threshold implies that some hardship

14. *Ibid.* at paras 12, 18.
15. *Ibid.* at para. 22.
16. *Ibid.* at para. 23.
17. *Ibid.*
18. *Central Alberta Dairy Pool v. Alberta (Human Rights Commission)*, [1990] 2 SCR 489, 72 DLR (4th) 417 [*Dairy Pool*].

must be accepted in the interests of furthering equal opportunity;[19] and that the duty applies to unions as well as to employers.[20]

Finally, in its landmark decision, *British Columbia (Public Service Employee Relations Commission) v. B.C.G.E.U.* (hereinafter '*Meiorin*') the Court integrated its jurisprudence on employer defences to and remedies for direct and adverse impact discrimination so as to erase the legal consequences of distinguishing between them. Under the unified approach established in that decision, once a complainant has established a prima facie case either of adverse effect or direct discrimination the employer must satisfy the three-part test set out above. The court thus merged the BFOR defence developed under its direct discrimination jurisprudence with the duty to accommodate developed under its adverse impact jurisprudence. The Court reasoned that in practice the distinction between adverse impact and direct discrimination was often artificial,[21] and that attaching consequences to it did not serve the purposes of anti-discrimination law.[22] The Court specifically sought to eliminate any suggestion in earlier jurisprudence that the duty to accommodate served simply to offset unintentional adverse impacts, once proven, of otherwise legitimate employer rules or practices, stating that:

> Under the [previous] conventional analysis, if a standard is classified as being "neutral" at the threshold stage of the inquiry, its legitimacy is never questioned.
>
> [...]
>
> Although the practical result of the conventional analysis may be that individual claimants are accommodated and the particular discriminatory effect they experience may be alleviated, the larger import of the analysis cannot be ignored. It bars courts and tribunals from assessing the legitimacy of the standard itself....
>
> The right to be free of discrimination is reduced to the question of whether the mainstream can afford to confer proper treatment on those adversely affected, within the confines of its existing formal standard. If it cannot, the edifice of systemic discrimination receives the law's formal approval. This cannot be right.[23]

In the result, the Court upheld the award of a labour arbitrator reinstating Ms. Meiorin to her position as a firefighter. It agreed with the arbitrator that dismissing her for failing to meet the employer's physical fitness test constituted discrimination because women disproportionately failed the test and the test could not be justified as a BFOR. The test in question measured aerobic fitness levels, but the employer had not proven that the fitness standard in question was necessary to performing the essential duties of a firefighter.[24]

19. *Central Okanagan School District No 23 v. Renaud*, [1992] 2 SCR 970 at para. 19, 95 DLR (4th) 577 [*Renaud*].
20. *Ibid.*
21. By this time, the requirements for a BFOR defence to direct discrimination and for demonstrating compliance with the duty to accommodate were effectively the same. See *Meiorin, supra* note 5 at para. 38 (where the Court said that 'the employer must show that it could not have done anything else reasonable or practical to avoid the negative impact on the individual').
22. *Meiorin, supra* note 5 at paras 27-29, 39-49.
23. *Ibid.* at paras 39-42.
24. *Ibid.* at para. 82.

The Court thus made it clear that the lawfulness of employer practices depends upon meeting the duty to accommodate on an ongoing and proactive basis, and that eliminating adverse impacts resulting from failures to accommodate to the point of undue hardship is just as central to equality of opportunity as eliminating intentional disparate treatment.[25] Accommodation therefore must be 'designed in' to employer policies and practices. As the Court put it, a workplace standard or practice must 'accommodate factors related to the unique capabilities and inherent worth and dignity of every individual, up to the point of undue hardship'.[26] It is the measure or standard itself that must be reasonably necessary, and not simply its application. In this sense, accommodation is non-discrimination, and the duty is a direct correlate of the right to be free of discrimination in employment.[27]

As a result, the duty to accommodate applies to a wide range of protected personal characteristics. Statutes in all Canadian jurisdictions[28] prohibit discrimination on the basis of race, colour, religion, sex, national origin, age, physical or mental disability, marital status and sexual orientation. A majority also protect against discrimination on the basis of family status, political belief, one or more of 'record of criminal conviction' and 'pardoned criminal conviction' or source of income. In the

25. As the Court put it: '[t]he question should not be whether the discrimination is direct or indirect [i.e. adverse effect], but rather whether the individual or group discriminated against receives the same protection regardless of the manner in which that discrimination is brought about.' (*Ibid.* at para. 31).
26. *Ibid.* at para. 62.
27. In some recent lower court decisions, the Ontario Court of Appeal suggests that complainants need to establish that measures with disparate impacts are substantively discriminatory before an employer can be asked to meet the duty to accommodate. See especially *Ontario (Director of Disability Support Program) v. Tranchemontagne*, 2010 ONCA 593, 102 OR (3d) 97. This is inconsistent with *Simpsons-Sears* and with the Supreme Court of Canada's most recent pronouncement in *Moore v. British Columbia (Ministry of Education)*, 2012 SCC 61 at para. 33, [2012] 3 SCR 360. See Denise Reaume, 'Defending the Human Rights Codes from the Charter' (2012) 9 JL & Equality 67; Benjamin Oliphant, 'Prima Facie Discrimination: Is *Tranchemontagne* consistent with the Supreme court of Canada's Human Rights Code Jurisprudence' (2012) 9 JL & Equality 3 (for detailed arguments that the approach in *Tranchemontagne* is legally incorrect).
28. In Canada provincial governments have exclusive competence with respect to 'property and civil rights' – a category that includes employment relations, except in specific industries enumerated in the constitution as federal heads of power. See *Toronto Electric Commissioners v. Snider*, [1925] 1 WWR 785, [1925] 2 DLR 5 (JCPC); *Employees of the Canadian Pacific Railway in Empress Hotel, Victoria (City), Re*, [1950] 1 WWR 220, [1950] 1 DLR 721(JCPC). As a result, it falls largely to provincial governments to legislate against workplace discrimination. Every province and the federal government has enacted a comprehensive human rights statute prohibiting discrimination in a range of social and economic relations, including employment. See *Alberta Human Rights Act*, RSA 2000, c A-25.5 (for Alberta); *Human Rights Code*, RSBC 1996, c 210 (for British Columbia: *The Human Rights Code*, CCSM 1987, c H175 (for Manitoba); *Human Rights Act*, RSNB 2011, c 171 (for New Brunswick); *Human Rights Code*, RSNL 1990, c H-13.1 (for Newfoundland and Labrador); *Human Rights Act*, RSNS 1989, c 214 (for Nova Scotia); *Human Rights Code*, RSO 1990, c H.19 (for Ontario); *Human Rights Act*, RSPEI 1988, c.H-12 (Prince Edward Island); *Charter of Human Rights and Freedoms*, CQLR, c C-12 (for Quebec); *Saskatchewan Human Rights Code*, SS 1979, c S-24.1 (for Saskatchewan); *Canadian Human Rights Act*, RSC 1985, c H-6 (for the federal jurisdiction).

eyes of the law, there is no hierarchy among these prohibited grounds of discrimination.[29]

Anti-discrimination laws, and thus the duty to accommodate, apply to employers in all sectors of the economy and generally cover all aspects of employment relationships, broadly defined,[30] from pre-hiring to termination. The statutes apply broadly to both public and private sector employers without regard to the size of the employer.

§2.02 DEFINITION AND SCOPE OF REASONABLE ACCOMMODATION

The line of decisions from *Simpsons-Sears* to *Meiorin* has spawned an extensive jurisprudence interpreting and applying the duty to accommodate in myriad contexts. The duty now reaches well into the employment relationship. While there is no authoritative limitation or categorization of the types of accommodation that may be legally required, broadly speaking many if not most instances of accommodation involve one or more of: (1) the reformulation of rules, standards or other requirements; (2) modified work schedules; (3) modified duties; (4) access to leave; and (5) physical and technological adaptation of the workplace. When an employee is unable to perform all of the duties of a job because of a personal characteristic subject to the protections of anti-discrimination law, an employer must consider modifying those duties if the employee can perform the essential functions of the job.[31] In a number of recent decisions adjudicators have also ruled that even where an employee is no longer able to fulfil the essential requirements of his or her position, the employer must consider transfers to other positions[32] or whether job duties from other positions could be bundled to create a productive position.[33]

---

29. *Johnstone v. Canada (Border Services Agency)*, 2014 FCA 110 at para. 81, 372 DLR (4th) 730 [*Johnstone*].
30. Canadian human rights tribunals have tended to take a purposive approach to defining the employer-employee relationship, aiming to address discrimination in relationships of economic dependence in which a non-dependent party exerts sufficient control to eliminate it. Courts and tribunals have therefore tended to treat the traditional indicia of the employment relationship at common law as instructive, but not decisive of the issue. See generally Kevin D. MacNeill, *The Duty to Accommodate in Employment*, Rev ed (Toronto: Canada Law Book, 2003) at 3-4, 3-30 [MacNeill]. Evidence of economic dependency and administrative control has outweighed the conclusion at common law that the individual was an independent contractor. See e.g., *Sharma v. Yellow Cab Co.* (1983), 4 CHRR D/1432, 1983 CarswellBC 3536 (WL Can) (HRC) (for a case involving the absence of many of the traditional common law indicia of employment, including remuneration).
31. See e.g., *Ontario (Liquor Control Board) and OLBEU (Sanfilippo), Re* (2005), 80 CLAS 272 at para. 84, [2005] OGSBA No 36 (QL). See also *Bowater Canadian Forest Products Inc v. IWA-Canada, Local 2693*, 75 CLAS 73 at para. 41, [2003] OLAA No 597 (QL) (for a pronouncement by the arbitrator that there are situations where an employer is required to excuse a disabled employee from an essential function of a job).
32. *Re Peterborough Civil Hospital and ONA* (1981), 3 LAC (3d) 21, 1981 CarswellOnt 1955 (WL Can) (Arb Bd); *Calgary Co-operative Assn Ltd v. Calco Club* (1992), 24 LAC (4th) 308, 25 CLAS 566 (Alta Arb Bd); *McConnell v. Yukon (Public Service Commission)* (1998), 34 CHRR D/26, 1998 CarswellYukon 112 (WL Can) (Bd Adj).
33. See Leonard Marvy, 'Disability and the Duty to Accommodate: A Management Viewpoint', in W. Kaplan et al, (eds), *Labour Arbitration Yearbook* (Toronto: Lancaster House, 1998) at 129; Gary Hopkinson, 'Disability and the Duty to Accommodate: A Union Viewpoint', in W. Kaplan et al,

As noted above, the duty to make such accommodations extends only to the point at which the employer would face undue hardship. Adjudicators, employers, employees and unions must often grapple with where the at times ambiguous threshold of undue hardship lies.[34] The answer to this question is often very context-specific. In general terms, and subject to the stipulations of particular statutes, the relevant jurisprudence recognizes four sets of relevant criteria: (1) cost to the employer; (2) health and safety risks to employees, customers or other persons; (3) legitimate operational requirements; and (4) interference with collective agreement or employment contract rights of other employees. I will briefly consider each of these factors below. The application of these factors, especially cost and operational requirements considerations, will often vary according to the size and resources of the employer. In addition, tribunals will often assess the proportionality between hardship for the employer and the benefit to employee.[35]

[A] Costs to the Employer

While most accommodations cost little to implement, in a minority of cases accommodations can impose substantial costs.[36] In such cases the extent of legally required accommodations will depend upon wealth and size of employer. For example, the costs of hiring replacements to enable modified schedules can constitute an undue hardship, particularly for small employers.[37] In one case, a proposal to create indoor smoking facilities to accommodate workers addicted to nicotine presented an undue hardship even for a large employer.[38]

Regardless of the size and wealth of the employer, adjudicators have accepted the principle that reasonable accommodation does not require pay without productive work.[39] Where an employee is unable to perform productive work an employer may place him or her on leave without pay, subject to any contractual requirements to provide income replacement through disability benefits. Where an employee will remain unable indefinitely to resume productive employment even under modified duties or scheduling, and employer may terminate the employment relationship.

(eds), *Labour Arbitration Yearbook* (Toronto: Lancaster House, 1998) at 154-54; *Scott's No Frills v. UFCW, Local 1000A* (2011), 107 CLAS 244, 2011 CarswellOnt 7948 (WL Can) (Arb Bd).

34. See generally *MacNeill, supra* note 30 at ch 11-12.
35. *Dairy Pool, supra* note 18 at 521.
36. Kevin Banks, Richard P. Chaykowski & George A. Slotsve, 'Disability Accommodation in Employment: How Does an Aging Population Matter and What Might It Mean for Workplace Law and Policy?' 2013 17:2 CLELJ at n.88.
37. *Dairy Pool, supra* note 18 at 521. See especially *Mazuelos v. Clark*, 2000 BCHRT 1 at D/390, 2000 CLLC 230-013.
38. *Hamilton-Wentworth (Regional Municipality) v. CUPE, Local 167* (1994), 37 CLAS 197, 44 LAC (4th) 257 (Ont Arb Bd).
39. *Mitchell's Gourmet Foods Inc v. UFCW, Loc 248-P* (2004), 133 LAC 4th 210 at 273, 79 CLAS 38 (Sask Arb Bd).

[B] Health and Safety Risks

Substantial increased risks to the health or safety of the worker, his or her colleagues, customers or members of the public will amount to undue hardship. For example, each of the following have been found to constitute undue hardship: allowing workers with epilepsy or an addiction presenting a significant risk of relapse to perform safety-sensitive work in a manufacturing plant;[40] allowing a man whose facial hair, worn for religious reasons, prevented a gas mask that he must wear to safely shut down machinery from sealing properly, in turn presenting a risk to himself and others;[41] accommodating the Sabbath of religiously observant workers where doing so would require other workers in a manufacturing plant to work sixteen hour shifts, producing safety risks.[42] Where the employer demonstrated with evidence that the risk of cardiac arrest for firefighters over the age of 60 was elevated and could not be assessed on an individual basis, mandatory retirement for firefighters above that age was allowed.[43]

[C] Operational Requirements

Operational requirement considerations often overlap with considerations of cost or health and safety. For example, adjudicators have not required modified duties or modified schedules where to do so would be unworkable because employees are not interchangeable.[44] In an unusual case, an employer rule against religious preaching at work was upheld where an employee's insistence on preaching to his co-workers routinely upset them, and where the employer found it impossible to schedule him to work alone.[45] These instances appear to reflect an implicit judgment about the costs of hiring personnel to replace the employee seeking accommodation. There are also situations in which despite the low marginal cost of accommodation adjudicators will find undue hardship. A relatively common example arises where unsuccessful attempts have already been made to reintegrate a relapsing addict, and there is no assurance of future success.[46] These cases can be understood as either reflecting the operational requirements of the employer, or as an assessment of costs to the employer in light of the diminishing expected benefit to the employee.

---

40. *TCC Bottling Ltd v. RWDSU, Local 106* (1993), 29 CLAS 678, 32 LAC (4th) 73 (NB Arb Bd); *Kalbfleisch v. Carillo* (2002), 44 CHRR D/163, [2002] OHRBID No 16 (QL).
41. *Singh v. R* (1980), 27 LAC (2d) 295, 1980 CarswellOnt 2133 (WL Can) (Arb Bd).
42. *Roosma v. Ford Motor Co of Canada* (1988), 66 OR (2d) 18, 53 DLR (4th) 90 (Div Ct).
43. *Espey v. London (City)*, 2008 HRTO 412, 66 CHRR D/18 [*Espey*].
44. *Halliday v. Michelin North America (Canada) Ltd* (2006), 58 CHRR D/91, 2006 CarswellNS 652 (WL Can) (NS Bd Inq).
45. *Friesen v. Fisher Bay Seafood Ltd*, 2009 BCHRT 1, 2010 CLLC 230-029 [*Friesen*].
46. *Samuel, Son & Co v. USWA, Local 6398* (1995), 41 CLAS 15, 50 LAC (4th) 321(Ont Arb Bd); *Labatt Breweries Ontario v. Brewery, General & Professional Workers' Union, Local 30*, 107 LAC (4th) 126, 69 CLAS 132 (Arb Bd).

[D] Interference with Rights of Other Employees

Where an accommodation would interfere with collective agreement rights, other options must be explored first.[47] Substantial interference with employee job security rights generally amounts to undue hardship.[48] Similarly, accommodations that alter important aspects of other employees' duties – for example by removing the sedentary parts of a job involving heavy labour, requiring other employees to spend significantly more time 'on-call', or requiring other employees to frequently work short-staffed will often amount to undue hardship.[49] Conversely, interference with less substantial rights, for example rights to bid on vacancies or transfers, often will not.[50]

§2.03 AN ACCOMMODATED WORKPLACE FOR RELIGION OR BELIEF

Tribunals have required employers to adapt both work schedules and task assignments in light of the religious beliefs of employees. At least since *Simpsons-Sears* the duty to accommodate has required employers to adapt work schedules (to the point of undue hardship) to enable employees to observe religiously mandated days of rest such as the Sabbath. Employers are also required to provide employees of different religious faiths with equal opportunities to celebrate their religious holidays. One particular issue that courts and tribunals have grappled with arises out of the fact that employment legislation creates statutory holidays at Christmas and Easter. The Supreme Court of Canada has ruled that despite their religious origins these holidays are now secular, and that providing them while not creating holidays on the occasion of important dates in non-Christian religious calendars does not represent direct discrimination.[51] Nonetheless, it can have adverse impacts by making it more difficult for non-Christians than for Christians to celebrate important religious holidays. Courts and tribunals have ruled that employers must provide employees with unpaid time off to celebrate religious holidays, and opportunities for paid work time to make up for the resulting loss of income.[52] Employers who have provided employees with a menu of reasonable options to do so have been found to meet the duty to accommodate.[53] Courts and tribunals have required employers to permit scheduling changes and use of existing paid days off

---

47. See generally MacNeill, *supra* note 30 at 12:50:30.
48. See e.g., *Panabrasive Inc v. USWA, Local 8777*, 33 CLAS 541, 38 LAC (4th) 434 (Ont Arb Bd); *Canada Post Corp v. CUPW*, 30 CLAS 242, 32 LAC (4th) 289 (Arb Bd); *Dominion Colour Corp v. Teamsters Chemical, Energy & Allied Workers, Local 1880*, 57 CLAS 339, 83 LAC (4th) 330 (Ont Arb Bd).
49. See e.g., *Ottawa Civic Hospital v. ONA* (1995), 39 CLAS 463, 48 LAC (4th) 388 (Ont Arb Bd); *MacEachern v. St Francis Xavier University* (1994), 24 CHRR D/226 (NS Arb Bd); *Edgell v. Trail School District No 11* (1996), 97 CLLC 230-009, 1996 CarswellBC 2996 (WL Can) (HRC).
50. *Renaud, supra* note 19 at 984-985; *Greater Victoria School District No 61 v. BCTF* (1998), 55 CLAS 330, 78 LAC (4th) 289 (Arb Bd); *Peterborough Civic Hospital v. ONA* (1981), 3 LAC (3d) 21, 1981 CarswellOnt 1955 (WL Can) [*Peterborough*].
51. *R v. Big M Drug Mart Ltd*, [1985] 1 SCR 295, 18 DLR (4th) 321.
52. See *Markovic v. Autocom Manufactuing Ltd*, 2008 HRTO 64, [2008] 2008 CarswellOnt 5936 (WL Can).
53. *Ibid.* at para. 55.

to enable workers to take time off to observe religious holidays, consistently with the principle that the duty to accommodate does not require pay without work.[54]

Accommodating employees' religious needs may also involve modifying the tasks and duties that they are assigned. For instance, a Jehovah's Witness was relieved of the requirement to participate in administering blood transfusions where she worked as part of a team of nurses and there was always someone else available to perform the transfusions.[55] In another case dietary aides who were required to audit patient food were exempted from tasting the food due to religious reasons.[56] Similarly, an employer was found to have unlawfully terminated the employment of a Catholic woman on the grounds that she failed to approve social assistance for a person seeking to have an abortion. In this case the employer had not demonstrated that any of the challenges faced in ensuring that the complainant did not deal with such files would amount to undue hardship.[57]

The question of whether employers can impose neutrality policies as a response to religious expression of employees has received relatively little attention in the jurisprudence. As discussed above, tribunals have accepted the right of employees to refuse to perform tasks contrary to the tenets of their faith where the employer can assign those tasks to others without undue hardship. However, one tribunal found that an employer's insistence that an employee not preach to his or her colleagues was legally justified because of the objections of those colleagues to being subjected to such expressions of faith.[58] An employer rule requiring employees to refrain from preaching to or otherwise seeking to persuade customers or members of the public would likely be lawful for similar reasons. Of course, employer rules requiring employees to provide services to customers or members of the public without discrimination on the basis of religion would also generally be consistent with anti-discrimination law.

There has however been considerable debate recently in Canada over whether an employer can prohibit more subtle forms of religious expression in the workplace, such as the wearing of religious garb or symbols. This debate was sharpened by a proposal by the government of the province of Quebec to enact a 'Charter of Values' that would have prohibited the wearing of conspicuous religious symbols or garb by employees in the broader public sector, which includes public schools, and hospitals as well as the institutions of government and public service. The purported justification for the Charter of Values was to enact the secular values of Quebec in its public institutions, by having employees present a secular appearance to the public. This proposal sparked a good deal of criticism in legal circles. There is little doubt that such restrictions on

54. *Ibid.* at paras 28-29; See also *Chambly (Commission scolaire régionale) c Bergevin,* [1994] 2 SCR 525 at para. 26, 115 DLR (4th) 609, and *CUPE, Local 4400 v. Toronto District School Board* (2008), 178 LAC (4th) 182, 96 CLAS 90 (Ont Arb) in which an arbitrator reasoned that the duty to accommodate should not overwhelm the basis of the employment relationship, which is work for pay.
55. *Peterborough, supra* note 50.
56. *Victoria Hospital Corp v. London & District Service Workers' Union, Local 220* (1996), 45 CLAS 90, 57 LAC (4th) 221 (Ont Arb).
57. *Moore v. British Columbia (Ministry of Social Services) (Re)* (1992), 17 CHRR D/426, 1992 CarswellBC 3325 (HRC).
58. *Friesen, supra* note 45 at para. 74.

religious expression would adversely impact many members of religious minorities by forcing them to choose between employment and the tenets of their faith, or simply by restricting their capacity for religious self-expression. They would therefore require justification under the *Meiorin* test. Many legal experts are of the view that such adverse impacts could not be legally justified, because there is little evidence demonstrating a connection between the capacity of state personnel to be (and appear) religiously neutral in the fulfilment of their employment duties and the way they dress.[59] Moreover, since in both law and cultural practice religious identity is understood to be a private matter, it is difficult to see how the religious expression of most public sector employees could be attributed to the state. There is little evidence that the state cannot enact secular values where its employees wear religious garb or symbols. Such policies might therefore fail under the first or the third branch of the *Meiorin* test.

§2.04 AN ACCOMMODATED WORKPLACE FOR DISABILITY OR WORK INCAPACITY

The duty to accommodate applies to disability in all Canadian jurisdictions. Disability is the most frequently invoked ground of accommodation in Canadian case law. The concept of disability in Canadian human rights law extends to injury, illness and addictions,[60] and includes at least some temporary conditions though perhaps not 'normal ailments' such as the flu or a common cold.[61] In enforcing the duty adjudicators have required employers to provide workers with accommodations such as modified duties and schedules, leaves of absence, or furniture and other equipment needed to attend work or do the essential duties of a job.[62] For example, adjudicators have required accommodation of fatigue-inducing disabilities through shorter work hours,[63] and that a nurse with bipolar mood disorder be provided with a schedule that did not include night shifts.[64] Employers are often required to provide employees seeking treatment for addiction with unpaid leave to do so.[65] The duty to accommodate

---

59. See Sean Fine, 'Is Quebec's secular charter constitutional? Nine legal experts weigh in', *The Globe and Mail* (14 September 2003), online: <http://www.theglobeandmail.com/news/politics/is-quebecs-secular-charter-constitutional-nine-legal-experts-weigh-in/article14324825/?page=all>.
60. Russel W Zinn, *The Law of Human Rights in Canada: Practice and Procedure* (Toronto: Canada Law Book, 1996) at 5-10.1-5-13.
61. See the obiter dicta of the Supreme Court of Canada in *Québec (Commission des droits de la personne & des droits de la jeunesse) c Montréal (Ville)*, 2000 SCC 27 at para. 82, [2000] 1 SCR 665.
62. See MacNeill, *supra* note 30 at 13-77-13-78, 16-2, 17-1, 18-2, 20-1.
63. See e.g., *Korkola v. Maid Day! Maid Day! Inc*, 2013 HRTO 525; *UNA, Local 121-R v. Calgary District Hospital Group* (1994), 36 CLAS 70, 41 LAC (4th) 319 (Alta Arb Bd); *Greater Niagara General Hospital v. ONA* (1995), 40 CLAS 506, 50 LAC (4th) 34 (Ont Arb Bd).
64. *Shuswap Lake General Hospital and BCNU (Lockie), Re* (2002), 67 CLAS 264, 2002 CarswellBC 3994 (WL Can) (Arb Bd).
65. *Kemess Mines Ltd v. IUOE, Local 115* (2005), 139 LAC (4th) 305, 81 CLAS 154 (BC Arb Bd).

physical disabilities may require employers to provide mechanical lifting devices,[66] ergonomic chairs,[67] hearing aids,[68] or lumbar support braces.[69]

§2.05 AN ACCOMMODATED WORKPLACE FOR AGE

There are relatively few instances in which adverse employment impacts on the basis of age per se can be justified as BFORs. Age is seldom in and of itself relevant to the requirements of an occupation or to the ability of an employer to compensate an employee for work. Rather, it is reductions in physical and mental capacity that may be associated with age that are relevant to such matters. Since such capacities may vary widely among individuals at any given age, limiting the opportunities of employees based on age will often amount to stereotyping that cannot be legally justified as reasonably necessary. As a general matter, it is widely accepted that decisions to afford or deny opportunities to aging or younger workers must be based on individualized assessment.[70] Thus, for example, mandatory retirement of school bus drivers at age 65 constituted discrimination on the basis age.[71] Legislatures across Canada have responded to the logic of such arguments, and to political pressures inherent in an aging population by removing exceptions in anti-discrimination law that previously permitted mandatory retirement (usually at age 65). Nonetheless, mandatory retirement remains permissible under anti-discrimination law's *Meiorin* test where an employer can demonstrate that individualized assessment would pose an undue hardship. As noted above, a number of decisions involving firefighters have upheld mandatory retirement at age 60.[72] One court has also suggested that mandatory retirement at age 60 might constitute a BFOR where later retirement dates would have a substantial negative impact on the career earnings potential of younger employees, under a seniority-based career progression compensation system.[73]

§2.06 FAMILY STATUS AND FAMILY RESPONSIBILITIES

In Canada, family status is a protected ground under the human rights codes of all jurisdictions except those of two provinces.[74] Equal opportunity without discrimination on the basis of family status protects the ability of family members to meet legally

66. *Air Canada v. IAM & AW* (1998), 53 CLAS 208, 74 LAC (4th) 233 (Arb Bd).
67. *Wernick v. Federal Reserve Bank of New York*, 01 F.3d 379 (2nd Cir. 1996).
68. *Thunder Bay Catholic District School Board v. OECTA* (2011), 106 CLAS 134, 209 LAC (4th) 223 (Ont Arb Bd). See also *Toronto (City) and CUPE, Local 79 (Wilson), Re* (2001), 66 CLAS 117, 2001 CarswellOnt 10096 (WL Can) (Arb Bd).
69. *Chen (Applicant) and Ingenierie Electro-Optique Exfo Inc*, 2009 HRTO 1465, [2009] OHRTD No 1579 (QL).
70. For a general discussion, see Pnina Alon-Shenker (CLELJ).
71. *Mortland v. Peace Wapiti School Division No 76*, 2015 AHRC 9, 2015 CLLC 230-038.
72. *Espey*, *supra* note 43. See also *Dairy Pool*, *supra* note 18 (although the standard at issue was found not to be bona fide occupational requirement, the result of that case turned on the lack of evidence rather than the illegitimacy of the claim that the evidence was adduced to support).
73. *Adamson v. Air Canada*, 2014 FC 83, 13 CCEL (4th) 1.
74. Tarnopolsky, *supra* note 7 at 12-3-12-6.

mandated or otherwise essential care-giving responsibilities towards one's children or aging parents.[75] Further, pregnancy and childbirth discrimination are either explicitly prohibited or recognized as sex discrimination in all jurisdictions.[76]

Accordingly, employers have a duty to accommodate pregnancy and family care-giving responsibilities of employees. Meeting this duty can entail providing leaves of absence, modified schedules or modified duties up to the point of undue hardship on the employer. For example, parents of young children may be relieved of rotating day and night shifts, or other shift schedules that prevent them from obtaining child care during their working hours.[77]

§2.07 BEYOND REASONABLE ACCOMMODATION

In Canada there are relatively few legal requirements for accommodation beyond those imposed by anti-discrimination law. Such requirements are found in three sources: (1) minimum employment standards; (2) workers' compensation laws applying in cases of work-related illness or injury; and (3) recent statutes requiring employers to proactively enhance the accessibility of work for persons with disabilities. Each is briefly surveyed below.

[A] Employment Standards

Employment standards legislation in all Canadian jurisdictions entitles employees to at least fifteen weeks of unpaid leave for pregnancy, thirty-five weeks of such leave during the first year of the life of a child by birth or following an adoption, and eight weeks of such leave to care for a family member who has a serious medical condition with a significant risk of death within twenty-six weeks.[78] This latter form of leave is commonly referred to as compassionate care leave. Canada's unemployment insurance system provides a basic level of income support during such periods of leave, a level to which employers may add voluntarily or by contract.

In addition, employment standards statutes in most Canadian jurisdictions provide employees with entitlements to leave ranging between three and twelve days for family responsibilities including attending to the needs of family members purposes range between days.[79]

75. *Francis Lyndon Devaney v. ZRV Holdings Limited and Zeidler Partnership Architect*, 2012 HRTO 1590, 75 CHRR D/142; *Hoyt v. Canadian National Railway*, 2006 CHRT 33, 2006 CLLC 230-035; *Seeley v. Canadian National Railway*, 2014 FCA 111, 15 CCEL (4th) 324; *Johnstone, supra* note 29.
76. Tarnopolsky, *supra* note 7 at 12-3-12-6; *Brooks v. Canada Safeway Ltd*, [1989] 1 SCR 1219, 59 DLR (4th) 321.
77. *SMS Equipment Inc v. CEP, Local 707*, 2015 ABQB 162, 250 ACWS (3d) 329.
78. Richard N. Block, 'Work-Family Legislation in the United States, Canada, and Western Europe: A Quantitative Comparison' (2007) 34:2 Pepp L Rev 333 at 347.
79. By way of exception, Saskatchewan and Quebec provide up to twelve weeks of leave without pay for family and medical purposes, while Alberta, Nunavut, the Yukon and Northwest Territories and the federal jurisdiction provide none at all. *Ibid.*

Outside the first year of child rearing, the Canadian legislative fabric clearly leaves a gap between compassionate care leave and the relatively short periods of leave available for other family medical or other caring responsibilities. As a result employees may increasingly have recourse to the duty to accommodate in cases of conflict between work and family responsibilities.

In most jurisdictions employment standards legislation provides also employees with access to between three and twelve days of leave without pay in the case of illness.[80] This modest level of protection leaves employees who cannot characterize their temporary illness as a disability and whose employers have rigid attendance requirements legally vulnerable to dismissal.

[B] Workers' Compensation Statutes

In several jurisdictions workers' compensation statutes impose on employers positive obligations to assist employees with injuries or illnesses arising out of or in the course of employment to return to work as soon as they are ready to do so.[81] These obligations are similar to those imposed by the duty to accommodate, but may also include cooperating with case workers tasked by government operated workplace safety and insurance agencies with seeking to return injured workers to active employment. From the employee's perspective these provisions have the advantage of being proactively administered rather than requiring a complaint to a human rights tribunal for enforcement.

[C] Accessibility Statutes

There is little legislation in Canada systematically requiring employers to proactively change their hiring and employment practices to remove barriers to equal opportunity. Accessibility Standards established by regulation under the *Accessibility for Ontarians with Disabilities Act* require employers to:

80. Notable exceptions include the federal jurisdiction, Saskatchewan, and Quebec, which provide up to 12, 12 and 26 weeks of unpaid sick leave respectively. *Ibid.*
81. The federal jurisdiction, Manitoba, Ontario, Quebec, Yukon, Nova Scotia, New Brunswick, Prince Edward Island and Newfoundland and Labrador impose a statutory obligation on employers to return injured employees to work. All except Quebec exclude employees with less than a year's service with the employer from the statutory protection. Ontario, Nova Scotia, Prince Edward Island, Newfoundland and Labrador and the Yukon exempt employers employing less than twenty employees; New Brunswick exempts employers employing less than ten employees; Manitoba exempts employers employing fewer than twenty-five employees. See *Workplace Safety and Insurance Act, 1997*, SO 1997, c 16, s 41 (for Ontario); *Workers' Compensation Act*, SNS 1994-95, c 10 ss 89-101 (for Nova Scotia); *Workers' Compensation Act*, RSNB 1973, c W-13, s 42.1 (for New Brunswick); *Workers Compensation Act*, SPEI 1994, c 67, s 86.1-86.12 (for Prince Edward Island); *Workplace Health, Safety and Compensation Act*, RSN 1990, c W-11, s 89-89.4 (for Newfoundland and Labrador); *The Workers Compensation Act*, RSM 1987, c W200, s 49.3 (for Manitoba); *An Act Respecting Industrial Accidents and Occupational Diseases*, CQLR c A-3.001 (for Quebec), Schedule II, ss 32, 234, 251; *Canada Labour Code*, RSC 1985, c L-2, s 239.1 (for the federal jurisdiction); *Canada Labour Standards Regulations*, CRC, c 986, s 34.

(1) notify employees and the public about the availability of accommodation for applicants with disabilities in their recruitment processes;
(2) notify job applicants, when they are individually selected to participate in an assessment or selection process, that accommodations are available upon request in relation to the materials or processes to be used;
(3) when making offers of employment, notify the successful applicant of its policies for accommodating employees with disabilities;
(4) inform employees of its policies used to support its employees with disabilities, including, but not limited to, policies on the provision of job accommodations that take into account an employee's accessibility needs due to disability;
(5) at the request of an employee consult with the employee to provide or arrange for the provision of accessible formats and communication supports for:
    (a) information that is needed in order to perform the employee's job; and
    (b) information that is generally available to employees in the workplace.
(6) develop and have in place a written process for the development of documented individual accommodation plans for employees with disabilities;
(7) develop and have in place a return to work process for its employees who have been absent from work due to a disability and require disability-related accommodations in order to return to work.[82]

The government of Manitoba is working to establish employment accessibility standards under the *Accessibility for Manitobans Act*.[83] The Employment Equity Act in the federal jurisdiction requires employers to identify and eliminate employment barriers against persons in designated groups (women, aboriginal peoples, persons with disabilities and members of visible minorities) that result from the employer's employment systems, policies and practices. It also requires them to institute positive policies and practices and make reasonable accommodations to ensure that persons in designated groups achieve a degree of representation in each occupational group in the employer's workforce that reflects their representation in the Canadian workforce, or in those segments of the Canadian workforce that are identifiable by qualification, eligibility or geography and from which the employer may reasonably be expected to draw employees.[84]

§2.08 CONCLUDING OBSERVATIONS

In a paper published in 2013, two colleagues and I found that that about 35% of employed persons with disability in Canada do not receive needed accommodations, and that the causes of the problem are often systemic but quite likely preventable. Likely causes included lack of information, stereotyping, rules and norms that

82. See O Reg 191/11, ss 20-32.
83. CCSM c A1.7.
84. *Employment Equity Act*, SC 1995, c 44, s 5.

unnecessarily disadvantage persons with disability, and the allocation of accommodation costs to private employers unwilling to assume them.

We also concluded that there are good reasons to believe that anti-discrimination law's reach is insufficient to ensure that Canadians with disabilities can count on receiving needed accommodation at work. Determining whether an anti-discrimination statute has been violated can be very complex and therefore time-consuming and expensive.[85] Relatively few workers are likely to have the financial and emotional resources to pursue a complaint, particularly where discrimination occurs at the point of hire, as hiring and pay gap studies suggest it often does.[86] Relatively few non-unionized employees are willing to challenge their employer by bringing a complaint during the life of the employment relationship, for fear of reprisals of various types.[87]

Two major public reviews of human rights enforcement, in Ontario in 1992 and in the federal jurisdiction in 2001, concluded that the complaint-driven model was an out-dated and ineffective way of addressing forms of discrimination that are systemic - that is, embedded in pervasive economic incentives, or in cultural stereotypes or workplace norms, rather than being individual acts of prejudice.[88] Both of those reports went on to recommend other options (most of which were not implemented), as did the Organization for Economic Co-operation and Development in a recent report on Canada's approach to integrating persons with disabilities into the workforce.[89]

Canada's experience with the duty to accommodate offers important insights into the centrality of reasonable accommodation to genuine equality of opportunity. It demonstrates the possibility and the implications of implementing reasonable accommodation of a wide range of intrinsic personal characteristics and choices fundamental to human dignity through employer obligation and duties. But Canadians might well

85. A range of factors must be considered in determining whether accommodation has to be provided, including the employee's physical and mental abilities, potential effects on health and safety, 'financial cost, disruption of a collective agreement, problems of morale of other employees, [and] interchangeability of work force and facilities' (*Dairy Pool, supra note* 18 at para. 439). See Jean R Sternlight, 'In Search of the Best Procedure for Enforcing Employment Discrimination Laws: A Comparative Analysis' (2004) 78 Tulane L Rev 1401 (for a good discussion of the difficulties that such complex factors pose for the adjudication of human rights claims).
86. See Banks et al, *supra* note 2.
87. See Canada, Federal Labour Standards Review Commission, *Fairness At Work: Labour Standards for the 21st Century* (Ottawa: HRSDC, 2006) at chap 9, s 2a (for a notation that that '92% of all complaints under Part III were filed by workers who were no longer employed in the same workplace. This striking statistic suggests that some workers are so concerned that they will be fired that they abandon their statutory rights'). See also Ian B Mackenzie, 'Legal Rights for Persons with Disabilities in Canada: Can the Impasse Be Resolved?' (1997) 29 Ottawa L Rev 153 at 177; Catherine R Albiston, 'Mobilizing Employment Rights in the Workplace' in Laura Beth Nielson & Robert L Nelson (eds), *Handbook of Employment Discrimination Research* (New York: Springer, 2008) 301 at 304.
88. Ontario Human Rights Code Review Task Force, *Achieving Equality: A Report on Human Rights Reform* (Toronto: Ontario Human Rights Commission, 1992); Canadian Human Rights Act Review Panel, *Report of the Canadian Human Rights Review Panel* (Ottawa: Canadian Human Rights Act Review Panel, 2001).
89. See Organisation for Economic Co-Operation and Development, *Sickness, Disability and Work: Breaking the Barriers* (OECD, 2010) at chap 5-6 (for the recommendations).

look abroad for additional and innovative approaches to implementing reasonable accommodation. They might in particular learn from legal systems treating reasonable accommodation as an objective to foster through public policy programmes supporting proactive adaptation of workplaces so as to reasonably accommodate employees.

CHAPTER 3

Reasonable Accommodation in Australia: Displacing the Normative Worker?

Anna Chapman

§3.01 INTRODUCTION

Like many Western countries, Australia has a breadwinner tradition within Australian law, workplace cultures and arrangements, as well as the domestic sphere. The Australian breadwinner framework has its origins most obviously in a 1907 court decision in which the basic (or minimum) wage in Australia was set according to the needs of the average labourer, who was conceptualised as a male breadwinner providing financial support to himself, his homemaker wife and children.[1]

Scholarship has shown how this breadwinner/homemaker framework became normative in the Australian labour law system for most of the twentieth century. This structure can be revealed at various points within Australian labour law, including the setting of a lower female basic wage in 1919 on the assumption that women workers were single and childless, and supported themselves alone.[2] A breadwinner/homemaker norm is also apparent in debates during the first half of the twentieth century regarding the reduction of standard working hours. The underlying assumption in these debates was that a worker's waking hours were spent either in labour market engagement or in leisure. No calculation was made for the worker to

1. *Ex parte H V McKay* (1907) 2 CAR 1 (known as the Harvester decision).
2. Rosemary Hunter, 'Women Workers and Federal Industrial Law: From *Harvester* to Comparable Worth' (1988) 1 *Australian Journal of Labour Law* 147; Anna Chapman, 'Work/Family, Australian Labour Law, and the Normative Worker', in Joanne Conaghan and Kerry Rittich (eds), *Labour Law, Work and Family: Critical and Comparative Perspectives*, Oxford University Press, 2005, 79.

spend time on domestic and care responsibilities, as these were assumed to be attended to by his homemaker wife.[3]

In these various ways the paradigmatic worker of Australian labour law was gendered male, and without substantial care responsibilities. Sandra Berns has identified him as the 'unencumbered' worker.[4] He was conceptualised as being in a full-time permanent employment relationship from his young adult years until retirement. He was not seen as having any need for adjustment to his working arrangements due to, for example, his responsibilities to care for children, or his disability. Indeed, the workplace, workplace cultures and legal frameworks, were all designed and developed over the course of the twentieth century around his work patterns, abilities and domestic arrangements.

Legal developments in Australia over the last ten years or so potentially challenge the normativity of the vision of the standard worker of the Australian labour law framework, and of collective work relations. Since 2005 a number of legal mechanisms have developed through which a worker can seek to have adjustments made to their individual work arrangements. Modifications might include, for example, an alteration in hours of work in order to accommodate a worker's responsibilities to care for children or an elderly relative, or that an employer provide special computer equipment or additional training for a worker with a disability. The most firmly established right to reasonable accommodation relates to the attribute of disability, where workers with a disability have a legal right across Australia to expect that their employer will provide them with adjustments in their working arrangements to the extent that such accommodation is reasonable. Less well recognised in the Australian legal system is a right to reasonable adjustment in relation to being a parent or carer. There is also a right to request (but not an enforceable right to receive), reasonable accommodation that arises due to the worker being of an older age, or because he or she is experiencing domestic violence. No explicit statutory obligation exists anywhere in Australia to provide reasonable accommodation in relation to religion or belief.

These developments in the last ten years or so prompt questions about whether the post 2005 mechanisms of reasonable accommodation have the capacity to dislodge the legatee of the breadwinner tradition from his central role in Australian law and workplace relations. Does the mechanism of adjustment itself suggest a further entrenching of the normativity of existing arrangements? As Sara Charlesworth has written, claims by workers for reasonable accommodation focus on the 'individual "special" needs' of the worker, and the '"lack of fit"' of the 'individual worker with a seemingly fixed organisation of work'.[5] Law focuses on the worker's particular circumstances and the accommodation they seek, and not only might this deflect attention away from the ways in which the existing arrangements are based on a model of an unencumbered and abled subject worker, it may further entrench that model as

---

3. Anna Chapman, 'Industrial Law, Working Hours, and Work, Care and Family' (2010) 36 *Monash University Law Review* 190.
4. Sandra Berns, *Women Going Backwards: Law and Change in a Family Unfriendly Society*, Ashgate Publishing, 2002.
5. Sara Charlesworth, 'Managing Work and the Family in the "Shadow" of Anti-discrimination Law' (2005) 23 *Law in Context* 88 at 90.

normative. Existing arrangements are always the benchmark from which the worker's difference is measured and the assessment of reasonable accommodation is made.

These are ambitious questions, and they are not able to be fully addressed in this chapter. However, it is shown in this chapter that although on their face, the Australian legal mechanisms look to offer important potential, they are beset by weaknesses, particularly in relation to their enforcement, and that these weaknesses seriously undermine the ability of the Australian reasonable adjustment mechanisms to displace the remaining vestiges of the breadwinner tradition of the twentieth century, in favour of a fully subjective vision of the worker.

The Australian legal developments of reasonable accommodation have taken place within two separate spheres of Australian law - anti-discrimination law and labour law. These two fields of legal regulation have separate traditions within the Australian system and perhaps surprisingly, developments in one sphere have not tended to greatly influence legal change in the other sphere. This may explain the piece-meal character of the different Australian initiatives on reasonable adjustment. This chapter examines each of these fields of law in turn, commencing with anti-discrimination law. Anti-discrimination law in Australia exists at both the Commonwealth (or national) level, as well as at the State and Territory level. The Commonwealth level is examined first.

§3.02 ANTI-DISCRIMINATION LAW

[A] Commonwealth Level

The only anti-discrimination statute at the Commonwealth level that contains an explicit obligation on employers to provide reasonable adjustments to workers is the Disability Discrimination Act 1992 (Cth) (DDA). As the title of the DDA indicates, the duty applies in relation to disability, which is broadly defined in the Act.[6] There is no obligation at the Commonwealth level to reasonably accommodate in relation to, for example, care or family responsibilities, or any other attribute such as age, religion or belief.[7]

The duty to provide reasonable adjustment came into the DDA scheme after its enactment, and only after some false starts. As enacted in 1992, the DDA did not contain an explicit requirement on employers to reasonably accommodate the needs of workers with disabilities. However some early decisions of tribunals and courts

6. DDA s 4 definition of 'disability'; Lee Ann Basser and Melinda Jones, 'The Disability Discrimination Act 1992 (Cth): A Three Dimensional Approach to Operationalising Human Rights' (2002) 26 *Melbourne University Law Review* 254 at 261.
7. Recommendations have been made to amend the Sex Discrimination Act 1984 (Cth) to enact a duty on employers to reasonably accommodate a worker's care responsibilities and pregnancy, but these recommendations have not be actioned by the government: Senate Standing Committee on Legal and Constitutional Affairs, House of Representatives, *Effectiveness of the Sex Discrimination Act 1984 in Eliminating Discrimination and Promoting Gender Equality*, 2008, recommendation 14; Australian Human Rights Commission, *Supporting Working Parents: Pregnancy and Return to Work National Review - Report*, 2014, 12.

interpreted the Act as implicitly imposing such an obligation on employers.[8] That approach though was cast into doubt by Australia's highest court in the 2003 decision of *Purvis v. New South Wales*. In this case the High Court appeared to express the view that the concept of discrimination in the DDA at that time did not require positive action, or reasonable accommodation, by an employer.[9]

For a number of reasons *Purvis v. New South Wales* received considerable legal and public attention, and in the following year the Commonwealth government referred the DDA to the Productivity Commission for review. The Productivity Commission is a government-funded independent research and advisory body, staffed largely by Commissioners with backgrounds in economics. From this perspective the Commission made a strong recommendation in favour of the introduction of a duty of reasonable adjustment into the DDA:

> The Commission considers that substantive equality is a sound basis for disability discrimination legislation. It therefore endorses the concept of reasonable adjustment as a means to this end, and recommends that it be included explicitly in the Act as a stand alone duty. This would mean that failure to provide reasonable adjustment could itself be unlawful discrimination and the subject of a complaint.
>
> ...
>
> The Commission considers that the task of eliminating discrimination cannot he adequately addressed in the absence of a duty to make reasonable adjustments. If disability discrimination legislation only went as far as formal equality, it would entrench existing disadvantages.[10]

A few years after the Commission handed down its report a Labor government was elected federally and two years later in 2009 a number of amendments were made to the DDA, one of which was to the effect that a failure to make reasonable adjustments can amount to discrimination.[11] The drafting of the 2009 amendments embedded this positive duty, rather clumsily, in both the prohibition on direct discrimination and the prohibition on indirect discrimination.[12] It was not drafted as a stand-alone duty, as the Productivity Commission had recommended. The new rules provide that direct discrimination is prohibited where the employer does not make 'reasonable adjustments' for a worker with a disability, and the failure to make the reasonable adjustments had the effect that the worker was treated less favourably than a person without the disability in similar circumstances.[13] Indirect discrimination is prohibited where a person with a disability cannot comply with a condition or

8. See e.g., *McNeill v. Commonwealth of Australia* (1995) EOC 92-714; *Randell v. Consolidated Bearing Co (SA) Pty Ltd* [2002] FMCA 44.
9. *Purvis v. New South Wales* (2003) 217 CLR 92 at 105-6, 127 (McHugh and Kirby JJ); 155 and 159 (Gummow, Hayne and Heydon JJ).
10. Productivity Commission, Australian Government, *Review of the Disability Discrimination Act 1992*, Report No 30 (2004), Overview, pp XL-XLI, 193.
11. DDA s 5(2), s 6(2).
12. Belinda Smith, 'Fair and Equal in the World of Work: Two Significant Federal Developments in Australian Discrimination Law' (2010) 23 *Australian Journal of Labour Law* 199 at 205; Therese MacDermott, 'Affirming Age: Making Federal Anti-discrimination Regulation Work for Older Australians' (2013) 26 *Australian Journal of Labour Law* 141 at 145.
13. DDA s 5(2).

requirement unless the employer makes 'reasonable adjustments' and the employer's failure to do so disadvantages the person with a disability.[14] The DDA provides a defence (in relation to both direct and indirect discrimination) where an employer is able to establish that the worker could not perform the 'inherent requirements' of the position, even after reasonable adjustments have been provided.[15]

The Explanatory Memorandum released by Parliament to explain these 2009 amendments to the DDA asserted that the Bill's new positive duty to make reasonable adjustments is consistent with the requirement of reasonable accommodation in the UN Convention on the Rights of Persons with Disabilities (CRPD).[16] This Convention had been ratified by the Australian government in 2008, and was used to provide constitutional support for the 2009 amendments.

The DDA identifies that 'reasonable adjustments' are all adjustments that do not impose an 'unjustifiable hardship' on the employer.[17] In making this assessment, 'all relevant circumstances of the particular case must be taken into account', including the following matters:

(a) the nature of the benefit or detriment likely to accrue to, or to be suffered by, any person concerned;[18]
(b) the effect of the disability of any person concerned;
(c) the financial circumstances, and the estimated amount of expenditure required to be made, by the [employer];
(d) the availability of financial and other assistance to the [employer];
(e) any relevant action plans given to the Commission under section 64.[19]

It is clear that the DDA requires a balancing process of weighing up various matters. Factors to be taken into account go beyond financial considerations, and involve balancing the respective rights and interests of the worker, the employer and more broadly, 'any person concerned'.[20] The concept of unjustifiable hardship itself suggests that some hardship will be justifiable and will not enliven the defence. As Belinda Smith points out, 'it is the net cost – gross costs of adjustments less financial or other assistance and benefit that might accrue to the employer and others including the community – that would need to be unjustifiable in all the circumstances.'[21] The onus

14. DDA s 6(2). It is not indirect discrimination if the requirement or condition is reasonable, having regard to the circumstances of the case: s 6(3).
15. DDA s 21A(1)(b). In such circumstances the employer is lawfully entitled to discriminate against the worker.
16. Commonwealth Parliament, *Explanatory Memorandum to the Disability Discrimination and Other Human Rights Legislation Amendment Bill 2008*, [35], [39].
17. DDA s 4.
18. A legislative note to s 11(1) states: 'Example: One of the circumstances covered by paragraph (1)(a) is the nature of the benefit or detriment likely to accrue to, or to be suffered by, the community.'
19. DDA s 11(1). Part 3 of the DDA provides that certain employers may, if they choose to do so, prepare and lodge an Action Plan with the Australian Human Rights Commission in order to achieve the objectives of the Act.
20. DDA s 11(1)(a).
21. Smith above n 12, at 207.

is on the employer to establish the 'unjustifiable hardship' defence where it wishes to rely on it.[22] This appears to create in practice a presumption that an adjustment will be reasonable unless the employer proves otherwise.

On their face these provisions may appear to have significant potential to displace the normative worker who does not have a disability. They enact Australia's international responsibilities under the Convention on the Rights of Persons with Disabilities, and articulate the key legal obligation to provide 'reasonable adjustments' through a broadly worded concept of 'unjustifiable hardship'. There are limitations though. Importantly, the drafting of the obligation to provide reasonable adjustments as embedded within both direct and indirect discrimination is awkward and unwieldy, especially to those unfamiliar with the jurisdiction. In addition, several scholars have provided strong critiques of the enforcement structures of anti-discrimination law, and these criticisms apply equally to the DDA.[23] The process of pursuing a claim is slow, and the financial and psychological pressures on a claimant are great. There is no public enforcement agency in anti-discrimination law, and trade unions may have limited resources to assist a worker with their claim. In addition, where workers pursue their claim to court and are unsuccessful, they face the very real possibility that they may be required to pay the employer's legal costs.[24]

Most claims under the DDA do not proceed to a hearing on their merits, with the majority settling through a process of conciliation conducted by the Australian Human Rights Commission (AHRC).[25] Conciliation outcomes are confidential. Anecdotally some lawyers express the view that conciliation potentially leads to large payments in favour of workers, and this is especially so where the employer faces a reputational loss should the claim proceed to a public forum. Given the nature of the claim process, successful outcomes may be highly individualised rather than systemic.

In research conducted for this chapter less than a half a dozen court decisions were identified that were hearings on their merits regarding an alleged contravention of the 2009 reasonable adjustments provisions in the DDA in the context of work relations. The fact that so few decisions appear to have been handed down on the 2009 reasonable adjustments provisions suggests that workers may face a number of inbuilt headwinds in pursuing their claims to court.

Of the decisions that have been made, two stand out. In both the claimants were successful, with one claimant receiving a substantial damages order of approximately AUD 175,000.[26] For these two resilient workers who successfully pursued their claims

22. DDA s 11(2).
23. See e.g., Beth Gaze and Rosemary Hunter, *Enforcing Human Rights: An Evaluation of the New Regime*, Themis Press, 2010; Dominique Allen, 'Behind the Conciliation Doors: Settling Discrimination Complaints in Victoria' (2009) 18 *Griffith Law Review* 776.
24. Neil Rees, Simon Rice and Dominique Allen, *Australian Anti-Discrimination Law*, Federation Press, 2014, [13.10.1]ff.
25. Australian Human Rights Commission, *Annual Report 2013-2014*, 2014, 132.
26. *Huntley v. State of NSW* [2015] FCCA 1827. This figure comprised AUD 75,000 for pain and suffering and breach of contract plus approximately AUD 100,000 for loss of wages, other monetary work entitlements, loss of promotion opportunities and medical costs. In *Watts v. Australian Postal Corporation* (2014) 222 FCR 220 the judge indicated she would award AUD 10,000 for pain and suffering, and left it to the parties to draft orders to compensate for the

to a hearing, the outcomes suggest that the 2009 DDA reasonable adjustment provisions have caused the normative (non-disabled) worker to be displaced, at least in relation to their employment arrangements at that time. One of these decisions - *Watts v. Australian Postal Corporation* - provides a good example of this. The case was brought by a worker who had suffered a psychological injury during the course of her employment as a manager with the Australian Postal Corporation (Australia Post). Due to this injury she had spent a considerable amount of time away from the workplace on leave, and then returned to restricted duties. While Watts was on restricted duties, Australia Post required her to provide evidence as to whether she was fit to return to her management position, and if so, what modifications might be required to allow her to do so. Australia Post was not satisfied with the report that Watts provided from her psychologist, and it directed her to take sick leave and not attend for work. At the hearing Australia Post asserted that it was not satisfied that Watts was fit to perform the role of manager, and no adjustments that were reasonable would allow her to do so.

In reaching a judgment in favour of Watts the court drew on the Convention on the Rights of Persons with Disabilities and the Productivity Commission report that lead to the 2009 amendments, and especially the idea that the amendments are aimed at achieving substantive equality for people with disabilities. The court determined that there was much that Australia Post could have done by way of reasonable adjustment for Watts, without causing unjustifiable hardship to itself. For example, it could have limited her working hours, altered her supervision arrangements, modified the requirements for face-to-face meetings, and ameliorated deadlines that were too tight. In addition, Australia Post could have made changes to the kind of work Watts performed, including minimising conflict situations and not requiring her to lead teams. The evidence was that Watts required adjustments for approximately three months only.[27]

Notably *Watts v. Australian Postal Corporation* involved a Commonwealth government statutory agency. The other successful claim by a worker – in *Huntley v. State of NSW* – was brought against a state government. In these two cases, against large government employer organisations, the courts did require a relatively high level of investigation, careful consideration and then action by the employer to bring about alterations and modifications for the worker with a disability. For the two claimants, the 2009 DDA reasonable adjustment rules did provide a mechanism that displaced, in that claimant's employment arrangements, the normative vision of the abled subject worker of Australian law. In addition, the impact of these two decisions may extend beyond the two claimants, as court outcomes are likely to shape settlements reached in conciliation.

[B] State and Territory Anti-discrimination Law

In relation to the attribute of disability, State and Territory anti-discrimination statutes largely mirror the Commonwealth DDA in their legislative form. All Acts contain

claimant's economic loss. There is no further order in this litigation, suggesting that the parties settled the matter after the judgment on the merits of the claim was handed down.

27. *Watts v. Australian Postal Corporation* (2014) 222 FCR 220 [229].

variously worded provisions that require employers to make reasonable adjustment for workers with a disability. Most of these State and Territory anti-discrimination statutes articulate the limits of the accommodation required through a concept of 'unjustifiable hardship', or a related term.[28]

Leaving aside the attribute of disability, State and Territory anti-discrimination legislation is not consistent on the obligations of employers to provide reasonable accommodation or adjustment for workers. The Acts differ in their approach and scope.

Some State and Territory anti-discrimination statutes have been interpreted to require reasonable accommodation in relation to the attributes of being a parent or having care responsibilities. For example, the Anti-Discrimination Act of New South Wales appears to impose an obligation on employers to provide some level of accommodation in relation to care responsibilities. This arises through the context of indirect discrimination claims, where the New South Wales tribunal has interpreted the Act to require employers to at least consider and sometimes to make reasonable efforts to accommodate an employee's request to alter their work arrangements for care reasons.[29]

Two Acts stand apart from other State and Territory anti-discrimination legislation on the duty to accommodate. They are the Northern Territory Act and the Victorian Act. The Anti-Discrimination Act of the Northern Territory is the broadest in Australia in terms of coverage. It imposes an obligation on employers to provide reasonable accommodation in relation to 'a special need that [a] person has because of an attribute', and does so in relation to all attributes covered in the Act.[30] This statute is unique in Australia in requiring accommodation on a full range of discriminatory criteria.[31] Notably though, there are no decisions on these unique Northern Territory rules, indicating that they have not been argued before a tribunal or court.

The Victorian Equal Opportunity Act is also worthy of examination as it contains the most fully articulated accommodation requirements of all State and Territory legislation.[32] The scheme requires reasonable accommodation for parents and carers (enacted in 2008) and reasonable accommodation in relation to disability (from

28. See e.g., Anti-Discrimination Act 1977 (NSW) s 49D; Equal Opportunity Act 1984 (WA) s 66Q; Anti-Discrimination Act 1998 (Tas) s 45.
29. See e.g., *Tleyji v. The TravelSpirit Group Pty Ltd* [2005] NSWADT 294 [105]; *Reddy v. International Cargo Express* [2004] NSWADT 218 [84].
30. Anti-Discrimination Act 1992 (NT) s 24, s 58. See also s 35(1)(b)(ii) on 'inherent requirements' of the work.
31. The attributes in this Act are: race, sex, sexuality, age, marital status, pregnancy, parenthood, breastfeeding, impairment, trade union or employer association activity, religious belief or activity, political opinion, affiliation or activity, irrelevant medical record, association with a person who has one of these attributes: Anti-Discrimination Act 1992 (NT) s 19(1).
32. In addition, the Equal Opportunity Act 2010 (Vic) (EO Act) contains a limited positive duty on employers to take 'reasonable and proportionate' measures to eliminate discrimination: s 15. This is not enforced through a complaint process. Rather, the Victorian Equal Opportunity & Human Rights Commission may conduct an investigation. At the time of writing it does not appear that the Commission has conducted any such investigations.

2010).[33] These provisions are stand-alone protections, and are independent of, and additional to, any claim of direct or indirect discrimination.[34] They are bolstered by the enactment of new legislative objectives in 2010 which cite that a purpose of the Victorian Act is to bring about 'substantive equality'.[35] In this sense the accommodation requirements in the Victorian Equal Opportunity Act appear to be the most clearly and strongly expressed of all Australian anti-discrimination statutes.

A slightly different drafting approach has been taken in each set of provisions. In relation to parental or care responsibilities, the Act provides that an employer must not, in relation to the 'work arrangements' of the worker, 'unreasonably refuse to accommodate the responsibilities that the [claimant] has as a parent or carer'.[36] As for disability, the Act requires that an employer make 'reasonable adjustments' for a worker with a disability who requires adjustments 'in order to perform the genuine and reasonable requirements of the employment'.[37] A defence exists in relation to the attribute of disability. It arises where the worker 'could not or cannot adequately perform the genuine and reasonable requirements of the employment even after the adjustments are made'.[38]

Both sets of provisions use the concept of reasonableness to delineate the scope of an employer's obligation to accommodate. In coming to an assessment of reasonableness, the Act requires that all relevant facts and circumstances must be considered, in addition to a list of matters. The list of factors in relation to both parental or care responsibilities and disability is very similar, and is similar to the list in the DDA: the worker's circumstances and their needs; the nature of the worker's role; the nature of the adjustment or arrangement that is needed in order to accommodate the worker; the size and nature of the workplace and the organisation; the financial circumstances of the employer; the impact of making the adjustment on other workers (both in terms of benefit and disadvantage); any potential impact on efficiency, productivity and

33. A review into the Victorian Equal Opportunity Act recommended that Victoria follow the lead of the 2009 changes to the DDA, and of the 2004 Productivity Commission report: Julian Gardner, *An Equality Act for a Fairer Victoria: Equal Opportunity Review Final Report*, 2008, 89-94.
34. EO Act s 7(1). The 2010 Act replaced a 1995 Act of the same title.
35. EO Act s 3. In addition, the Charter of Human Rights and Responsibilities Act 2006 (Vic) (Charter) provides that all Victorian legislation must, so far as is possible consistently with its purpose, be interpreted in a way that is compatible with the human rights set out in the Charter. These rights include equality before the law, and the 'right to enjoy ... human rights without discrimination', and the right to 'equal and effective protection against discrimination' (Charter s 8(2), (3)).
36. EO Act s 17, s 19, s 22, s 32. The concept of 'work arrangements' is defined in s 4 to mean arrangements that apply to the worker or that apply in the workplace. The Act provides some illustrative examples: working additional daily hours in return for a shorter working week; occasionally working from home; having a later start time on one day; rescheduling a regular staff meeting; flexible start, finish or break times; and, flexible attendance arrangements: s 17, s 19, s 22, s 32. The concepts of 'parent' and 'carer' are defined in s 4.
37. EO Act s 20(1). The concept of 'disability' is defined in s 4 and is similar to the broad definition that exists under the DDA.
38. EO Act s 20(2), s 23. In such circumstances the employer is lawfully entitled to discriminate against the worker.

customer service; and, the consequences on the worker of not making the adjustment.[39]

This provides for a balancing of interests – of the worker, the employer, other workers and potentially customers as well. It is clear that none of the factors in the list are determinative, and other factors not on the list may be important in particular cases.[40] The Act provides some examples that an employer may be able to reasonably accommodate a worker in relation to their parent or care responsibilities, through altering their hours of work, allowing them to work from home for part of the week, or rescheduling a regular meeting so that they can attend.[41] In relation to disability, the Act provides some illustrative examples of what might be reasonable adjustments: providing a ramp for access to a building; providing a particular software package; modifying work instructions or reference manuals; allowing a person to be absent during work hours for rehabilitation or treatment; and, allowing a person to take breaks more frequently.[42]

Like the DDA, it appears that most claims under the Victorian Equal Opportunity Act are settled confidentially.[43] Notably though, it appears that approximately twice as many claims reach a hearing on their merits under the Victorian reasonable adjustment provisions as reach that stage of litigation under the 2009 DDA provisions. This may be because the Victorian cases relate to both parental and care responsibilities, as well as to disability. In contrast to the outcomes of the fewer DDA cases though, no decisions were identified where claimants were successful under the Victorian adjustment provisions. Workers were unsuccessful for a variety of reasons, including simply that the tribunal weighed up the factors to consider in coming to a view on reasonableness and concluded on the evidence before it that the rejection by the employer was not unreasonable.[44] In one case a worker failed because he had not provided sufficient medical evidence about his disability and its impact on his work.[45] In another case the worker failed to establish that he 'require[d]' adjustment due to his disability (as the Act specified), as the evidence indicated only that the requested adjustment was a good idea and a sensible initiative.[46] In one case on parent and care responsibilities, the tribunal determined that the worker had not made her request for accommodation to

39. EO Act s 17(2); s 20(3), (4).
40. The Explanatory Memorandum to the 2008 Victorian Bill suggested some additional factors: when the proposed work arrangement is to commence, and how long it is to continue; the information that has been provided by the worker regarding her or his circumstances; the accrued entitlements of the worker; and, whether there are any legal constraints effecting the ability of the employer to reorganise the worker's work: Victorian Parliament, *Explanatory Memorandum to the Equal Opportunity Amendment (Family Responsibilities) Act 2008 (Vic)*, 5.
41. EO Act s 19(1).
42. EO Act s 20(2).
43. See e.g., Victorian Equal Opportunity and Human Rights Commission, *Annual Report 2013/2014*, 2014, 24.
44. *Richold v. Department of Justice (Vic)* [2010] VCAT 433; *Tate v. Department of Human Services (Human Rights)* [2015] VCAT 507; *Weber v. Deakin University (Human Rights)* [2014] VCAT 1440.
45. *Muller v. Toll Transport Pty Ltd* [2014] VCAT 472.
46. *Bevilacqua v. Telco Business Solutions (Watergardens) PL (Human Rights)* [2015] VCAT 269.

her employer clearly enough.[47] In relation to disability too, the Victorian tribunal has indicated that workers bear responsibility for articulating their request and the reasons for it clearly enough so that an employer can properly assess the feasibility of accommodating the worker:

> The concept of 'reasonable adjustment' does not mean an employer must simply comply with an employee's demands. It surely must be a product of proper consultation by parties armed with appropriate (in this case) medical information and advice and appropriate knowledge of the genuine and reasonable requirements of the particular job. That much is clear from [the relevant sections] of the Act. It is not for the respondent to work out what is required in an information vacuum. There must be some initiative from the worker. The comprehensive requirements of [the Act] make it clear considerable information is required in determining reasonability – 'all relevant facts and circumstances' must be considered. That obviously requires a proper understanding of the requirements of an employee ... having regard to the nature and specifications of his employment and having regard to the nature and difficulties of his disability.[48]

Although the Victorian Equal Opportunity Act contains the clearest and the strongest requirements on an employer to reasonably accommodate a worker, both in relation to being a parent or other carer as well as in relation to disability, the cases indicate that workers are not faring well in litigation. This appears to be for a number of reasons, including that the concept of reasonableness is being interpreted by the Victorian tribunal in ways that give more weight to the employer's interests than the employee's needs. So, although on paper the Victorian Act appears to offer potential to displace the breadwinner legatee, in practice this set of anti-discrimination rules is more limited.

§3.03 LABOUR LAW

Neither the DDA, nor State and Territory anti-discrimination legislation sets out a procedural framework for a worker to request an adjustment, and then for a process of information, consideration and decision by the employer to follow. As is apparent from the discussion above, this lack of a procedural framework in Victoria has worked against the interests of some workers, who appear to have floundered in knowing how to articulate their request, and what types of information they ought to provide to their employer.[49]

In contrast to anti-discrimination law, Australian labour law does provide a procedural framework for employees to request an adjustment to work arrangements. The origins of the current legislation lie in a 2005 test case brought by the Australian

47. *Richold v. Department of Justice (Vic)* [2010] VCAT 433.
48. *Muller v. Toll Transport Pty Ltd (2)* (Human Rights) [2014] VCAT 472 at [74]. This was applied in *Bevilacqua v. Telco Business Solutions (Watergardens) PL (Human Rights)* [2015] VCAT 269 [204]-[205].
49. *Richold v. Department of Justice (Vic)* [2010] VCAT 433; *Muller v. Toll Transport Pty Ltd (2)* (Human Rights) [2014] VCAT 472.

Council of Trade Unions.[50] In this test case the tribunal granted a limited right to request accommodation, identifying its decision as a 'cautious' one.[51] The provision was that upon return from parental leave following the birth of a child, an employee was entitled to request to move from full-time to part-time work, and this request must be granted unless the employer had 'reasonable grounds' to refuse. In its deliberations the tribunal drew on the United Kingdom right to request scheme. The effects of the decision were short lived, as soon after it was handed down the legislative framework was rewritten in a wide-sweeping manner (by the incoming conservative government) and the practical effect of the test case was largely curtailed.[52]

A Labor government was elected federally in 2008. Under pressure to reinstate the right to request lost through the previous government's legislative changes, a mechanism facilitating employee requests for accommodation of care responsibilities was enacted with the Fair Work Act 2009 (Cth) (FW Act).[53] Under the FW Act, eligible workers may request a change in their 'working arrangements'.[54]

When it was enacted in 2009 this right was initially limited to care responsibilities to pre-school aged children and children under 18 with a disability. It was however extended in 2013 to apply in a broader range of situations.[55] Those broader circumstances cover a wide range of responsibilities to care for others (be they children, family members, friends or other people), and also relates to the worker having a disability, being 55 years of age or older,[56] and where the worker is dealing with a situation of domestic violence.[57] The Act picks up the 2005 test case standard explicitly to provide that in order to avoid doubt, an employee who is returning to work after taking leave in relation to birth or adoption of a child may request to move from full-time to part-time work.[58]

As noted above, and in contrast to anti-discrimination law, the FW Act contains a procedural framework for the process of requesting an adjustment or change, and then the employer considering the request, and providing a response to the employee. Under the FW Act the employee's request must be in writing and set out details of the

50. Parental Leave Test Case 2005 (2005) 143 IR 245.
51. Parental Leave Test Case 2005 (2005) 143 IR 245 [394].
52. Sue Williamson and Marian Baird, 'Family Provisions and Work Choices: Testing Times' (2007) 20 Australian Journal of Labour Law 53. The legislative changes were enacted through the Workplace Relations Amendment (Work Choices) Act 2005 (Cth). This Act amended the then Workplace Relations Act 1996 (Cth).
53. Fair Work Act 2009 (Cth) (FW Act) Part 2-2 Div 4.
54. FW Act s 65(1). The concept of 'working arrangements' is undefined, although the statute provides the following examples: hours of work, patterns of work and location of work.
55. FW Act s 65(1A). Fair Work Amendment Act 2013 (Cth). An extension of care arrangements had been recommended in John Edwards, Ron McCallum and Michael Moore, *Towards More Productive and Equitable Workplaces: An Evaluation of the Fair Work Legislation*, 2012, 99. See also Australian Human Rights Commission (AHRC), Investing in Care: Recognising and Valuing Those Who Care, Vol. 1, Research Report, 2013, 37-38.
56. An extension to older workers was recommended by the Advisory Panel on the Economic Potential of Senior Australians, *Realising the Economic Potential of Senior Australians – Turning Grey into Gold*, 2011, recommendation 15.
57. An extension to family violence situations was recommended in: Australian Law Reform Commission, *Family Violence – Commonwealth Laws, Discussion Paper 76*, 2011, proposal 16-1.
58. FW Act s 65(1B).

changes sought and the reasons for those changes.[59] The Fair Work Ombudsman, which is the inspectorate under the FW Act, publishes on its internet site a very useful template letter of request, with examples of wording, to assist employees. It also produces a best practice guide for employers.[60] The Act requires the employer to provide a written response to the employee's request within twenty-one days, and where the employer refuses the request, the response must include details of the reasons for the refusal.[61] The employer is only entitled to refuse a request on 'reasonable business grounds'.[62] When it was enacted the FW Act contained no further explanation of the meaning of this phrase 'reasonable business grounds'. However the amendments in 2013 introduced a non-exhaustive list of matters that are stated to constitute 'reasonable business grounds':

> (a) that the new working arrangements requested by the employee would be too costly for the employer;
> (b) that there is no capacity to change the working arrangements of other employees to accommodate the new working arrangements requested by the employee;
> (c) that it would be impractical to change the working arrangements of other employees, or recruit new employees, to accommodate the new working arrangements requested by the employee;
> (d) that the new working arrangements requested by the employee would be likely to result in a significant loss in efficiency or productivity;
> (e) that the new working arrangements requested by the employee would be likely to have a significant negative impact on customer service.[63]

Importantly, and unlike the concept of reasonableness in the context of the anti-discrimination law, the FW Act does not appear to envisage a process of balancing the employee's interest in being accommodated against the interests of the employer. Indeed, the employee's interests are absent in this list of 'reasonable business grounds'. The list is simply one of employer concerns. It does not direct employers to take into account the detriment to the employee, and the community, in not providing the accommodation sought. In addition, the legislation uses many open textured tests such as 'too costly', 'impractical' and 'significant negative impact on customer service'. These phrases leave a wide scope of interpretation open to the employer.

The FW Act request mechanism contains an important and substantial limitation. This is that it has a partial enforcement framework only. The obligation on the employer to provide a written response within twenty-one days, and to provide details of the reasons for a refusal, is enforceable under the FW Act. However, the central requirement that an employer is only permitted to reject a request on 'reasonable

59. FW Act s 65(3).
60. See http://www.fairwork.gov.au/employee-entitlements/flexibility-in-the-workplace/flexible-working-arrangements (accessed 9 September 2015).
61. FW Act s 65(4), (6).
62. FW Act s 65(5).
63. FW Act s 65(5A).

business grounds', is not legally challengeable as a contravention of the Act.[64] In other words, the merits of an employer's refusal of a request cannot be reviewed by a tribunal or court.

This lack of legal enforceability of the FW Act right to request is likely to take effect to undermine its capacity to displace the unencumbered able worker of Australian law. In effect, provided employers respond to each request made, and do so within twenty-one days setting out details of their reasons, they are in practice free to reject all requests, however reasonable those requests might objectively be. It must be said though that the limited ability to enforce the statutory right to request is somewhat ameliorated in that some Enterprise Agreements negotiated under the FW Act do contain reasonable accommodation clauses, and a breach of one of those clauses is legally enforceable under the FW Act as a breach of the Enterprise Agreement. It is however unknown how many Enterprise Agreements contain such an accommodation clause, and how widely those clauses are drawn. Even prior to the enactment of the statutory right in 2009 it appears that some employers were granting accommodation to workers, pursuant to, for example, organisational policies on family-friendly initiatives. These issues raise interesting, and as yet unexplored, questions about the interaction of law and practice on this issue in Australian workplaces. It suggests that law is lagging behind employer practices that may be motivated more by the need to attract and retain staff than the legal framework. The impact of all of this on the continuing position of the breadwinner legatee in work organisation and workplace culture is unclear.

§3.04 CONCLUSION

This chapter has explored legal initiatives in Australia over the past ten years or so that provide rights to individual workers to request accommodation in their work arrangements. These mechanisms are tied to the attributes of disability, parent and care responsibilities, and to a more limited extent, being of an older age and experiencing domestic violence. The chapter has shown that each mechanism is beset by limitations and deficiencies that undermine the capacity of the legal framework to displace the normative legatee of the breadwinner tradition. Together the provisions may provide more potential in this regard, as gaps in one scheme, such as the lack of a procedural framework in anti-discrimination law, may be filled by another scheme, such as the right to request under the FW Act. In addition, legislation can play an educative role, establishing the government's statement of desirable employer practices, and this may perform some role in reconceptualising the subject worker and work relationship in Australia. Nonetheless, as the chapter shows, it appears that the impact of these Australian reasonable accommodation provisions may be quite limited.

64. For an exploration of this partial enforcement system, see Anna Chapman, 'Is the Right to Request Flexibility Under the Fair Work Act Enforceable?' (2013) 26 *Australian Journal of Labour Law* 118.

CHAPTER 4

Disability and Reintegration in Work: Interplay between EU Non-discrimination Law and Labour Law

Frank Hendrickx

§4.01 INTRODUCTION

With the adoption of Directive 2000/78, the concept of disability discrimination was introduced in European Union (EU) law. The origins are found in the Amsterdam Treaty, which introduced a new Article 6a in the (then existing) EC Treaty, allowing the Union to 'take appropriate action to combat discrimination based on sex, racial or ethnic origin, religion or belief, disability, age or sexual orientation'. With these new competences, the focus in EU employment discrimination law shifted towards other forms of discrimination. It led to Council Directive 2000/78EC of 27 November 2000, establishing a general framework for equal treatment in employment and occupation[1] and Council Directive 2000/43EC of 29 June 2000 implementing the principle of equal treatment between persons irrespective of racial or ethnic origin.[2]

With the adoption of the Charter of Fundamental Rights of the European Union (CFEU),[3] the principle of non-discrimination on the ground of disability was confirmed. The promotion of the non-discrimination principle, including protection against disability discrimination, as a fundamental right is significant. The Court of Justice of the European Union (CJEU) repeatedly stated that the respect for fundamental rights is one of the general principles of Union law and that there can be no doubt that the elimination of labour market discrimination forms part of those fundamental human

1. *OJ* 2 December 2000, L303/16.
2. *OJ* 19 July 2000, L180.
3. *OJ* 30 March 2010, C83/389.

rights.[4] With regard to disability, the CFEU is particularly referring to the 'integration of persons with disabilities'. It is provided that the Union recognises and respects the right of persons with disabilities to benefit from measures designed to ensure their independence, social and occupational integration and participation in the life of the community.[5]

It is assumed that disability discrimination has taken a rather modest start at the level of the Member States' case law, although there is a steadily growing attention and concern, and thus a growing number of cases.[6] The potential impact of the EU legislation in the area of disability discrimination may, however, be important, not the least for labour law.

This contribution focuses on the interplay between the concept of disability discrimination and labour law. Although the concept of disability discrimination exists for about a decade and a half, it can still be seen as relatively new at the level of the EU. The case law of the CJEU is, nevertheless, slightly growing and the academic debate is gaining pace.

The Belgian case may illustrate the possible impact of EU disability discrimination legislation on national labour law. The case law of the Belgian 'Cour de Cassation' (Supreme Court) is under debate. In its judgment of 5 January 1981, known as the *Collman*-decision, the Court stated that a permanent work incapacity which makes it definitely impossible for an employee to perform the agreed work constitutes a case of force majeure terminating the employment contract.[7] The case law created the theory of terminating 'force majeure' ('Act of God') in case of permanent work incapacity. This theory is based on labour law provisions which provide that an employment contract can be terminated by reason of 'force majeure'. It can be assumed that discrimination law is going to have an important impact on this case law, since it offers additional protection on the grounds of disability. The termination of an employment contract, be it on the basis of force majeure, will need to pass the test of the non-discrimination standard relating to disability. The role of reasonable accommodation may throw a different light on the debate. Employers may receive the obligation to search for solutions and adaptations of the work or the workplace, and only if this is considered impossible or unreasonable, the termination of the employment contract would be lawful.

However, the impact question seems to have a broader relevance than the strict framework of (disability) discrimination law. The idea of adapting work or the workplace, basically an inclusive strategy, is neither uncommon nor new for labour law. Disability discrimination law and labour law have shared objectives. The idea of integration and the connected 'integrative function' of labour law is an important

4. *Cf.* ECJ 15 June 1978, 149/77, *Defrenne v. Sabena (Defrenne III)*, E.C.R. 1978, 1365, para. 26 (sex discrimination case).
5. Article 26 CFEU.
6. C. Hießl & G. Boot, 'The Application of the EU Framework for Disability Discrimination in 18 European Countries', *ELLJ* 2013, 119-134.
7. Cass. 5 January 1981, *RW* 1980-81, 2401.

function of labour law and receives increased attention.[8] In the evolution of labour law in the EU, a broader social and employment policy discourse including the notion of 'employability' has arisen. Ideas concerning activation, inclusive labour markets and integration are all used in modern social and employment policy debate.[9] This is certainly relevant with regard to workers suffering from disability, or seen broader, dealing with a situation of work incapacity due to medical reasons.

The relationship between disability discrimination law and broader labour law and labour market objectives is made explicit in the Preamble of Directive 2000/78. Preamble 6 refers to the Community Charter of the Fundamental Social Rights of Workers (1989) with specific reference to 'the social and economic integration disabled people'. Preambles 7 and 8 refer to European employment policy and specifically to the Employment Guidelines stressing 'the need to foster a labour market favourable to social integration by formulating a coherent set of policies aimed at combating discrimination against groups such as persons with disability'. Preamble 27, furthermore, refers to Recommendation 86/379/EEC of 24 July 1986 on the employment of disabled people in the Community,[10] in which the Council established a guideline framework setting out examples of positive action to promote the employment and training of disabled people, and in its Resolution of 17 June 1999 on equal employment opportunities for people with disabilities,[11] affirming the importance of giving specific attention *inter alia* to recruitment, retention, training and lifelong learning with regard to disabled persons.

There seem to be mutually influencing forces. The horizon of discrimination law and the 'integrative function' of labour law both lead to the need to match workforce diversity with employability and the employers' organisational or business needs, increases the importance of the notion of reasonable accommodation as it operates in employment discrimination law, but also increasing the importance of integration and inclusion.

Discrimination law appears as a catalyst for new approaches and avenues in labour law. Notions such as 'adaptability' and 'employability' not only require workers to adapt to new labour market circumstances, but are also directed towards employers' duties to accommodate work and the workplace to the worker's situation. Employment discrimination law gives shape to an accommodated workplace. This serves the functions of labour law.

It is the purpose of this contribution to further analyse the concept of disability discrimination, including a duty to make reasonable accommodation, and labour law. To organise the discussion, three (perhaps challenging) questions are formulated. They are formulated in an almost rhetorical manner, as they serve as hypotheses which need to be examined further:

---

8. B. Hepple, 'The Future of Labour Law', *Ind. L.J.* 1995, 322/ F. Hendrickx, 'Foundations and Functions of Contemporary Labour Law', *ELLJ* 2012, No. 2, 108-129.
9. See e.g., the Framework Agreement on Inclusive Labour Markets, 25 March 2010, concluded by the European social partners.
10. *OJ* L225, 12 August 1986, 43.
11. *OJ* C186, 2 July 1999, 3.

- Is the social model in disability discrimination law not inevitable, as it fits better into a labour law model than the medical model?
- Is it still possible, seen the rise of the social model, to maintain the distinction between disability and illness?
- Should it not be so that, since the United Nations (UN) Convention promotes the social model, it should be preferably relied upon, more than the EU directive?

§4.02 FROM A MEDICAL MODEL TO A SOCIAL MODEL

Workers are protected against discrimination based on disability. But what is a disability? One of the problems is that EU Directive 2000/78 does not provide a definition of what constitutes a disability. The CJEU has developed a notion of disability. This case law is, however, evolving. It can be seen to develop from a medical model towards a social model. While the 'medical model' of disability focuses on the impairment itself, the 'social model' refers to disability resulting from an impairment in combination with barriers created by the context, the environment or society, while the medical approach of disability focuses on the person's impairment.[12]

In *Chacon Navas*, the CJEU established a definition of disability for the first time. It held that 'the concept of "disability" must be understood as referring to a limitation which results in particular from physical, mental or psychological impairments and which hinders the participation of the person concerned in professional life' (paragraph 43). The question in this case was whether an illness could qualify as a disability. The Court, furthermore, specified that:

> the importance which the Community legislature attaches to measures for adapting the workplace to the disability demonstrates that it envisaged situations in which participation in professional life is hindered over a long period of time. In order for the limitation to fall within the concept of 'disability', it must therefore be probable that it will last for a long time.[13]

The Court clearly wanted to make a distinction between a disability and an illness. It stated that 'there is nothing in Directive 2000/78 to suggest that workers are protected by the prohibition of discrimination on grounds of disability as soon as they develop any type of sickness.'[14] It concluded that 'it follows from the above considerations that a person who has been dismissed by his employer solely on account of sickness does not fall within the general framework laid down for combating discrimination on grounds of disability by Directive 2000/78'.[15]

12. N. Betsch, 'The Ring and Skouboe Werge Case: A Reluctant Acceptance of the Social Approach of Disability', *ELLJ* 2013, 135.
13. Paragraph 45.
14. Paragraph 46.
15. Paragraph 47.

With the concept of *Chacon Navas*, the Court is seen to have used a medical model of disability discrimination law. In order to determine the concept of disability, the Court focused on the impairment(s) of a person concerned. However, in *HK Danmark* the Court left this approach in favour of a social model. In this case, the Court still referred to its reasoning in *Chacon Navas*, but added that 'the concept of "disability" must be understood as referring to a limitation which results in particular from physical, mental or psychological impairments which in interaction with various barriers may hinder the full and effective participation of the person concerned in professional life on an equal basis with other workers.'[16]

In *FAO*,[17] a case concerning a dismissal of a childminder who claimed that his dismissal was motivated by the fact that he suffered from obesity, the CJEU referred back to the issue of qualification and definition. The Court reasoned that 'obesity cannot as such be regarded as a ground in addition to those in relation to which Directive 2000/78 prohibits discrimination'.[18] The Court specified that the 'concept of "disability" must be understood as referring not only to the impossibility of exercising a professional activity, but also to a hindrance to the exercise of such an activity. Any other interpretation would be incompatible with the objective of that directive, which aims in particular to enable a person with a disability to have access to or participate in employment.'[19] The Court went on to say that 'the concept of "disability" within the meaning of Directive 2000/78 does not depend on the extent to which the person may or may not have contributed to the onset of his disability.'[20] The Court then held that:

> in the event that, under given circumstances, the obesity of the worker concerned entails a limitation which results in particular from physical, mental or psychological impairments that in interaction with various barriers may hinder the full and effective participation of that person in professional life on an equal basis with other workers, and the limitation is a long-term one, obesity can be covered by the concept of 'disability' within the meaning of Directive 2000/78.[21]

The Court said that 'such would be the case, in particular, if the obesity of the worker hindered his full and effective participation in professional life on an equal basis with other workers on account of reduced mobility or the onset, in that person, of medical conditions preventing him from carrying out his work or causing discomfort when carrying out his professional activity'.[22]

This case law leads to a discussion on how broad the concept of disability can be interpreted and how the distinction with the concept of 'illness' is to be made, or, alternatively, whether the distinction between disability and illness should not be abandoned. This is further discussed below.

16. Paragraph 38.
17. CJEU 18 December 2014, C-354/13, *Fag og Arbejde (FOA) v. Kommunernes Landsforening (KL)*.
18. Paragraph 37.
19. Paragraph 54.
20. Paragraph 56.
21. Paragraph 59.
22. Paragraph 60.

§4.03 IMPACT OF THE UN CONVENTION

It is remarkable to note how the case law of the CJEU is strongly influenced by the UN Convention on the Rights of Persons with Disabilities (CRPD), adopted on 13 December 2006.

The UN CRPD has a broad and integrated approach of disability, encompassing various areas and sectors of individual and societal life, including the aim to cover all persons with a disability.[23] The CRPD takes a human rights approach based on human dignity. It aims 'to promote, protect and ensure the full and equal enjoyment of all human rights and fundamental freedoms by all persons with disabilities, and to promote respect for their inherent dignity'.[24] Unlike Directive 200/78, it provides a definition of what constitutes a disability: 'Persons with disabilities include those who have long-term physical, mental, intellectual or sensory impairments which in interaction with various barriers may hinder their full and effective participation in society on an equal basis with others'.[25] The Convention promotes a wide variety of rights and obligations, relating to accessibility, the right to life, access to justice, liberty and security, integrity of the person, freedom from exploitation, liberty of movement, participation rights, and so on.

The CRPD thus covers much more than the provision of an equal treatment provision. Equality is, nevertheless, a key concept. The CRPD lays down a general principle of equal treatment. According to Article 5, state parties must recognise that all persons are equal before and under the law and are entitled without any discrimination to the equal protection and equal benefit of the law. Furthermore, state parties must prohibit all discrimination on the basis of disability and guarantee persons with disabilities equal and effective legal protection against discrimination.

States are also required to take all appropriate steps to ensure that reasonable accommodation is provided.[26] According to Article 2 of the CRPD, 'reasonable accommodation' means 'necessary and appropriate modification and adjustments not imposing a disproportionate or undue burden, where needed in a particular case, to ensure to persons with disabilities the enjoyment or exercise on an equal basis with others of all human rights and fundamental freedoms'.

Furthermore, the principle of equality stands central in the provision of specific obligations and rights in relation to work and employment. The Convention brings this in relation with the right to work and seems to integrate this in an employment law discourse. According to Article 27, the signatory states recognise 'the right of persons with disabilities to work, on an equal basis with others'. This includes, according to the same article, 'the right to the opportunity to gain a living by work freely chosen or accepted in a labour market and work environment that is open, inclusive and accessible to persons with disabilities'. States are required to safeguard and promote the realisation of the right to work by taking various appropriate steps. The Convention

23. See e.g., Preambles j and k CRPD.
24. Article 1 CRPD.
25. Article 1 CRPD.
26. Article 5, para. 3 CRPD.

expressly mentions that this also includes measures for 'those who acquire a disability during the course of employment'. It is worth to mention requirements to 'ensure that reasonable accommodation is provided to persons with disabilities in the workplace'[27] and to 'promote professional rehabilitation, job retention and return-to-work programmes for persons with disabilities'.[28]

The CPRD has exercised an important influence in the EU legal order. This is not only due to the fact that the EU Member States signed the Convention but also because the Convention was approved on behalf of the EU by Council Decision 2010/48/EC of 26 November 2009.[29] It has does become an integral part of EU law and it has allowed the CJEU to rely on it in order to interpret the concept of disability discrimination as provided in Directive 2000/78.

In *HK Danmark*, the Court explicitly referred to the CRPD, stating that it 'acknowledges in recital (e) that "disability is an evolving concept and that disability results from the interaction between persons with impairments and attitudinal and environmental barriers that hinders their full and effective participation in society on an equal basis with others". Thus the second paragraph of Article 1 of the convention states that persons with disabilities include "those who have long-term physical, mental, intellectual or sensory impairments which in interaction with various barriers may hinder their full and effective participation in society on an equal basis with others".'[30]

The Court made clear that, due to Decision 2010/48, the CRPD is 'from the time of its entry into force, an integral part of the EU legal order'.[31] It follows, according to the Court, 'that Directive 2000/78 must, as far as possible, be interpreted in a manner consistent with that convention.'[32]

The influence of the CRPD is obviously much wider than the area of disability discrimination law. Seen its broad scope, it has a strong impact on labour law as a whole. This also means that the CRPD will have its influence on EU (and national) labour law provisions, understood in their wider sense. It is, for example, relevant to refer to the provisions relating to health and safety at work, such as Council Directive 89/391/EEC of 12 June 1989 on the introduction of measures to encourage improvements in the safety and health of workers at work.[33] The influence of the CRPD on health issues at work, including the adaptation of work or the workplace, will thus not only become visible through disability discrimination law only.

§4.04 DISCUSSIONS ON WHAT IS A DISABILITY VERSUS ILLNESS

From a labour law perspective, promoting equal treatment and reasonable accommodation for the disabled, may appear as a too restrictive approach. The wider issue in

27. Article 27, para. 1, i CRPD.
28. Article 27, para. 1, k CRPD.
29. *OJ* 2010, L23.
30. Paragraph 3.
31. Paragraph 30.
32. Paragraph 32.
33. *OJ* L183, 19 June 1989.

labour law concerns work incapacity and the question how medical profiles or problems of workers can be reconciled with the demands and requirements of the agreed work and the workplace. There is thus a close link between the issue of work incapacity in labour law and the principle of non-discrimination on the grounds of disability. However, the question whether all types of work incapacity may come into the scope of protection of EU disability discrimination law, runs into the limits of the concept of disability as approached by the CJEU, as explained before.

The question is to what extent the evolving concept of disability can be widened in order to expand the scope of protection offered by disability discrimination law and, in this way perhaps, serving better the integrative function of labour law. Labour law should be concerned with all workers suffering from medical problems, not only with disabled workers in the strict sense.

The definition of what is a disability and what is not, which is evidently determining the question whether an individual finds protection under Directive 2000/78 or not, is sometimes defined as a 'threshold requirement'.[34] It raises the problem that some persons may suffer from an illness which is limiting them in their professional life, but which is not of such a nature that they are viewed by a court as being disabled. They might thus be seen as 'not disabled enough'.[35]

This leads to a strange situation. Some persons may wish to be (seen as) 'disabled' in order to receive the protection of Directive 2000/78. It seems, indeed that disability discrimination law only comes into play when a disability is established. It appears that only when someone is 'disabled', he or she should be 'enabled' by the anti-discrimination provisions, for example through provisions on reasonable accommodation. When somebody is not disabled, there would be no need to provide this protection. It is however not necessarily fair to exclude persons without a disability from this enabling provisions of anti-discrimination law.

At the level of EU case law, the CJEU's decision in *Glatzel*[36] may be referred to as a case where it became clear that there might be a thin line between what constitutes a disability and what not. Mr Glatzel lost his driving licence by a court judgment on the ground that he had driven under the influence of alcohol. In a later stage, Mr Glatzel applied for a new driving licence including a licence for driving heavy goods vehicles. This was refused on the ground that an ophthalmological examination had revealed that Mr Glatzel suffered from unilateral amblyopia, involving a substantial functional loss of vision in one eye. Mr Glatzel was able to detect only hand movements with his right eye. The visual acuity in Mr Glatzel's right eye did not satisfy the requirements laid down by German law for the issue of a driving licence for vehicles in the heavier categories.

In discussing the minimum standards for drivers of heavy goods vehicles in light of the principle of equality before the law, non-discrimination on grounds of disability, and the integration of persons with disabilities, the Court examined whether Mr Glatzel

34. L. Waddington, '"Not-Disabled Enough": How European Courts Filter Non-discrimination Claims through a Narrow View of Disability', *Eur. J. Human Rights*, 2015, No. 1, 14.
35. L. Waddington, *supra*, 2015, 15.
36. CJEU 22 May 2014, C-356/12, *Wolfgang Glatzel v. Freistaat Bayern*.

suffered from a disability. The Court reasoned 'that while, according to the information in the order for reference, the visual acuity in Mr Glatzel's worse eye is very weak, the fact remains that when he uses both eyes, he has a binocular visual acuity of 1,0, that is, 'full' acuity. In that regard, the Court does not have sufficient information to ascertain whether such impairment constitutes a 'disability' within the meaning of Article 21 (1) of the Charter'.[37] This reasoning is criticised, as the Court arguably did not involve a social model of disability discrimination law, as it seemed looking at the impairment suffered by the person concerned instead of paying attention to barriers following from the wider environmental context.[38]

The Court, nevertheless, did not avoid a discussion on the interaction between the disability and the context of driving heavy vehicles. The Court held that 'as regards the necessity of the minimum standards for vision of drivers of power-driven vehicles, it is essential, in order to ensure road safety, that the persons to whom a driving licence is issued possess sufficient physical capabilities, in particular with respect to their vision, in so far as physical defects may have significant consequences'.[39] In this context, the Court referred to the case of *Prigge and Others* which it decided in the context of age discrimination.[40] The Court held that 'it is well known that vision is essential for the purposes of driving power-driven vehicles and, accordingly, the more that function is reduced, the more it becomes necessary to take into consideration requirements relating to road safety.'[41]

The national case law may solve the issue by giving a broad interpretation to the concept of disability, perhaps broader than the CJEU has defined it. Although this may not seem logic, this is in line with the provisions of Article 8 of Directive 2000/78 stating that Member States may introduce or maintain provisions which are more favourable to the protection of the principle of equal treatment than those laid down in the Directive.

The Belgian case law may, again, serve as an example where the distinction between a disability and a work incapacity due to illness becomes rather small. The Labour Tribunal of Leuven accepted that the need to take care of a newborn daughter with a severe abnormality constitutes a disability, even if the worker himself does not have a disability.[42] This court obviously made use of the concept of associative discrimination accepted by the CJEU before.[43] A couple of cases of the Labour Court of Antwerp have triggered a lot of attention. Referring to the case law of the CJEU, the labour court considered situations of workers who suffered from medical problems which made them possibly (partly or fully) incapable for work. In the context of work

37. Paragraph 47.
38. C. O'Brien, 'Driving Down Disability Equality?', 21 *MJ* 4, 2014, 727-728.
39. Paragraph 54.
40. Cf. CJEU 13 September 2011, C-447/09, *Reinhard* Prigge, Michael Fromm en Volker Lambach / Deutsche Lufthansa AG.
41. Paragraph 54.
42. Labour Tribunal Leuven 10 December 2013, AR nr. 12/1064/A, *NB Arbeidsrecht 2013/10* (Summary S. De Groof).
43. CJEU 17 July 2008, C-303/06, *Coleman*.

in an industrial laundry, the fact that due to a medical problem in the foot, a worker was not able anymore to perform standing work, was considered a handicap.[44] In another case, the Labour Court of Antwerp accepted that the definitive, physical incapacity of a cleaner to perform cleaning work above shoulder level should be regarded as a disability in the sense of Directive 2000/78.[45] With regard to the performance of a function as dock worker, the same labour court judged that the situation of insulin-dependent diabetes constitutes a disability.[46]

It is clear that the case law developed in light of a broader discussion in Belgian labour law with regard to the termination of the employment contract due to work incapacity. For example, with qualifying a worker's incapacity for work as a disability, the courts may require that employers make reasonable accommodation first before they invoke 'force majeure' (see above) or terminate the contract. Nevertheless, the case law also shows that the concept of disability may be quite useful in cases of medical screening in order to determine an employee's fitness to work.

Due to the fact that Member States may be inclined to widen the concept of disability to situations that are rather referred to as illness, but need protection for reasons of fairness, and given the fact that the CJEU itself does not exclude situations of illness from the concept of disability, the question is whether it is useful to maintain the distinction between disability and illness.

§4.05 SOCIAL MODEL AS A LABOUR LAW MODEL

From the discussion undertaken above, it seems clear that the step from the medical model to the social model of disability is an inevitable one. The social model is more proper to a labour law understanding of integration. It also seems more appropriate in terms of a labour market policy model searching for strategies of employability and inclusion.

In this respect, as the social model of disability looks at the context and the interaction of a person with the environment, it is interesting to refer to the opinion of Advocate-General Bot in *Glatzel*, who argued that:

> disability must not be understood according to the degree of the deficiency at issue, but must be determined having regard to the end result occasioned by that deficiency in a given social context or environment. Accordingly, attention must be focussed on that consequence and not on the deficiency in itself. Where the interaction between a deficiency – or an impairment to use the term employed by the Court – and a particular environment has the effect of restricting the activity of the person concerned so that he is no longer able to participate fully and effectively in professional life on an equal basis with other workers, that person may be said to have a disability.[47]

44. Labour Court Antwerp 12 May 2009 AR 2070100.
45. Labour Court Antwerp 23 April 2010, AR 2007/AA/448 and AR 2007/AA/450.
46. Labour Court Antwerp 21 November 2011, AR 2010/AA/334, *NB Arbeidsrecht* 2011/9.
47. Opinion of Advocate General Bot, delivered on 18 July 2013, Case C-356/12 *Wolfgang Glatzel v. Freistaat Bayern* (para. 35).

If understood in this way, many health problems which lead to a deficiency for work, may be caught by health and safety or work incapacity provisions in labour law. It is exactly the goal of these parts of labour law to take care that people are employed and remain in work that is fit for them, seen their medical profile or medical condition. In this sense, health and safety law is designed to adapt work to the person and has by nature an inclusive goal. This is confirmed by the provisions of the EU framework directive on health and safety.[48] With regard to determining the relation between a person's medical condition or medical profile and labour law, the area of medical screening for fitness to work is concerned. Employment and pre-employment medical examination has the aim to 'place and maintain employees in an occupational environment adapted to their physiological and psychological capacities'.[49]

Ideas in labour law are evolving to thinking in terms of ability and capability instead of disability. According to the OECD, 'to improve the integration of disabled persons, societies need to change the way they think about disability and those affected by it. The term "disabled" should no longer be equated automatically with "unable to work". Disability should be recognised as a condition, but it should be *distinct* from eligibility for, and receipt of, benefits, just as it should not *automatically* represent an obstacle to work.'[50] The 'work capacity' or the 'remaining work capacity' is becoming as important as the provision of benefit schemes in terms of people's incapacity to work.[51]

§4.06 CONCLUSIONS

The central idea of this contribution is that disability discrimination law and labour law are strongly interwoven and serving shared objectives: an inclusive labour market where integration of workers stands central. This can be based on a right to work perspective, or on a non-discrimination perspective, but both serve the logic of the integrative function of labour law. The rise of the concept of reasonable accommodation in discrimination law seems to be an example of the growing concern of conceiving employability and employment security of workers in terms of an 'accommodated workplace'. This concern has been present in labour law since a long time, although often elaborated through work incapacity law or health and safety law, subjects that are often not popular in broader labour law scholarship or seen as (too) technical subjects, although of high relevance in our modern labour markets. In these areas of labour law, integration and adapting work to the person are leading principles. The evolution of labour law, driven by labour market and employment policy views but also building on its own functions, shows that these fields need to receive renewed attention. Thinking of health issues, including disability, in terms of ability and

48. *OJ* L183, 19 June 1989.
49. J. Pachman, 'Evidence Base for Pre-employment Medical Screening', *Bull. World Health Org.* 2009, 529-534.
50. OECD, *Transforming Disability into Ability: Policies to Promote Work and Income Security for Disabled People*, OECD Publishing, Paris, 2003, 156.
51. Cf. OECD, *Sickness, Disability and Work: Breaking the Barriers*, OECD Publishing, Paris, 2010, 105.

capability, is necessary. Disability discrimination law is a reinforcing factor to move this debate ahead.

The questions of this contribution were posed in a rather challenging way. However, it would seem that the social model in disability discrimination law is inevitable. Compared to the medical model, the social model fits much better into a labour law model which takes into account contextual elements of the work environment to determine whether a worker is capable or incapable for work. Health issues in labour law are viewed from a model of inclusion.

Due to this social model, seen as familiar to the labour law model, it seems difficult to maintain the distinction between disability and illness. This is not only due to the case law (both of the CJEU as national case law) on disability. When workers suffer from medical or health problems relating to their current work, or broader, on the labour market, the integrative logic of labour law would require that people who suffer from illness but not from disability, are not set aside.

Finally, it may be that the CRPD has ultimately a stronger influence than EU Directive 2000/78. The CRPD promotes the social model of disability. It includes a duty to make reasonable accommodation and offers a rich array of measures promoting labour market participation of disabled workers. Since it is not only signed by the EU Member States themselves, but also adopted by the EU, it potentially has an important impact and may steadily start to exercise its influence in different labour law areas.

CHAPTER 5

Accommodating 'Reasonable Accommodation': Encouraging Liability Evasion over Employment Integration?

Alan C. Neal

§5.01 INTRODUCTION

Shortly after the Council of the European Union (EU) had adopted a 'framework Directive' establishing an EU-level model for achieving equal treatment in employment,[1] and before that instrument had been duly implemented into the legal systems of the Member States of the Union,[2] this author made a presentation to a Swedish colloquium in which I criticised the approach being taken at the European level as regards 'disability discrimination' within that framework.[3]

By way of placing my criticism into context, I suggested that Anglo-American Common Law experience from the preceding decade had given rise to an increasingly effective 'promotional' model for influencing the treatment of disabled persons at work. I suggested that this established model appeared to stand in stark contrast to an

1. Council Directive 2000/78/EC of 27 November 2000 establishing a general framework for equal treatment in employment and occupation.
2. Article 18 of Directive 2000/78/EC provided that: 'Member States shall adopt the laws, regulations and administrative provisions necessary to comply with this Directive by 2 December 2003 at the latest or may entrust the social partners, at their joint request, with the implementation of this Directive as regards provisions concerning collective agreements'. However, that Article went on to allow that: 'In order to take account of particular conditions, Member States may, if necessary, have an additional period of 3 years from 2 December 2003, that is to say a total of 6 years, to implement the provisions of this Directive on age and disability discrimination', subject to an annual reporting obligation during such an additional period.
3. Subsequently published as Alan C. Neal, 'Disability Discrimination at Work', in A. Numhauser-Henning (ed.), *Legal Perspectives on Equal Treatment and Non-Discrimination* (Kluwer, 2001) 343 ff.

essentially 'penal' regime constituting the new EU approach to the issue. In the course of introducing a 'European-level model', I put forward the proposition that normative compliance was being placed above functional integrative outcomes – what I characterised as part of a broader 'positive re-integration' ethos – for disabled persons seeking to participate in the labour market. Such a shift, I suggested, carried the potential to diminish existing incentives to make employers consider practical means by which disabled workers or job applicants might be accommodated into employment. In particular, I expressed the fear that a fledgling move in the direction of a 'disability risk assessment' ethos ran the danger of being stopped in its tracks, to be replaced by a return to a mindset confined to achieving 'merely the penalisation and sanctioning of identifiable "unlawful" acts'. Such a prospect, I concluded, could serve to limit the impact of regulatory initiatives in relation to disabled persons seeking to participate (fully or at all) in the world of work, and fall disappointingly short of what I considered to be the 'new and imaginative regulatory techniques' which are called for in order to penalise those who discriminate, to shift attitudes, to raise awareness of disability as an issue in employment relations, and to promote the integration of disabled persons into the active workforce.

Having observed 'disability discrimination' litigation in the United Kingdom courts and tribunals at first hand,[4] both under the pre-'framework' Directive regime and since implementation of that Directive's provisions,[5] the initial impression is that my expressed fears of a decade and a half ago have, indeed, subsequently come to pass. Furthermore, it is suggested that other elements of the arrangements stipulated by Directive 2000/78/EC – in particular the 'one size fits all' nature of the so-called principle of equal treatment applied to all of the protected characteristics addressed by the Directive[6] – have contributed towards a situation in which ostensibly 'hard law' normative provisions are relatively easy to evade, while relatively 'softer' approaches focused upon 're-integrative' objectives have been effectively sidelined.

The following brief comment begins with a consideration of the 'Anglo-American model' developed prior to the advent of Directive 2000/78/EC. That is followed by a comparison of approaches to so-called reasonable accommodation, and consideration of some of the implications following from separating out that element of the legislative arsenal from the generally-stated 'principle of equal treatment'. Remarks are then made in relation to the founding of the EU model upon that 'principle of equal treatment', before a concluding observation touches upon the significance of the shift from 'promotional' to 'penal' regulatory techniques as part of the struggle to address problems encountered by disabled persons seeking to participate in the modern world of work, and the absence of indications from early jurisprudence emanating from the

4. The author sits as an Employment Judge in the London Central Region of the Employment Tribunals of England and Wales, and, since 1996, has been the Convenor of the European Association of Labour Court Judges.
5. Initially, by way of The Disability Discrimination Act 1995 (Amendment) Regulations 2003 (S.I. 2003 No. 1673), which came into force on 1 October 2004. The modern United Kingdom provisions are now contained in the Equality Act 2010.
6. See Art. 2 of the Directive.

Court of Justice of the European Union (CJEU) of any more pro-active approach to integrating disabled persons within the workforce.

§5.02 INSPIRATION DRAWN FROM THE UNITED STATES OF AMERICA AND THE EMERGENCE OF AN ANGLO-AMERICAN 'COMMON LAW' APPROACH TO DEALING WITH ISSUES TOUCHING DISABLED MEMBERS OF THE WORKFORCE

[A] Leading the Way: The Americans with Disabilities Act 1990

The introduction by the United States of America of legislation to address challenges perceived to be associated with disabled persons active or seeking to be active in the workforce was accomplished initially through the Americans With Disabilities Act of 1990,[7] which noted that 'individuals with disabilities continually encounter various forms of discrimination, including outright intentional exclusion, the discriminatory effects of architectural, transportation, and communication barriers, overprotective rules and policies, failure to make modifications to existing facilities and practices, exclusionary qualification standards and criteria, segregation, and relegation to lesser services, programs, activities, benefits, jobs, or other opportunities',[8] and declared that 'the Nation's proper goals regarding individuals with disabilities are to assure equality of opportunity, full participation, independent living, and economic self-sufficiency for such individuals'.[9]

The American statute extended its coverage specifically to 'employment', and included within its framework the general rule that:

> No covered entity shall discriminate against a qualified individual with a disability because of the disability of such individual in regard to job application procedures, the hiring, advancement, or discharge of employees, employee compensation, job training, and other terms, conditions, and privileges of employment.[10]

For the purposes of the application of that general rule, the expression 'qualified individual with a disability' was defined to mean 'an individual with a disability who, with or without reasonable accommodation, can perform the essential functions of the employment position that such individual holds or desires.' Thus was introduced the notion of 'reasonable accommodation', which was said to be capable of including:

> (A) making existing facilities used by employees readily accessible to and usable by individuals with disabilities; and (B) job restructuring, part-time or modified work schedules, reassignment to a vacant position, acquisition or modification of equipment or devices, appropriate adjustment or modifications of examinations,

7. The original version of the Act has subsequently been amended – in particular, through the Americans With Disabilities Amendments Act of 2008 – in the light of case-law developments in this field.
8. Title 42, Chapter 126, section 12101, subsection (5).
9. Subsection (5).
10. A 'covered entity' was defined so as to include 'an employer, employment agency, labor organization, or joint labor-management committee'.

training materials or policies, the provision of qualified readers or interpreters, and other similar accommodations for individuals with disabilities.

Importantly, the notion of 'discrimination', constituting the mischief to which the Act was directed, was stated to include:

> (A) not making reasonable accommodations to the known physical or mental limitations of an otherwise qualified individual with a disability who is an applicant or employee, unless such covered entity can demonstrate that the accommodation would impose an undue hardship on the operation of the business of such covered entity; or (B) denying employment opportunities to a job applicant or employee who is an otherwise qualified individual with a disability, if such denial is based on the need of such covered entity to make reasonable accommodation to the physical or mental impairments of the employee or applicant.

The Act made explicit, in its presentation of potential defences to liability under the general rule, that:

> It may be a defense to a charge of discrimination under this chapter that an alleged application of qualification standards, tests, or selection criteria that screen out or tend to screen out or otherwise deny a job or benefit to an individual with a disability has been shown to be job-related and consistent with business necessity, and such performance cannot be accomplished by reasonable accommodation, as required under this subchapter.

Within the regime thus established by the 1990 Act a 'covered entity' faced an obligation to make 'reasonable accommodation' for a qualified individual with a disability, subject only to the possibility of establishing that 'the accommodation would impose an undue hardship on the operation of the business of such covered entity' (the 'undue hardship' defence).[11]

[B] Bringing the American Model to Europe: The United Kingdom's Disability Discrimination Act 1995

Five years after the enactment of the American provisions relating to disability discrimination in the world of work, the United Kingdom Parliament passed a

11. The statute dealt with that potential defence in terms that: 'In general the term "undue hardship" means an action requiring significant difficulty or expense, when considered in light of the factors set forth in subparagraph (B).' Those factors were provided for such that: 'In determining whether an accommodation would impose an undue hardship on a covered entity, factors to be considered include (i) the nature and cost of the accommodation needed under this chapter; (ii) the overall financial resources of the facility or facilities involved in the provision of the reasonable accommodation; the number of persons employed at such facility; the effect on expenses and resources, or the impact otherwise of such accommodation upon the operation of the facility; (iii) the overall financial resources of the covered entity; the overall size of the business of a covered entity with respect to the number of its employees; the number, type, and location of its facilities; and (iv) the type of operation or operations of the covered entity, including the composition, structure, and functions of the workforce of such entity; the geographic separateness, administrative, or fiscal relationship of the facility or facilities in question to the covered entity.'

Disability Discrimination Act 1995, which came into force on 30 May 1996. The underlying model adopted owed much to the American experience with the Americans With Disabilities Act 1990, while the new Act also drew inspiration from existing United Kingdom experience in the fields of race discrimination[12] and sex discrimination[13] – much of which had itself drawn inspiration from Title VII of the American Civil Rights Act 1964 – and equal pay.[14]

As with the American model, the new Disability Discrimination Act extended its scope of protection to the employment field, and provided that it was unlawful for an employer to discriminate against a disabled person in various respects where that disabled person was an employee or a job applicant.[15] In common with its American counterpart, the United Kingdom legislation also dealt with the primary challenge of discrimination against disabled persons through the statutory prohibition of what had come to be known as 'direct discrimination'. There was no echo in this new area of disability discrimination of the 'indirect discrimination' mechanism which had earlier been introduced and developed for the fields of race discrimination and sex discrimination. However, the 1995 Act provided for an employer defence of 'justification' where such direct discrimination (less favourable treatment for a reason which relates to the disabled person's disability) had taken place – although only if the reason for the employer's failure to comply with the primary duty not to discriminate was 'both material to the circumstances of the particular case and substantial'.[16] No such defence of 'justification' was to be found in the 'direct discrimination' provisions of the Race Relations Act or the Sex Discrimination Act already in force for those aspects of discrimination at work.

Significantly, however, the defence of 'justification' was sharply limited by reason of the operation of another phenomenon drawn from the American experience

12. In the form of the Race Relations Act 1965 and then the Race Relations Act 1968, which latter measure extended the scope of the statutory protections to the employment field. The 1968 Act was eventually replaced by the Race Relations Act 1976, which also introduced a statutory body, the Commission for Racial Equality, charged with duties '(a) to work towards the elimination of discrimination; (b) to promote equality of opportunity, and good relations, between persons of different racial groups generally; and (c) to keep under review the working of this Act and, when they are so required by the Secretary of State or otherwise think it necessary, draw up and submit to the Secretary of State proposals for amending it.'
13. By way of the Sex Discrimination Act 1975, which also established a specialised agency in the guise of the Equal Opportunities Commission, charged with the duties: '(a) to work towards the elimination of discrimination; (b) to promote equality of opportunity between men and women generally; and (c) to keep under review the working of this Act and the Equal Pay Act 1970 and, when they are so required by the Secretary of State or otherwise think it necessary, draw up and submit to the Secretary of State proposals for amending them.'
14. Initially by way of the Equal Pay Act 1970, which was never brought into force in its original form but which subsequently found itself (in much amended form) brought to life by Schedule I of the 1975 Sex Discrimination Act with effect from Christmas Day 1975. This measure can also be seen to have drawn upon American experience, particularly in respect of that country's Equal Pay Act 1963, which introduced amendments into the Fair Labor Standards Act 1938.
15. Section 4.
16. Section 5(3).

– the duty of the employer in particular circumstances[17] 'to take such steps as it is reasonable, in all the circumstances of the case, for him to have to take' in order to prevent arrangements or any feature having the effect of placing a disabled person at a substantial disadvantage in comparison with persons who are not disabled. This 'duty to make adjustments', imposed subject to a 'test of reasonableness', invoked strong overtones of the American obligation for an employer (or other 'covered entity') to make 'reasonable accommodation'. However, the United Kingdom legislator had also taken the step of making it clear that recourse to the potential defence of 'justification' could not, in the normal case, be relied upon unless any duty to make adjustments to which the employer might be subject had been properly complied with.[18] Only if the employer could first justify the failure to comply with the 'duty to make adjustments' would it then be open to seek to justify the discriminatory treatment itself.[19]

In consequence, therefore, the arrangements introduced into the United Kingdom in 1996 made any opportunity for an employer to argue 'justification' for treating a disabled person less favourably than non-disabled persons by reason of that person's disability exceedingly difficult to access unless proper consideration had been given to the possibility of making 'reasonable adjustments' (and the employer could show that to have been the case) and a justification could be shown for any decision or failure to discharge the duty to make adjustments in the particular case.

This, I suggested in my Swedish presentation of a decade and a half ago, gave rise to a situation in which 'the whole decision-making frame of reference of the employer is affected, since the issue of potential discrimination to the disadvantage of disabled persons has to be addressed throughout the management process'. I also suggested that this arguably constituted a significantly more radical approach than 'the mere utilisation of the "indirect discrimination" mechanism to identify action which can then be subjected to legal penalty alongside other acts of "direct discrimination"'. Likening the approach to regimes for regulating and sanctioning health and safety duties at work (notably, through the process of the 'risk assessment'),[20] I argued that this 'duty to make adjustments' approach requires a thoroughgoing reconsideration of the entire policy-forming and decision-making practices of the employer. In consequence, it was

17. This duty arose under the provisions of section 6 where: '(a) any arrangements made by or on behalf of an employer, or (b) any physical feature of premises occupied by the employer, place the disabled person concerned at a substantial disadvantage in comparison with persons who are not disabled'.
18. Section 5(6) made further provision for Regulations to be made setting out circumstances in which *inter alia* failure to comply with a section 6 duty was to be taken to be justified or where such a failure was to be taken not to be justified.
19. Unless that discriminatory less favourable treatment would have been justified even if the employer had complied with the duty to make adjustments.
20. The approach favoured both at the level of the European Union and at the national level in the United Kingdom. See the provisions of the EU's health and safety 'framework' Directive 89/391/EEC. See also the 'risk assessment' regime introduced as part of the United Kingdom's implementation measures by the Management of Health and Safety at Work Regulations 1992, under the umbrella of the Health and Safety at Work Act 1974. Those regulations need to be seen in conjunction with the Guidance document, *Managing for Health and Safety* (HSG65), first published in 1991, and associated Approved Codes of Practice issued by the Health and Safety Executive (HSE).

suggested, an employer who fails to take into consideration even the possibility of there being disadvantage to disabled persons would find it difficult, if not impossible, to bring home a 'justification' argument. Although I expressed the view that it was probably going too far to suggest that the 1995 arrangements introduced a duty for United Kingdom employers to undertake a 'disability risk assessment', I concluded that:

> it is hard to see how a future failure to re-visit procedures for recruitment selection, redundancy selection, capability discipline/dismissal, or a wide range of other interfaces between established 'general' individual employment rights and obligations raised in relation to potential disability discrimination by both the 1995 Act and the associated Codes of Practice can now be defended by a Respondent employer or employing organisation.

§5.03 DEVELOPMENT OF A DISTINCTIVE 'EU' APPROACH

[A] An Early Swedish 'Straw in the Wind': The Act on Discrimination in Working Life against Persons Suffering from Disability 1999

Before turning to what is now the Europe-wide framework of regulation to address the challenges of disability discrimination, a brief passing mention should be made of the experience witnessed in Sweden under the provisions of that country's Act on the Prohibition of Discrimination in Working Life against persons suffering from disability of 1999.[21]

The approach adopted by the 1999 Swedish legislation built upon an established 'penal' approach to specified forms of discrimination already developed in relation to sex discrimination twenty years earlier.[22] Thus, the provisions of the statute dealt in the language of 'direct' and 'indirect' discrimination, and included powers to establish a special 'Ombudsman for Handicapped Persons' – a common feature of regulatory promotional and enforcement measures in Sweden.[23]

There was no strongly-worded 'duty to make adjustments', or obligation for an employer to make 'reasonable accommodation' in this Swedish framework, although a provision under the rubric of 'support and adaptation measures' evidently envisaged an expectation that such measures could be addressed in the context of managing employment arrangements at large.[24]

In consequence, it can be seen that the Swedish innovations made right at the end of the twenty-first century, and just prior to the final elaboration of the EU's draft

21. *Lag om förbud mot diskriminering i arbetslivet på grund av funktionshinder* (SFS 1999:132). For contemporaneous consideration of this area of regulation in Sweden, see A. Inghammar, 'Discrimination of People with Disabilities', in A. Numhauser-Henning (ed.), *Normative Aspects of Disability and Work in a Swedish, English and EC Context* (The Hague, 2001) 323-349.
22. See *Lag om jämställdhet mellan kvinnor och män i arbetslivet*, the Act on Equality between Women and Men at Work (SFS 1979:1118), which came into force on 1 January 1980.
23. See Art. 17 of the 1999 Act.
24. See Art. 6 of the Act.

Directive on a framework for combating discrimination at work,[25] were already demonstrating a path somewhat different from that which had developed in the Anglo-American legal systems during the previous decade.

[B] The 'EU Model' under the Provisions of Directive 2000/78/EC

As is well known, the model introduced by the 'framework' Directive 2000/78/EC placed an emphasis upon 'penal' mechanisms, through the traditional approach of prohibiting both acts of 'direct discrimination' and measures of 'indirect discrimination'. This prohibition was then formulated as the so-called principle of equal treatment,[26] and made applicable to all of the forms of discrimination falling within the scope of the Directive.[27]

Alongside that approach, however, is provision specific to discrimination concerning disabled persons, to require 'reasonable accommodation' on the parts of employers – although this appears as a self-standing obligation upon employers, rather than as an integrated element in a co-ordinated promotional framework for addressing problems of disabled persons in the workforce.[28]

The social policy objectives of the Directive were set out in its Preamble, which made specific mention of persons with disability. Thus it was declared that: 'The Employment Guidelines for 2000 agreed by the European Council at Helsinki on 10 and 11 December 1999 stress the need to foster a labour market favourable to social integration by formulating a coherent set of policies aimed at combating discrimination against groups such as persons with disability',[29] while also recognising that: 'The provision of measures to accommodate the needs of disabled people at the workplace plays an important role in combating discrimination on grounds of disability'.[30]

25. The timing was not coincidental. Thus, the European Commission's eventual Proposal for a Council Directive establishing a general framework for equal treatment in employment and occupation (2000/C 177 E/07) was submitted on 6 January 2000 – reflecting the outcome of steady preparation since the introduction of legislative powers in relation to discrimination contained in new Arts 12 and 13 of the EC Treaty as provided for by the Treaty of Amsterdam. See also the picture painted in the Annual Report from the Commission, *Equal Opportunities for Women and Men in the European Union 1998* (COM (1999) 106 final).
26. Supplemented by a provision endorsing 'positive action', contained in Art. 7.1 of the Directive, to the effect that: 'With a view to ensuring full equality in practice, the principle of equal treatment shall not prevent any Member State from maintaining or adopting specific measures to prevent or compensate for disadvantages linked to any of the grounds referred to in Article 1'.
27. Specifically, the 'protected characteristics' of religion or belief, disability, age and sexual orientation as regards employment and occupation. The area of discrimination by reference to sex had been developed at the European Union level in the wake of the equal pay requirement established by Art. 119 of the Treaty of Rome 1957 – in particular, through Council Directive 76/207/EEC of 9 February 1976 on the implementation of the principle of equal treatment for men and women as regards access to employment, vocational training and promotion, and working conditions. Measures directed towards the issue of discrimination on the grounds of racial or ethnic origin were set out in Council Directive 2000/43/EC of 29 June 2000 implementing the principle of equal treatment between persons irrespective of racial or ethnic origin.
28. See Art. 5 of the Directive.
29. Preamble, para. (8).
30. Preamble, para. (16).

Nevertheless, although some mention was made of the 'social integration' imperative for the European labour market, this was nothing like as explicit as the American declarations to be found in the 'Findings and purpose' section of the Americans With Disabilities Act 1990.[31] Nor, arguably, did the language of the Directive indicate the strength of purpose encapsulated within the United Kingdom legislation's 'Section 6 duty' to make reasonable adjustments. On the other hand, under the rubric of 'Positive action', the Directive did provide that:

> With regard to disabled persons, the principle of equal treatment shall be without prejudice to the right of Member States to maintain or adopt provisions on the protection of health and safety at work or to measures aimed at creating or maintaining provisions or facilities for safeguarding or promoting their integration into the working environment.[32]

Distinct from the American and United Kingdom forerunners, the European Directive made its Article 5 provision on 'reasonable accommodation for disabled persons' subordinate to the 'principle of equal treatment',[33] and provided for a variety of 'exit gateways' to enable employers to avoid liability. The duty itself was expressed in terms that employers 'shall take appropriate measures, where needed in a particular case, to enable a person with a disability to have access to, participate in, or advance in employment, or to undergo training'. However, no such duty arose if 'such measures would impose a disproportionate burden on the employer'.[34]

[C] 'Feedback Effects' for United Kingdom Disability Law

The coming into force of Directive 2000/78/EC brought the United Kingdom legislator face-to-face with the inevitability that the post-1995 framework for addressing disability discrimination at the workplace would need to be adjusted in order to deliver the effects set out in the Directive. That task of adjustment was eventually achieved through the enactment of the Disability Discrimination Act 1995 (Amendment) Regulations 2003, which significantly modified provisions contained in the Disability Discrimination Act 1995.

31. As, for example, in subpara. (5), which recognises that: 'individuals with disabilities continually encounter various forms of discrimination, including outright intentional exclusion, the discriminatory effects of architectural, transportation, and communication barriers, overprotective rules and policies, failure to make modifications to existing facilities and practices, exclusionary qualification standards and criteria, segregation, and relegation to lesser services, programs, activities, benefits, jobs, or other opportunities;...'.
32. See Art. 7.2.
33. 'In order to guarantee compliance with the principle of equal treatment in relation to persons with disabilities, reasonable accommodation shall be provided.'
34. Although Art. 5 does go on to provide that: 'This burden shall not be disproportionate when it is sufficiently remedied by measures existing within the framework of the disability policy of the Member State concerned.' – whatever that may mean.

Thus, the original section 6 in the 1995 Act was repealed with effect from 1 October 2004 and, in its place, a new section 4A was inserted.[35] At the same time, the old section 5(2) was replaced by a new section 3A(2).[36]

Subsequently, the provisions relating to disability discrimination in the United Kingdom have been placed together with statutory measures dealing with the entirety of the 'protective characteristics' established by the EU's framework arrangements, now contained in the Equality Act 2010, as the so-called disability stream of protection offered by that statute.

§5.04 COMMENT

The introduction of an EU-wide framework for regulating issues arising in the context of disability discrimination has seen the adoption of an approach to 'reasonable accommodation' which is different from the model developed during the 1990s in the Anglo-American systems which had been at the forefront of introducing protective measures in this area. Experience in the context of the United Kingdom's regulatory framework has led to the proposition that a 'penally sanctioned compliance' approach has been favoured over a 'promotional' model designed to encourage the integration of disabled persons into the active workforce.

In particular, the introduction of a prohibition against what is generally referred to as 'indirect discrimination' as part of the so-called principle of equal treatment, coupled with the formulation of a duty to make reasonable accommodation as, to all intents and purposes, a self-standing duty has shifted the emphasis from what it has been argued could have been a development towards a form of 'disability risk assessment' regime to a situation in which employer approaches to litigation strategy concentrate much more upon defending against allegations of non-compliance rather than upon establishing pro-active integrative policies in relation to persons with disabilities.

Observed trial behaviour following amendment of United Kingdom legislative provisions as a result of that Member State's obligation to implement the provisions of Directive 2000/78/EC as compared with litigation conduct under the original regime introduced by the Disability Discrimination Act 1995 suggests some anecdotal evidence to this effect. Furthermore, indications in decided case law since the introduction of a

---

35. Providing that:

    '(1) Where –

    (a) a provision, criterion or practice applied by or on behalf of an employer, or
    (b) any physical feature of premises occupied by the employer,places the disabled person concerned at a substantial disadvantage in comparison with persons who are not disabled, it is the duty of the employer to take such steps as it is reasonable, in all the circumstances of the case, for him to have to take in order to prevent the provision, criterion or practice, or feature, having that effect.'

36. Which provided that: 'For the purposes of this Part, a person also discriminates against a disabled person if he fails to comply with a duty to make reasonable adjustments imposed on him in relation to the disabled person'.

Directive-compliant framework for the United Kingdom suggest a marked shift away from the expectation that the employer should take the initiative in relation to evaluating relevant circumstances affecting a disabled person and coming up with an appropriate course of action to satisfy the duty to make adjustments. Instead, we increasingly find a situation in which the complainant disabled person is expected to set out what 'should be', or 'should have been', actions to be taken by the employer in discharge of the duty to make reasonable accommodation, followed by attempts on the parts of respondent employers to argue either that such suggested specific actions do not form part of the employer's duty or that the complainant disabled person has failed to establish with sufficient clarity what it is the employer should be, or have been, expected to do.

The consequence of this, it is suggested, is, most obviously, that the 'integrative' or 're-integrative' ambitions of the Anglo-American model to combat disability discrimination have been subordinated to the 'equal treatment' principle which runs through the generality of EU regulatory arrangements to combat discrimination in relation to all of the 'protected characteristics' placed under the umbrella of framework Directive 2000/78/EC in conjunction with Directive 2000/43/EC. This placing together of the specific regime designed to combat disability discrimination with the approach taken in respect of discrimination in relation to other 'protected characteristics' also, it is suggested, reinforces a more general 'dilution' of protection through the EU model. This is particularly the case when compared with the arrangements which had been operated in the United Kingdom, where a 'floor of rights' approach has been the norm, as opposed to a broadly proclaimed 'principle of equal treatment'. When combined with a general tendency towards the enforcement and promotion of the interests of persons experiencing any of the 'protected characteristics' through a unified state established body, such as an 'equality commission' or an 'equality and human rights commission', responsible for all kinds of discrimination, this further removes the particular sensitivity of the regulatory framework for particular categories of 'protected characteristic' such as disability.

The direction of travel embraced by the EU model in relation to 'disability accommodation' is particularly striking when set against the evident priority accorded to the 'integration/promotion model' of dealing with disadvantage for disabled persons at or seeking work accorded by instruments such as the UN Convention on the Rights of Persons with Disabilities (CRPD) and the EU's own Charter of Fundamental Rights of the EU.[37] However, in the light of recent comments at the level of the CJEU, there have apparently been awakened suggestions in certain quarters that the 'promotional' and 'labour market integration' components of the declared objectives to which

37. The Charter of Fundamental Rights of the European Union was first signed in Nice on 7 December 2000 (OJ 2000/C 364/01, 18.12.2000). An identical version was signed in Strasbourg on 12 December 2007 (OJ 2007/C 303/01, 14.12.2007) and has acquired its current standing in the wake of the coming into force of the Treaty of Lisbon 2009. Article 26 of the Charter declares that the EU 'recognises and respects the right of persons with disabilities to benefit from measures designed to ensure their independence, social and occupational integration and participation in the life of the community'.

Directive 2000/78/EC is addressed might now be given more impetus that had earlier appeared to have been the case.

The trigger for such a ray of optimism lies primarily in the judgment of the CJEU in Joined Cases C-335/11, *HK Danmark (Ring) v. Dansk almennyttigt Boligselskab* and C-337/11, *HK Danmark (Werge) v. Dansk Arbejdsgiverforening (Pro Display A/S, in liquidation)*.[38] In particular, the apparent willingness of the Luxembourg Court to permit express reference to be made to the UN CRPD as an interpretative aid to dealing with matters arising within the scope of Directive 2000/78/EC has attracted significant attention.[39] At the same time, great faith appears to be placed in other quarters upon the potential which is said to reside in declarations contained in the Charter of Fundamental Rights of the EU in the post-Lisbon era. It has to be said, however, that this author remains sceptical, on the basis of the evidence to date, of any such optimism in relation to either of those two instruments.

Certainly, it cannot be denied that, if one looks at the observations of the Court of Justice in the *HK Denmark* case, the frame of reference adopted drew directly and heavily upon the UN Convention framework, so that:

> 53. In accordance with the second paragraph of Article 2 of the UN Convention, 'reasonable accommodation' is 'necessary and appropriate modification and adjustments not imposing a disproportionate or undue burden, where needed in a particular case, to ensure to persons with disabilities the enjoyment or exercise on an equal basis with others of all human rights and fundamental freedoms'. It follows that that provision prescribes a broad definition of the concept of 'reasonable accommodation'.
>
> 54. Thus, with respect to Directive 2000/78, that concept must be understood as referring to the elimination of the various barriers that hinder the full and effective participation of persons with disabilities in professional life on an equal basis with other workers.

The importance of the EU's adherence to an international human rights order established through an UN Convention was emphasised by the Luxembourg Court,

38. Joined Cases C-335/11, *HK Danmark (acting on behalf of Jette Ring) v. Dansk almennyttigt Boligselskab* and C-337/11, *HK Danmark (acting on behalf of Lone Skouboe Werge) v. Dansk Arbejdsgiverforening (acting on behalf of Pro Display A/S, in liquidation)*. Judgment of the Court delivered on 11 April 2013.

39. UN Convention on the Rights of Persons with Disabilities, adopted on 13 December 2006 (See resolution A/RES/61/106, passed during the sixty-first session of the General Assembly, New York). That Convention eventually entered into force on 3 May 2008. The European Union acceded to the UN Convention on 30 March 2007 (see IP/07/446), the first day on which that instrument was opened for signature. That act of accession on behalf of the European Union was approved by Council Decision 2010/48/EC of 26 November 2009 concerning the conclusion, by the European Community, of the United Nations Convention on the Rights of Persons with Disabilities (OJ L 23, 27.1.2010, p. 35). The Convention declares (in Art. 2) that 'reasonable accommodation' means: 'necessary and appropriate modification and adjustments not imposing a disproportionate or undue burden, where needed in a particular case, to ensure to persons with disabilities the enjoyment or exercise on an equal basis with others of all human rights and fundamental freedoms'. Article 27 of the Convention further provides that: 'States Parties recognise the right of persons with disabilities to work, on an equal basis with others; this includes the right to the opportunity to gain a living by work freely chosen or accepted in a labour market and work environment that is open, inclusive and accessible to persons with disabilities…'.

making it clear that such a source of regulation constitutes an obligatory and important point of reference for any consideration of the obligations arising for employers in relation to disabled persons active or seeking to be active in the European labour market.[40]

The practical question, however, remains to be answered as to whether, in the light of the emerging jurisprudence of the Court of Justice, the direction of travel can justifiably be said to be towards the promotion of labour market integration for disabled persons - and, even more aspirationally, whether there might be said to be any optimistic future for something akin to the 'disability risk assessment' approach to reasonable accommodation.

A recent revisiting of this area has been seen in the Luxembourg Court's judgment of 18 March 2014 in Case C-363/12, *Z. v. A Government department, The Board of management of a community school*, while some additional consideration is to be found in the Court's broadly contemporaneous judgment, handed down on 22 May 2014, in Case C-356/12, *Wolfgang Glatzel v. Freistaat Bayern.*[41]

Thus, it was confirmed in Case C-363/12 - which had been referred under Article 267 by an Equality Tribunal in Ireland - that the provisions of the UN Convention are 'from the time of its entry into force, an integral part of the European Union legal order'.[42] Furthermore, echoing the approach laid down in the *HK Denmark* case, 'the UN Convention is capable of being relied on for the purposes of interpreting Directive 2000/78, which must, as far as possible, be interpreted in a manner that is consistent with that Convention'.[43]

However, since the Court came to the conclusion that the complainant's circumstances did not amount to a 'disability' within the scope of the EU Directive's provisions,[44] it was not necessary to test directly the area of 'reasonable accommodation' and its inter-relationship with either the UN Convention or the EU Charter.

40. Thus, at paras 28 and 29 of the judgment, the Court confirmed that: '28. It should be noted, as a preliminary point, that, by virtue of Article 216(2) TFEU, where international agreements are concluded by the European Union they are binding on its institutions, and consequently they prevail over acts of the European Union (Case C-366/10, *Air Transport Association of America and Others* [2011] ECR I-13755, paragraph 50 and the case-law cited)... 29. It should also be recalled that the primacy of international agreements concluded by the European Union over instruments of secondary law means that those instruments must as far as possible be interpreted in a manner that is consistent with those agreements (Joined Cases C-320/11, C-330/11, C-382/11 and C-383/11, *Digitalnet and Others* [2012] ECR, paragraph 39 and the case-law cited)'.
41. As with the other (as yet, still very limited) jurisprudence of the Court in the field of disability discrimination, these cases have been primarily concerned with clarifying the scope of the protected notion of 'disability'. The line of authority emerges from consideration of the issue in Case C-13/05, *Chacón Navas.*
42. See para. 73 of the judgment, making reference to Case 181/73, *Haegeman*, at para. 5, and to the *HK Danmark* case (*supra*), at para. 30.
43. See para. 75.
44. As expressed in the view of the Court, 'the concept of "disability" within the meaning of Directive 2000/78 presupposes that the limitation from which the person suffers, in interaction with various barriers, may hinder that person's full and effective participation in professional life on an equal basis with other workers' - something not satisfied in the facts of the particular case'. (See para. 80).

In relation to the former of those instruments, the Court reaffirmed that:

> while the validity of an act of the European Union may be affected by the fact that it is incompatible with rules of international law... where such invalidity is pleaded before a national court, the Court of Justice verifies whether certain conditions are satisfied in the case before it, in order to determine whether, pursuant to Article 267 TFEU, the validity of the act of European Union law concerned, in light of the rules of international law relied on, may be ascertained.[45]

However:

> in a situation where the nature and the broad logic of an international treaty permit the validity of the act of European Union law to be reviewed in the light of the provisions of that treaty, it is still necessary that the provisions of that treaty which are relied on for the purpose of examining the validity of the act of European Union law appear, as regards their content, to be unconditional and sufficiently precise,[46]

and, furthermore, that these give rise to an entitlement or protection 'which is not subject, in its implementation or effects, to the adoption of any subsequent measure'.[47] So far as the UN Convention is concerned, though:

> it is apparent from Article 4(1) of the UN Convention that it is, in particular, for the States Parties to adopt all appropriate legislative, administrative and other measures for the implementation of the rights recognised in that Convention. In addition, under Article 4(3) of the UN Convention, in the development and implementation of legislation and policies to implement that Convention, and in other decision-making processes concerning issues relating to persons with disabilities, States Parties are to closely consult with and actively involve persons with disabilities, including children with disabilities, through their representative organisations,[48]

leading to the Court adopting the position of the Advocate General that '...so far as the obligations imposed by [the UN] Convention are addressed to Contracting Parties, that international agreement is "programmatic".'.[49] All of these factors led the Court to the conclusion that:[50]

> In those circumstances, without there being any need to examine the nature and broad logic of the UN Convention, it must be held that the provisions of that Convention are not, as regards their content, provisions that are unconditional and sufficiently precise within the meaning of the case-law cited in paragraphs 85 and 86 of the present judgment, and that they therefore do not have direct effect in European Union law. It follows from this that the validity of Directive 2000/78 cannot be assessed in the light of the UN Convention.

The operative part of the judgment thus limited itself to the clarification that '...the validity of [Directive 2000/78/EC] cannot be assessed in the light of the UN

45. Paragraph 84.
46. Paragraph 85.
47. Paragraph 86.
48. Paragraph 87.
49. Paragraph 88.
50. Paragraph 90.

Convention, but that directive must, as far as possible, be interpreted in a manner that is consistent with that Convention'.

Meanwhile, so far as the EU Charter might be concerned, the Court in Case C-363/12 settled for a much more robust approach, holding simply that '...it is not necessary to examine the validity of Directive 2000/78 in the light of Article 10 TFEU and Articles 21, 26 and 34 of the Charter'.

Consequently, the only directly-relevant pronouncements to date on this latter instrument are to be drawn from the judgment of the Court, delivered on 22 May 2014, in Case C-356/12, *Wolfgang Glatzel v. Freistaat Bayern*. Yet, even there, the prospects for relying directly upon declarations contained in the Charter of Fundamental Rights of the EU received something of a dampening, given that the view was expressed that:[51]

> although Article 26 of the Charter requires the European Union to respect and recognise the right of persons with disabilities to benefit from integration measures, the principle enshrined by that article does not require the EU legislature to adopt any specific measure. In order for that article to be fully effective, it must be given more specific expression in European Union or national law. Accordingly, that article cannot by itself confer on individuals a subjective right which they may invoke as such.[52]

Given these (albeit limited) indications from the Court, the pessimistic conclusion has to be that the mechanism of 'reasonable accommodation' in the framework Directive appears to have been consigned to the realm of 'soft' aspiration, rather than grasped as a potent tool for integrating disabled persons into the active labour market. The rejection of the Anglo-American model, and the embracing of the one-size-fits-all 'principle of equal treatment', has seen the EU turn its back on an opportunity to place effective pressure upon employers to consider 'pro-active' measures to enable disabled workers to play a full part in the labour market. Instead, the choice of a generic model developed primarily on the back of experience in the field of gender discrimination has deprived the regulatory tools deployed in the particular field of 'disability discrimination' of what might be suggested is the necessary nuanced application appropriate to this delicate and controversial area.

Nor would the development of a protective back up for disabled workers through creative use of key declarations contained in the Charter of Fundamental Rights of the EU appear to be something to which immediate recourse may be had – still less the 'programmatic' framework embodied in the UN CRPD.

So, no pro-active integrative instruments, and little or nothing to encourage the development of a 'disability risk assessment' culture in enterprises faced with disabled workers or disabled persons seeking access to employment. All in all, not an attractive prospect, and certainly nothing to inspire confidence in those suffering from disabilities

51. Paragraph 78 of the judgment.
52. And note the reliance of the CJEU upon the observations in Case C-176/12 *Association de mediation sociale* – a case involving consideration of Art. 27 of the Charter (information and consultation for workers or their representatives) – at paras 45 and 47.

who wish to access or to play a full part in the modern European labour market that there is anything more than 'empty words' in the proposition that:[53]

> The provision of measures to accommodate the needs of disabled people at the workplace plays an important role in combating discrimination on grounds of disability.

53. Preamble to Council Directive 2000/78/EC of 27 November 2000 establishing a general framework for equal treatment in employment and occupation, para. (16).

CHAPTER 6

Non-discrimination, Reasonable Accommodation and Swedish Law: With a Special Focus on Disability

Mia Rönnmar

§6.01 INTRODUCTION

This chapter presents a discussion and analysis of reasonable accommodation in the context of Swedish non-discrimination law, with a special focus on disability. The legal analysis covers statutory and case law developments, and is set against the backdrop of the complex interplay between international law, EU law and national law.

After an introduction to the EU law framework, the outline of the chapter is as follows. Section §6.02 explores Swedish non-discrimination law. Section §6.03 presents an analysis of Swedish disability discrimination law and reasonable accommodation in context, including recent domestic and international case law developments and links between reasonable accommodation and regulation on active measures, working environment and employment protection. Finally, section §6.04 provides some concluding remarks.

Sweden has been a member of the EU since 1995, and EU law developments are naturally crucial for the development and content of Swedish law. Non-discrimination law is a central and well-developed part of EU law, and has gradually extended its reach beyond working life. Primary law is complemented by a number of non-discrimination law directives, and the Court of Justice of the European Union (CJEU) and its case law has contributed greatly to the development of EU non-discrimination law. This development has been described by Hepple as a move towards comprehensive and transformative discrimination and by Bell as a widening and deepening of non-discrimination law.[1]

Article 21 of the EU Charter of Fundamental Rights (legally binding and primary law since the Lisbon Treaty) contains an open list of discrimination grounds and states that:

> [a]ny discrimination based on any ground such as sex, race, colour, ethnic or social origin, genetic features, language, religion or belief, political or any other opinion, membership of a national minority, property, birth, disability, age or sexual orientation shall be prohibited.[2]

The EU shall adopt a proactive mainstreaming approach in all its activities and policies to eliminate inequalities, to promote equality between men and women and to combat discrimination.[3]

The (2000/78/EC) Employment Equality Directive (just like the (2000/43/EC) Race Directive) was adopted in 2000, following the Amsterdam Treaty and the widened competence in the equality field through the inclusion of Article 13 EC, now Article 19 TFEU. The Employment Equality Directive lays down a general framework for combating discrimination on the grounds of religion or belief, disability, age or sexual orientation, as regards employment and occupation. The Employment Equality Directive encompasses prohibitions on direct and indirect discrimination, harassment, and instruction to discriminate, as well as provisions on positive action and active measures, and a rule on a reversed burden of proof.[4]

In relation to disability, Article 5 of the Employment Equality Directive regulates the issue of reasonable accommodation and states that 'employers shall take appropriate measures, where needed in a particular case, to enable a person with a disability to have access to, participate in, or advance in employment, or to undergo training, unless such measures would impose a disproportionate burden on the employer'. In *Coleman*[5] a woman was found to have suffered discrimination when she was treated less favourably and harassed because of her son's disability – so-called *transferred discrimination*. The CJEU held that the Employment Equality Directive 'which seeks to combat all forms of discrimination on grounds of disability in the field of employment

1. See B. Hepple, 'Equality at Work', in B. Hepple & B. Veneziani (eds), *The Transformation of Labour Law in Europe, A Comparative Study of 15 Countries 1945-2004* (Hart Publishing, Oxford 2009) and M. Bell, 'The Principle of Equal Treatment; Widening and Deepening', in P. Craig & G. de Búrca (eds), *The Evolution of EU Law* (Oxford University Press, Oxford 2011).
2. The CJEU has also held that EU law encompasses a general principle of non-discrimination on grounds of age; see C-144/04 *Werner Mangold v. Rudiger Helm* [2005] ECR I-09981 and Case C-555/07 *Seda Kücükdeveci v. Swedex GmBH & Co* [2010] ECR I-00365.
3. Articles 8 and 10 TFEU.
4. Discrimination on grounds of age (even direct discrimination) can be justified to a greater extent than discrimination on other grounds, and Art. 6 provides for specific justification of differences of treatment on grounds of age. See A. Numhauser-Henning & M. Rönnmar (eds), *Age Discrimination and Labour Law. Comparative and Conceptual Perspectives in the EU and Beyond* (Kluwer Law International, Alphen aan den Rijn 2015) for a thorough analysis of age discrimination in an EU law perspective, including the CJEU's now quite extensive case law in this area, and a comparative law perspective.
5. Case C-303/06 *Coleman* [2008] ECR I-5603.

and occupation, applies not to a particular category of person but by reference to the grounds mentioned in Article 1'.[6]

The EU, as well as its Member States, has signed the United Nations Convention on the Rights of Persons with Disabilities (CRPD). In *HK Danmark*[7] the CJEU aligned its interpretation both of the concept of disability and the duty of reasonable accommodation with the UN Convention. The Court declared that the Convention formed an integral part of the EU legal order, wherefore the Employment Equality Directive must 'as far as possible, be interpreted in a manner consistent with that Convention'.

The CJEU interpreted the concept of disability and developed its reasoning in relation to its earlier judgment in *Chacón Navas*.[8] The CJEU stated that:

> the concept of 'disability' must be understood as referring to a limitation which results in particular from physical, mental or psychological impairments which, in interaction with various barriers, may hinder the full and effective participation of the person concerned in professional life on an equal basis with other workers.

This has been seen as a shift on the part of the CJEU from a medical or individual model of disability to a social model of disability.[9,10]

In *HK Danmark* the CJEU interpreted Article 5 in conformity with the UN Convention and held that a reduction in working hours may constitute one of the accommodation measures referred to in Article 5. Accommodation measures are not only material but also organizational and the list of appropriate measures in recital 20 in the preamble to the Employment Equality Directive is not exhaustive. The CJEU stated that it is up to the national court to assess whether a reduction in working hours

6. Paragraph 50.
7. Joined Cases C-335/11 and C-337/11 *HK Danmark* EU:C:2013:222. Compare also Case C-152/11 *Johann Odar v. Baxter Deutschland GmbH* EU:C:2012:772 and Case C-356/12 *Glatzel* EU:C:2014:350.
8. Case C-13/05 *Chacón Navas* [2006] ECR I-6488.
9. See L. Waddington, 'HK Danmark (Ring and Skouboe Werge): Interpreting EU Equality Law in Light of the UN Convention on the Rights of Persons with Disabilities', *European Anti-Discrimination Law Review*, November 2013, Issue 17, pp. 13-23, and A. Bruce, *Which Entitlement and for Whom? The Convention on the Rights of Persons with Disabilities and Its Ideological Antecedents* (Lund University, Lund 2014).
10. On the issue of illness the CJEU stated that 'if a curable or incurable illness entails a limitation which results in particular from physical, mental or psychological impairments which in interaction with various barriers may hinder the full and effective participation of the person concerned in professional life on an equal basis with other workers, and the limitation is a long-term one, such an illness can be covered by the concept of "disability" within the meaning of Directive 2000/78', para. 41. However, the Court, also with reference to *Chacón Navas*, held that '[i]llness as such cannot be regarded as a ground in addition to those in relation to which Directive 2000/78 prohibits discrimination', para. 42. – On the issue of obesity the CJEU held in the case of *Kaltoft* that EU law must be interpreted as not laying down a general principle of non-discrimination on grounds of obesity as such, as regards employment and occupation and that obesity does not in itself constitute a disability. However, 'in the event that, under given circumstances, the obesity of a worker concerned entails a limitation which results in particular from physical, mental or psychological impairments that in interaction with various barriers may hinder the full and effective participation of that person in professional life on an equal basis with other workers, and the limitation is a long-term one, obesity may be covered by the concept of "disability" within the meaning of Directive 2000778' (para. 59); see Case C-354/13 *Kaltoft* EU:C:2014:2463.

represents a disproportionate burden on the employer. In this context, account should be taken of financial and other costs, the scale and financial resources of the undertaking and the possibility of obtaining public funding and other assistance. The CJEU also clarified that the concept of disability comes before the determination and assessment of the appropriate accommodation measures, and the measures are therefore 'the consequence, not the constituent element, of the concept of "disability"'.[11]

In 2008 a proposal was put forward for extending protection against discrimination on the grounds of disability, age, religion or belief and sexual orientation to areas beyond working life, in parallel with the protection provided by the Race Directive. In 2014 the Juncker Commission declared that this proposal had been made a top priority. However, the proposal is still pending.[12]

The overall aim of the European Disability Strategy 2010-2020 is to 'empower people with disabilities so that they can enjoy their full rights, and benefit fully from participating in society and in the European economy'.[13] Accessibility[14] is identified as one of the eight main areas for action. In line with this, the Commission presented a proposal in December 2015 for a directive on the approximation of the laws, regulations and administrative provisions of the Member States as regards accessibility requirements for products and services.[15] The proposal aims to aid the EU and the Member States in achieving their commitments under the UN CRPD, while contributing to the proper functioning of the international market and removing and preventing barriers for the free movement of accessible products and services.

§6.02 SWEDISH NON-DISCRIMINATION LAW

The Swedish labour law and industrial relations system is characterized by self-regulation, cooperation between the social partners and autonomous collective bargaining. Wages and terms and conditions of employment are generally set by collective bargaining, but labour law legislation is also frequent. Most labour law legislation is of a so-called *semi-compelling* nature, and allows for collectively bargained deviations, to the advantage and detriment of employees. The trade union organization rate is about 70%, and the collective bargaining coverage rate is about 90%. Rules on information, consultation and co-determination complement collective bargaining.

11. Joined Cases C-335/11 and C-337/11 *HK Danmark* EU:C:2013:222, paras 45 and 46.
12. See COM(2008) 426 final. See further L. Waddington, 'Future Prospect for EU Equality Law: Lessons to Be Learnt from the Proposed Equal Treatment Directive', *European Law Review*, 2011, vol. 36, Issue 2, pp. 163-184.
13. See Communication from the Commission to the European Parliament, the Council, the European Economic and Social Committee and the Committee of the Regions, *European Disability Strategy 2010-2020: A Renewed Commitment to a Barrier-Free Europe*, COM(2010) 636 final.
14. Defined here as meaning that people with disabilities have access, on an equal basis with others, to the physical environment, transportation, information and communications technologies and systems (ICT), and other facilities and services.
15. See European Commission, *Proposal for a Directive of the European Parliament and of the Council on the Approximation of the Laws, Regulations and Administrative Provisions of the Member States as regards the Accessibility Requirements for Products and Services*, COM(2015) 615/2.

In the area of non-discrimination, EU law and Swedish law interact in a dynamic way. In a comparative perspective, Nordic and Swedish non-discrimination law is characterized by an early and strong focus on active measures in the area of gender equality.[16] EU law has strongly influenced the development and content of Swedish non-discrimination law through a number of factors: its constant change, the case law of the CJEU, the emphasis on substantive equality, an increasing number of protected discrimination grounds, a widened scope and a strengthened fundamental-rights perspective. At the same time, Swedish law is still characterized by independence, and in some aspects has gone further than EU law requires. This is the case, for example, when it comes to active measures, transgender as a separate discrimination ground, a ban on age discrimination beyond working life and the new ban on inadequate accessibility.

The first Gender Equality Act was adopted in 1979, and was subsequently reformed, *inter alia* under the influence of EU law. The protection against discrimination in working life was greatly strengthened in 1999 when Sweden - before the adoption of the Race Directive and the Employment Equality Directive - introduced three new acts against discrimination on grounds of ethnicity, religion or other belief,[17] disability[18] and sexual orientation.[19]

In 2008, parallel to the development at EU level towards new and more discrimination grounds and a widened scope of non-discrimination law, a Single Non-Discrimination Act was adopted in Sweden.[20] The Act was modelled on EU law, and implements the EU non-discrimination law directives. It replaced the earlier non-discrimination acts. The Act not only gathers different discrimination grounds but is also applicable in part outside the realm of working life - for example in goods and services, public employment services, education, health care, social services, and social security.[21] The Non-Discrimination Act covers protection against discrimination on grounds of sex, ethnicity, religion and other belief, sexual orientation, disability, age and transgender identity/expression.

An employer may not discriminate against a person who, with respect to the employer, is an employee; is enquiring about or applying for work; is applying for or carrying out a traineeship; or is available to perform work or is performing work as a temporary agency worker or as borrowed labour.[22] The Act contains prohibitions on direct and indirect discrimination, harassment, and instruction to discriminate, and provisions on a reversed burden of proof, positive action and active measures.[23]

16. See D. Schiek, L. Waddington & M. Bell, *Cases, Materials and Text on National; Supranational and International Non-Discrimination Law* (Hart, Oxford 2007) pp. 22 ff.
17. SFS 1999:130, which replaced an earlier act, SFS 1994:134.
18. SFS 1999:132.
19. SFS 1999:133.
20. SFS 2008:567. See Government Inquiry Report SOU 2006:22 and Government Bill prop. 2007/08:95.
21. See Governmental Bill prop. 2007/08:95 and Governmental Inquiry Report SOU 2006:22.
22. Chapter 2 section 1 of the Non-Discrimination Act.
23. See S. Fransson & E. Stüber, *Diskrimineringslagen. En kommentar*, 2 edn (Norstedts Juridik, Stockholm 2015).

However, like its EU counterpart, the Swedish legal development shows that a single non-discrimination legislation does not necessarily obviate the 'hierarchy' between different discrimination grounds and thus create the same possibilities to achieve substantial equality. In both Swedish and EU law important differences between different discrimination grounds persist when it comes to Treaty competence, scope, regulation of active measures and the scope for exemptions and justification.

The Equality Ombudsman (DO), a government agency, monitors the compliance with the Non-Discrimination Act. The Equality Ombudsman can also represent individuals in court disputes.[24] The Swedish Labour Court is the court of last instance in labour law disputes, including disputes on discrimination in working life.[25] The Labour Court is a tripartite body comprised of judges with judicial background and lay members from both sides of the labour market.[26] Before the Labour Court can deal with a legal dispute, local and central negotiation must have been conducted, and must have failed. An overwhelming number of disputes are resolved by negotiation between the parties.

§6.03 SWEDISH DISABILITY DISCRIMINATION LAW AND REASONABLE ACCOMMODATION IN CONTEXT

[A] Reasonable Accommodation and Case Law Developments

Swedish disability discrimination law is aligned with EU law, and the legislator, courts, Equality Ombudsman, social partners and legal scholars frequently refer to the Employment Equality Directive and case law from the CJEU. Sweden has signed the UN CRPD.

Only when it comes to disability does Swedish non-discrimination law contain a requirement for reasonable accommodation (and not for other discrimination grounds, such as age or religion or other belief).

The requirement for reasonable accommodation was introduced by the 1999 Act on Disability Discrimination in Working Life, and was later transferred into the Non-Discrimination Act.[27] Up until 1 January 2015 the Non-Discrimination Act provided that the bans on discrimination – such as the prohibition on direct and indirect discrimination – also applied in cases where the employer, through reasonable accommodation measures,[28] could put an employee, a job seeker or a trainee with a disability in a comparable situation with a person without such a disability.[29] (The new

24. Chapter 4 of the Non-Discrimination Act.
25. Cf. Art. 267 TFEU.
26. The Swedish Labour Court acts as the Supreme Court in labour law disputes. It is also the first, and only, instance in all proceedings filed by a trade union or an employer's organization.
27. Originally the requirement applied only in relation to job seekers, and in 2006 the scope of the requirement was widened to include employees and trainees; see Government Bill prop. 2005/06:207.
28. *Skäliga stöd- och anpassningsåtgärder*, reasonable support and adaptation measures.
29. Chapter 2 section 1 subsection 2 of the Non-Discrimination Act.

ban on inadequate accessibility,[30] which has replaced the previous requirement for reasonable accommodation, will be discussed in section §6.03[B]) Thus Swedish regulation of reasonable accommodation in disability discrimination law is characterized by continuity, and the preparatory works provide some guidelines as to the interpretation and application of the requirement for reasonable accommodation.[31]

The question of the accommodation measures an employer should consider and take, and whether or not they are reasonable, depends on the circumstances in each individual case. The assessment must thus be made on a case-by-case basis. In principle, the content and character of the measure should be influenced by the form and severity of the employee's disability in conjunction with the demands inherent in the employment relationship and the work tasks. The need for accommodation measures might relate to difficulties in performing the work tasks, or difficulties in accessing the workplace. In this context, the preparatory works refer to paragraph 20 in the Preamble to the Employment Equality Directive. For example, the measures can relate to occupational assistive devices and adjustments to the workplace, work organization, working time and work tasks.

The assessment of reasonableness is to be made with reference to factors such as the employer's economic situation, the managerial prerogative, the practical possibility of taking the measures in question, the form and degree of the disability and the form and duration of the employment relationship.[32] There is no obligation to take unreasonable or impossible measures or measures that meet with legal obstacles.[33] The managerial prerogative – and whether or not it is reasonable to restrict it – plays a key role in the assessment of reasonableness. Despite extensive labour law legislation, collective bargaining and strong trade unions, Swedish labour law is still based on a traditional and strong respect for the managerial prerogative.[34]

The case law on reasonable accommodation from recent years is rather limited. It relates to hiring[35] and dismissal.[36] In general, it has proven very difficult for employees and job seekers to argue – and prove – that employers have been in breach of their obligation to provide reasonable accommodation. In no case has the Labour Court handed down a judgment of discrimination.[37]

30. Chapter 1 section 4 p. 3 of the Non-Discrimination Act.
31. See Government Bill prop. 1997/98:179, Government Bill prop. 2007/08:95 and Government Bill prop. 2013/14:198.
32. A precondition for the employer's obligation to take reasonable accommodation measures is that the employer has knowledge of or should have knowledge that the job seeker or the employee is disabled. In order for the employer to be able to fulfil his or her obligation it might be necessary for the employee to inform the employer of his or her disability and convey his or her opinion about the need for accommodation measures. See Government Bill prop. 2007/08:95, p. 153.
33. Cf. Labour Court judgments AD 2012:51 and AD 2013:78.
34. For a comparative analysis of the role of the managerial prerogative in Swedish labour law, see M. Rönnmar, 'The Managerial Prerogative and the Employee's Obligation to Work. Comparative Perspectives on Functional Flexibility', *Industrial Law Journal*, 2006, vol. 35, Issue 1, pp. 56-74.
35. For example, Labour Court judgments AD 2010:13 and AD 2011:25.
36. For example, Labour Court judgments AD 2012:51, AD 2013:78 and AD 2014:26.
37. See S. Fransson & E. Stüber, *Diskrimineringslagen. En kommentar*, 2 edn (Norstedts Juridik, Stockholm 2015) pp. 144 ff.

In 2014, for the first time, the Committee on the UN CRPD had to respond to a complaint made in relation to a judgment from the Swedish Labour Court on disability discrimination in working life and the possible violation of Articles 5 and 27 of the Convention.[38]

In Labour Court judgment AD 2010:13 a visually impaired job seeker (supported in the dispute by the Equality Ombudsman) was not hired, because the employer (the state Social Insurance Agency) did not find it reasonable to take accommodation measures, such as re-programming a data-based case management system, reorganizing the work tasks and hiring an assistant, in order for the disabled job seeker to be able to perform the work.[39] The Labour Court, after having reviewed the measures at stake in the dispute and conducting a reasonableness assessment, agreed with the employer and found the measures unreasonable with reference to the large costs involved and the impact on the managerial prerogative and the work organization. Thus, the claimant did not possess the objective qualifications needed for the position in question, and was not discriminated against on grounds of her disability.

The complaint to the UN Committee was made by the disabled job seeker, who was supported in the claim by an NGO. The question before the Committee was whether the Labour Court judgment (and the direct application of the Act and the requirement for reasonable accommodation to the claimant's case) amounted to a violation of the claimant's rights under Articles 5 and 27 of the Convention on equality and non-discrimination and work and employment, respectively. The Committee recalled that the State parties have the responsibility to prohibit discrimination on the basis of disability with regard to all matters concerning all forms of employment, and to ensure that reasonable accommodation is provided to persons with disabilities in the workplace (paragraph 10.4). When assessing the reasonableness and proportionality of accommodation measures, State parties enjoy a certain margin of appreciation (paragraph 10.5). It is generally the duty of the courts of the State parties to evaluate facts and evidence in a particular case. The Committee considered that 'the Labour Court thoroughly and objectively assessed all the elements submitted by the author [claimant] and the Social Insurance Agency before reaching the conclusion that the support and adaptation measures recommended by the Ombudsman would constitute an undue burden for the Social Insurance Agency'. The Committee further considered that 'the author [claimant] did not provide any evidence which would enable it to conclude that the assessment conducted was manifestly arbitrary or amounted to a denial of justice' (paragraph 10.6). To conclude, the Committee found no violation of Articles 5 and 27 of the Convention.[40]

38. See Labour Court judgment AD 2010:13 and Committee on the Rights of Persons with Disabilities, Communication No. 5/2011 in November 2014.
39. The dispute related to the provision on reasonable accommodation in the 1999 Act on Disability Discrimination in Working Life.
40. In a dissenting opinion five Committee members found that there had been a violation of Arts 5 and 27, arguing, for example, that 'the judgment of the Labour Court reflects a wide interpretation of the notion of "undue burden", severely limiting the possibility for persons with disabilities of being selected for positions requiring the adaptation of the working environment to their needs' (para. 6).

This complaint is also a sign of the increased attention being paid to international law and human rights law instruments in Sweden as well as the increased recourse to international human rights bodies. This has also been the experience in relation to the so-called Laval case and the right to collective bargaining and collective action where Swedish trade unions have made complaints to supervisory bodies, such as the ILO Committee of Experts and the European Committee of Social Rights.[41]

[B] A New Ban on Inadequate Accessibility for People with Disabilities

On 1 January 2015 a new separate ban on discrimination – inadequate accessibility for people with disabilities – entered into force and replaced the previous requirement for reasonable accommodation applied in cases of alleged direct and indirect disability discrimination etc.[42]

The new ban has a wider scope than the previous requirement for reasonable accommodation. It applies to working life, but also beyond, in education, labour market policy activities, starting or running a business, membership of certain organizations, goods and services, public meetings, public events, health and medical care, social services, social insurance, etc.[43]

The aim of the ban is to increase accessibility for people with disabilities in order to achieve equality and increase participation. The ban on inadequate accessibility is independent from the bans on direct and indirect discrimination, but aimed at complementing them.[44]

Discrimination by way of inadequate accessibility is at hand when a person with a disability becomes disadvantaged through a failure to take measures for accessibility, to enable the person to come into a situation comparable with that of persons without this disability, where such measures are reasonable on the basis of accessibility requirements in legislation and with consideration to the financial and practical conditions, the duration and nature of the relationship or contact between the operator and the individual and other circumstances of relevance. The ban applies to a person with a disability, and not in cases of transferred discrimination.[45] The ban is sanctioned with damages (*diskrimineringsersättning*).

The preparatory works emphasize that the new ban is not meant to bring about any substantive legal changes in working life when it comes to the assessment of

---

41. See M. Rönnmar, 'The Impact of *Viking* and *Laval* in Swedish Labour Law and Industrial Relations', in J. Prassl & M. Freedland (eds), *EU Law in the Member States. Viking and Laval* (Hart Publishing Oxford, 2015) pp. 241-260.
42. Chapter 1 section 4 p. 3 of the Non-Discrimination Act. See Government Bill prop. 2013/14:198 and Government Inquiry Report 2010:20.
43. The new ban has a wider personal scope than the previous requirement for reasonable accommodation and also applies to trainees, see Government Bill prop. 2013/14:198, p. 74. However, the ban does not apply to a person who enquires about employment.
44. See S. Fransson & E. Stüber, *Diskrimineringslagen. En kommentar*, 2 edn (Norstedts Juridik, Stockholm 2015) pp. 138 ff.
45. Cf. Case C-303/06 *Coleman* [2008] ECR I-5603. See Government Bill prop. 2013/14:198, p. 62 and S. Fransson & E. Stüber, *Diskrimineringslagen. En kommentar*, 2 edn (Norstedts Juridik, Stockholm 2015) p. 139.

reasonable accommodation. Guidelines in earlier preparatory works are still relevant.[46] Even so, at present (before case law has developed) it is difficult to assess how this new ban in practice and in dispute resolution will interplay with the bans on direct and indirect discrimination.

[C] Reasonable Accommodation and Links to Active Measures, Working Environment and Employment Protection

In Sweden an individual-complaints-led approach, based on bans on discrimination and reasonable accommodation in relation to disability, is complemented by a more proactive and preventive approach, based on regulation of active measures in non-discrimination law and requirements for adaptation and rehabilitation within the framework of employment protection, working environment and social security regulation. Thus, the preparatory works to the Non-Discrimination Act highlight that although the underlying aims and substantive content of these regulatory frameworks differ to some degree, they aim to complement and strengthen each other.[47]

Regulation on *active measures* in the area of gender equality was introduced already in 1979, and in 1999 it was complemented by regulation on active measures in the area of ethnicity, religion or belief. The provisions on active measures are found in Chapter 3 of the Non-Discrimination Act.[48] At present there are no rules on active measures related to disability. Employers and employees are to cooperate on active measures to bring about equal rights and opportunities in working life regardless of sex, ethnicity, religion or other belief, and in particular to combat discrimination in working life on such grounds.[49] Employers are to conduct goal-oriented work to actively promote equal rights and opportunities in working life regardless of sex, ethnicity, religion or other belief, and active measures also relate to specific obligations – such as to help enable both female and male employees to combine employment and parenthood, to take measures to prevent and hinder any employee from being subjected to harassment or reprisals and to ensure that people have the opportunity to apply for vacant positions regardless of sex, ethnicity, religion or other belief. In order to discover, remedy and prevent unfair gender differences in pay and other terms of employment the employer is to conduct a wage survey every three years and draw up an action plan for equal pay. The employer also has to draw up a gender equality plan every three years.[50]

In 2014 a Government Inquiry proposed a reform aimed at achieving a stronger, wider and more effective regulatory framework for active measures.[51] The Inquiry

46. See Government Bill prop. 2013/14:198, p. 65 and p. 70.
47. See Government Bill prop. 2007/08:95.
48. Some rules on active measures also apply in the area of education.
49. Chapter 3 section 1 of the Non-Discrimination Act.
50. See Chapter 3 sections 10, 11 and 13 of the Non-Discrimination Act. The obligation to draw up these plans does not apply to employers who employed fewer than twenty-five employees at the start of the latest calendar year.
51. See Government Inquiry Report 2014:41. – For a comparative analysis of the regulation of positive measures within the framework of labour market policy aimed at the labour market

proposed to extend the employer's obligation to take active measures to all protected discrimination grounds, i.e., also to disability and age. Active measures are defined as prevention and promotion measures aimed at preventing discrimination in a given establishment and serving in other ways to promote equal rights and opportunities regardless of sex, transgender identity or expression, ethnicity, religion or other belief, disability, sexual orientation or age. A more comprehensive and *systematic* approach to active measures is proposed, and the employer is obliged to use a specific method directing the work on active measures. The employer must conduct prevention and promotion work by *investigating* the existence of any risks of discrimination or reprisals or any other obstacles to individuals' equal rights and opportunities; *analysing* the causes of any risks and obstacles discovered; *taking* the prevention and promotion measures that can reasonably be demanded; and *monitoring and evaluating* the measures. The proposed scope of the systematic work on active measures covers, for example, working conditions, rules and practice regarding pay, recruitment and promotion, training and other skills development and the reconciliation of employment and parenthood. The work on active measures should continue to take place in cooperation between employers and employees, and the employer must provide information to trade unions to which they are bound by a collective agreement. The obligation to draw up an action plan for equal pay and a gender equality plan is to be replaced by a yearly requirement to document the systematic work. The employers' actions in the area of active measures are to be monitored by the Equality Ombudsman and sanctioned by financial penalties.

The purpose of the Work Environment Act[52] (*inter alia* implementing the (89/391/EEC) Framework Directive on Health and Safety) is to prevent occupational illness and accidents and otherwise ensure a good *work environment*.[53] The work environment must be satisfactory, taking into account the nature of the work and social and technological developments in society, and working conditions must be adapted to people's differing physical and mental capabilities.[54] The employer is responsible for securing a healthy and safe work environment, and the employer's obligations entail both *general* and *individual work environment adaptation*.[55] Employers and employees must cooperate to create a good work environment, and the employer must systematically plan, direct and monitor activities in a manner that ensures that the work environment meets the prescribed requirements for a good work environment.[56] When it comes to individual work adaptation - closely linked to reasonable accommodation and rehabilitation - the employer must take into account the particular fitness of the employee to perform the work by adapting the working conditions or taking other

integration of people with disabilities, see A. Inghammar, *Funktionshindrad - med rätt till arbete? En komparativ studie av arbetsrättsliga regleringar kring arbete och funktionshinder* (Juristförlaget i Lund, Lund 2007).

52. SFS 1977:1160.
53. Chapter 1 section 1 of the Work Environment Act.
54. Chapter 2 section 1 of the Work Environment Act.
55. Cf. Government Bill prop. 1976/77:149 and Government Bill prop. 1990/91:140 p. 44.
56. Chapter 3 section 2a of the Work Environment Act.

appropriate measures. In the planning and organization of work, due account must be taken of the fact that people's fitness to perform working duties differs.[57]

Furthermore, Swedish work environment law contains a strong element of trade union influence. At every workplace where five or more employees are regularly engaged, one or more of the employees shall be appointed as health and safety officers, which are to be appointed by the local trade union; the union is bound by a collective agreement with the employer.[58] The health and safety officer shall represent the employees on work environment matters and strive for a satisfactory work environment.[59]

In Sweden statutory *employment protection* and the Employment Protection Act[60] apply to all employees, whether in private or public employment, from the first day of employment.[61] The employer may dismiss a permanent employee for personal reasons or for reasons of redundancy. The employer must have just cause for dismissal.[62] Coupled with this basic just-cause requirement are different rules obliging the employer (depending on whether the dismissal relates to personal reasons or reasons of redundancy) *inter alia* to negotiate with trade unions, give notice, provide the employee with alternative work, warn the employee, retrain the employee, apply seniority rules, and if necessary conditions are met, re-employ dismissed employees. Thus, in line with an *ultima ratio* principle, the employer must make an effort to avoid dismissing employees by first taking less radical measures. In order for any dismissal to be objectively justified, the employer must have tried and ruled out the possibility of providing the employee with alternative work (for which the employee is sufficiently qualified).[63] This duty is restricted to available positions. In comparison, Swedish employment protection – especially when it comes to dismissal for personal reasons, such as sickness, disability and work incapacity – is viewed as relatively strong.[64]

Redundancy is a broad concept, encompassing different reasons of an economic, organizational or other business-related character. The employer has a unilateral right

57. Chapter 3 section 3 of the Work Environment Act.
58. Chapter 6 section 2 of the Work Environment Act.
59. The health and safety officer shall participate in the planning of new premises, equipment, work processes and work organization. If a particular task involves immediate or serious danger to the life or health of an employee and if no immediate remedy can be obtained through representations to the employer, the health and safety officer may order the suspension of that work pending a decision by the Swedish Work Environment Authority, Chapter 6 section 7 of the Work Environment Act.
60. SFS 1982:80.
61. Some minor groups of employees, however, such as employees in an upper management position and the employer's family members, are excluded; section 1 subsection 2 of the Employment Protection Act.
62. Section 7 of the Employment Protection Act.
63. Section 7 subsection 2 of the Employment Protection Act.
64. However, in relation to dismissals for reasons of redundancy, the statutory employment protection (and accompanying collective bargaining) leaves much room for the managerial prerogative, and the possibility to flexible adjustment of the number of workers. See Labour Court judgments AD 2009:50, AD 2011:30 and AD 2012:11 and M. Rönnmar & A. Numhauser-Henning, 'Swedish Employment Protection in Times of Flexicurity Policies and Economic Crisis', *International Journal of Comparative Labour Law and Industrial Relations*, 2012, vol. 28, Issue 4.

to decide when and if a redundancy situation exists, and redundancy per se amounts to just cause.[65] The statutory seniority rules imply that the priority and selection of employees is to be made according to the last-in-first-out principle, i.e., according to each employee's total period of employment with the employer (and in the event of equal periods of employment, giving priority to senior age).[66] The employee has to have sufficient qualifications for the tasks which remain after the redundancy. The seniority rules are semi-compelling and the employer and the trade union may deviate from the statutory rules when determining the order of dismissals by concluding a local collective agreement.[67]

In Sweden it is a general rule that sickness or old age does not constitute just cause for dismissal. The employer is obliged to conduct a thorough investigation into the possibilities for adaptation and rehabilitation and finding alternative work for the employee.[68] In this context the employer's obligations are extensive and relate, for example, to the adjustment of the work environment, work organization, working time and work tasks. These obligations follow not only from regulation in the Employment Protection Act, but also from related regulation on individual work environment adaptation in the Work Environment Act and regulation on rehabilitation in the Social Insurance Code.[69] An employee can be dismissed only after such measures have been taken, the possibility to find alternative work has been tried and ruled out, and the employee can no longer perform work of any importance for the employer.[70]

In individual dismissal disputes, both as regards dismissal for redundancy and personal reasons, such as sickness and disability, the Employment Protection Act and

65. See for example Labour Court judgments AD 1993:61, AD 1993:101 and AD 1995:152.
66. Section 22 of the Employment Protection Act.
67. A so-called *avtalsturlista*. The principal restriction is that the decided order of dismissals must not go against so-called good labour market practice, or be blatantly discriminatory or offensive; see Labour Court judgments AD 1983:107, AD 1996:114 and AD 2002:37.(An employer with at the most ten employees, before the order of dismissals is determined, may exempt at most two employees who in the opinion of the employer are of particular importance for future activities, section 22 subsection 2 of the Employment Protection Act.) According to section 23 of the Employment Protection Act an employee who has reduced working capacity and therefore has been given special duties by the employer shall be given priority for continued work, notwithstanding the seniority rules, provided that this can be accomplished without serious inconvenience to the employer.
68. Cf. for example, Labour Court judgments AD 2013:78 and AD 2014:26.
69. SFS 2010:110 – The statutory sickness insurance regulation and unemployment insurance regulation have been reformed in order to enable an easier return to work. There has been a discussion about possible implications of these controversial reforms for dismissals for reasons of sickness. However, there have been no legislative changes to the employment protection regulation in this area, see further, for example, P. Norberg, 'The Swedish Social Security Reforms from 2008 and Their Impact on the National Sickness Insurance System: Some Reflections from an EU Law and Flexicurity Perspective', in M. Rönnmar (eds), *Labour Law, Fundamental Rights and Social Europe*, Swedish Studies in European Law, vol. 4, (Hart Publishing Oxford 2011) pp. 199-226.
70. Mandatory retirement is regulated through the '67-year rule', in sections 32a and 33 of the Employment Protection Act. An employee has a right to stay in employment up until the age of 67, when the employer may terminate the employment relationship after one month's notice and without having to provide objective grounds for dismissal. In the *Hörnfeldt* judgment by the CJEU, this Swedish system has been tried and found acceptable according to EU law, see C-141/11 *Hörnfeldt v. Posten Meddelande AB* EU:C:2012:421.

the Non-Discrimination Act may often be evoked at the same time. Case law from the Labour Court reflects this 'regulatory overlap' of two parallel sets of rules.[71] The Labour Court has clarified that the requirement for reasonable accommodation in the Non-Discrimination Act and the requirement for rehabilitation and work adaptation in cases of sickness in the Employment Protection Act are basically the same.[72] The non-discrimination rules are perhaps of particular importance when it comes to dismissals for reasons of redundancy. When an employee is dismissed for personal reasons the Labour Court must make a thorough examination of the employer's attempts to avoid dismissal (by work adaptation, rehabilitation and the provision of alternative work etc.) and the just cause of the dismissal. In contrast, as we have seen, redundancy amounts to just cause, and there is less room for legal scrutiny by the Court.[73]

§6.04 CONCLUDING REMARKS

The Swedish development in the area of non-discrimination reflects the trend towards comprehensive equality both generally, by way of an increasing number of protected discrimination grounds and an extended scope, and more specifically, by way of the extension of the ban on inadequate accessibility for people with disabilities and the ban on age discrimination to areas beyond working life, and the proposal to extend the employer's obligation to take active measures to all protected discrimination grounds.

The new ban on inadequate accessibility for people with disabilities, replacing the previous requirement for reasonable accommodation, is in line with EU policy, such as the European Disability Strategy 2010-2020 and the recent proposal for a

71. See, for example, Labour Court judgments AD 2005:32, AD 2012:51, AD 2013:78 and AD 2014:26.
72. See Labour Court judgments AD 2013:78 and AD 2014:26.
73. See in this context the early 'landmark' Labour Court judgment AD 2005:32, where a disabled employee, who had been diagnosed with multiple sclerosis, was dismissed three months after the time that the employer was informed about the illness. The employer claimed redundancy and made, in the course of applying the statutory seniority rules an exemption for two employees, who according to the employer was of particular importance for the continuance of the business, resulting in the disabled employee being dismissed. The issue in the dispute was whether the dismissal had been made in contravention of the Employment Protection Act or the 1999 Act on Disability Discrimination in Working Life. Since the dismissal was part of a reorganization and reduction of the business it was clear to the Labour Court that a redundancy situation was at hand. However, that was not enough to rule out that the dismissal had had a connection to the disability of the employee. According to the preparatory works the employer's decision to exempt two employees in this way was unilateral and could, in principle, not be legally scrutinized within the framework of the Employment Protection Act. However, the employer's decision could be tried against the ban on disability discrimination. Employers should not be allowed, by way of employment protection regulation, to circumvent non-discrimination regulation. The employees had, in principle, equal formal merits, while the employee in question had more extensive professional experience. The employer claimed that he lacked necessary personal qualities, and thus, sufficient qualities, required by the Employment Protection Act in order to be provided with alternative work. The Labour Court said that such arguments were typically hard for an employee to refute in a legal process. It had not been proven that the employee previously had received critique from the employer for his work. In conclusion, the Labour Court held that the employee had, through the dismissal, been directly discriminated against by the employer.

directive as regards accessibility requirements for products and services. However, the Swedish case law developments concerning reasonable accommodation in the area of disability discrimination shows that it has proven very difficult for job seekers and employees to succeed in litigation. This raises doubts on the effect of the requirement for reasonable accommodation and the strength of the protection against disability discrimination. At the same time, the 'elitist' design of bans on discrimination and the limitations of an individual-complaints-led-model are well-known, not least in the field of disability discrimination.[74]

Thus, there is a need also for a more proactive approach, represented by the mainstreaming strategy, active measures in non-discrimination law and requirements for adaptation and rehabilitation within the framework of work environment, employment protection and social security regulation – and Swedish law contains such elements. A combination of different approaches and regulation (including active labour market policy initiatives), is needed in order to achieve substantive and transformative equality and labour market integration of people with disabilities.

A recent comparative analysis of age discrimination and labour law in several EU Member States and countries from other continents reveals that there is still a strong emphasis on the individual-complaints-led model and on the bans against direct and indirect age discrimination. There are few examples of the regulation – and successful use – of a duty of reasonable accommodation, active measures or an adaption of the working time or work environment as a way to combat age discrimination and promote active ageing and a prolonged working life in light of a rapidly ageing population.[75]

To conclude, it will be interesting to follow future legal developments in Sweden. How will the new ban on inadequate accessibility for people with disabilities be applied in practice and interpreted in case law? How will the interplay between Swedish law and EU law and international law develop? And, will the relationship between non-discrimination law and other areas of law be characterized by synergy and mutual re-enforcement, or conflict and fragmentation?

74. See for example, A. Inghammar, *Funktionshindrad – med rätt till arbete? En komparativ studie av arbetsrättsliga regleringar kring arbete och funktionshinder* (Juristförlaget i Lund, Lund 2007).
75. See A. Numhauser-Henning & M. Rönnmar (eds), *Age Discrimination and Labour Law. Comparative and Conceptual Perspectives in the EU and Beyond* (Kluwer Law International, Alphen aan den Rijn 2015).

CHAPTER 7

Reasonable Accommodation of Disabled into the Modern Workplace in Poland

Andrzej Marian Świątkowski

§7.01 REINTEGRATION OF PERSONS WITH DISABILITIES

The legal situation of persons with disabilities (employees and persons seeking employment) is regulated by the Act of 27 August 1997 on occupational and social rehabilitation and on employment of persons with disabilities.[1] The Act was amended by an Act of 29 October 2010 on the amendment of the Act on occupational and social rehabilitation and on employment of persons with disabilities and on amendment of other acts.[2] The mentioned Act has been effective from 1 January 2011. The amendments include adaptation of the provisions on the protection of rights of persons with disabilities to the requirements introduced by a Council Directive 2000/78/EC of 27 November 2000 establishing a general framework for equal **treatment in employment and occupation.**[3] However, the above does not mean that before alignment of the Polish legislation with the EU standards the legal situation of persons with disabilities was different from this which was applicable until 31 December 2010. Under the former legal framework persons with disabilities were declared participation in the social life. It meant that such persons could play different social roles and overcome obstacles, in particular psychological, architectural, urban and transport obstacles as well as obstacles in communication with other, not disabled, members of the local,

1. Consolidated text: Journal of Laws Dz.U. of 20 June 2011, Journal of Laws Dz.U. No. 127, item 721 as amended.
2. Journal of Laws Dz.U. No. 226, item 1475.
3. Official Journal L 303 of 2 December 2000.

regional and national communities. Polish social policy[4] has been governed by a principle of social inclusion of persons with disabilities. It has been supplemented by a principle aimed at prevention and correction of negative consequences of social exclusion. The social exclusion of persons with disabilities was an effect of failure to fulfil a general obligation for inclusion of persons with disabilities into mainstream social activity or careless fulfilment by the public institutions and public and private companies of the applicable principle of social inclusion of persons with disabilities into the mainstream social life.

Before 1 January 2011 the Polish law applied a legal concept consisting in adaptation of a workplace to the needs and requirements of persons with disabilities, able to work and wishing to work.[5] The jurisprudence followed a principle that disability cannot be equated with inability to work caused by bodily injury and a lack of prognosis for recovering the ability to work after retraining of a disabled person.[6] It represented progress in comparison to the previous practice according to which employers were, in the first place, obligated by the legislature to satisfy needs consisting in separation or organization of an appropriate workplace for an employee injured as a result of an accident at work or occupational disease. Article 14(1) of the above-mentioned Act of 27 August 1997 granted to an employed person who was a victim of an accident at work or an occupational disease, who lost ability to work in a former workplace, a right to perform work in an appropriate workplace equipped with basic social facilities. The above right of the injured employee corresponds with an obligation of an employer to provide such appropriate workplace not later than three months from the date when the entitled employee notifies readiness to start work. The above right may be exercised only by employees injured as a result of an accident at work or an occupational disease who lost their ability to work in the former workplace and whose employment relationship was not terminated by the employer.[7] Article 14(1) of the Act of 27 August 1997 does not apply only in the case of employees injured as a result of an accident at work or occupational disease who caused such accident through their culpable conduct (Article 14(2)). Fault or intoxication of the injured employee absolves the employer from the above obligation expressed in Article 14(1). It must be stressed that the employer's obligation and the corresponding right of the injured employee are not absolute. An only legal sanction that may be applied against the employer who fails to separate or organize within three months an appropriate workplace for the employee injured as a result of an accident at work or occupational

4. R. Serafin, Praca a niepełnosprawność [*Work and Disability*], Praca i Rehabilitacja Niepełnosprawnych [*Work and Rehabilitation of Persons with Disabilities*], part 1, 2005, 5(85), pp. 9 ff.; part 2, 2005, 6(86), pp. 18 ff.
5. *Ibid*, Przystosowanie stanowiska pracy do potrzeb osób niepełnosprawnych [*Adaptation of a Workplace to the Needs of Persons with Disabilities*], Praca i Rehabilitacja Niepełnosprawnych [*Work and Rehabilitation of Persons with Disabilities*], 2005, 4(84), pp. 8 ff.
6. Judgment of the Polish Supreme Court *[Sąd Najwyższy]* of 17 February 2009. I UK 233/08 (second argument), LEX no. 736713.
7. Decision of the Polish Supreme Court of 12 December 2002 r., II UK 176/02, OSNP-insert 2003, No. 18, item 12, LEX no. 464672.

disease, is an obligation of the employer to make payment into the account of a State Fund for Rehabilitation of Persons with Disabilities *[Państwowy Fundusz Rehabilitacji Osób Niepełnosprawnych (PFRON)]* amounting to fifteen times the average remuneration for work (Article 23). The Act of 27 August 1997 grants to the injured employee a specific right and establishes a corresponding obligation; however at the same time the employer may be absolved from such obligation by termination of the employment relationship and payment of flat-rate compensation to a public body.

Provisions of the EU labour law – Article 1 and Article 5 of Directive 2000/78/EC, establishing a general framework for combating discrimination *inter alia* on the grounds of disability of employees and persons seeking employment, order the EU Member States to provide reasonable accommodation in the employment policy. This means an obligation to enact laws enabling a person with disability to have access to, participate in, or advance in employment, or to undergo training. Article 5 of Directive 2000/78/EC, a provision which is a basis for further actions undertaken by competent authorities of the Member States, does not specify the legal nature of the reasonable accommodation enabling fulfilment by the employers in particular Member States of a principle of equality of persons with disabilities, compliant with the European standards.

Other international model which constitutes a point of reference for compliance of national regulations prohibiting discrimination of persons with disabilities with applicable standards is a United Nations (UN) Convention on the Rights of Persons with Disabilities (CRPD) adopted by the UN General Assembly on 13 December 2006.[8] The Convention, ratified by Poland, entered into force on 25 October 2012.[9] The UN Member States ratifying that Convention recognized the right of persons with disabilities to work on an equal basis with other persons without disabilities. This includes the right to gain a living by work freely chosen by the employed person, accepted in a labour market and social environment. The choice of work is free which means that it is open and accessible to persons with disabilities. The States Parties shall safeguard and promote the realization of the above right by all persons, in particular by persons with disabilities (Article 27(1) of the Convention). By guaranteeing the persons with disabilities the right to choose work, the Member States were obligated, among others, to: (1) establish and enforce a prohibition of discrimination on the basis of disability with regard to all matters concerning all forms of employment, including conditions of recruitment, hiring and employment, continuance of employment, career advancement and safe and healthy working conditions (Article 27(1)(a)); (2) promote employment opportunities and career advancement for persons with disabilities in the labour market, as well as assistance in finding, obtaining, maintaining and returning to employment (Article 27(1)(e)); (3) employ persons with disabilities in the public sector (Article 27(1)(g)); (4) promote the employment of persons with disabilities in the private sector through appropriate policies and other preferential measures, which may include affirmative action programmes, incentives and other measures (Article

8. A/RES/61/106.
9. Journal of Laws, 2012, item 1169.

27(1)(h)); ensure that reasonable accommodation is provided to persons with disabilities in the workplace (Article 27(1)(i)).

According to the UN it is necessary because of the general obligation of the Member States to comply with the principles proclaimed in the UN Charter which considers dignity, worth and equal and inalienable rights of all people as the foundation of freedom, justice and peace in the world. Therefore, every person has the same rights and freedoms, regardless of any differences between people. Thus, disability cannot be a criterion for differentiation of vocational opportunities of persons with full and reduced ability. It is considered by the UN a result of interactions between persons with impairments and environmental barriers. In the fifth recital (letter e) of the preamble to the said UN Convention disability is considered a 'barrier that hinders full and effective participation in society of persons with disabilities on an equal basis with others'.

The main purpose of the UN CRPD is to ensure the full and equal enjoyment of all human rights and fundamental freedoms by all persons with disabilities, and to promote respect for their inherent dignity (Article 1(1)).

The purpose of this study is to allow lawyers specializing in the labour law and anti-discrimination law to become acquainted with the currently applicable provisions of the Act on occupational and social rehabilitation and on employment of persons with disabilities as amended by the Act of 29 October 2010, and to answer a fundamental question whether provisions of that Act, effective from 1 January 2011, guarantee to persons with disabilities sufficient fulfilment of the principle of equal treatment in labour relations and in employment.

§7.02 REASONABLE ACCOMMODATION OF WORKPLACES TO THE NEEDS OF PERSONS WITH DISABILITIES

The major innovation in implementation by the Polish laws of the principle of equal treatment of persons with disabilities is introduction in the Act of 27 August 1997 on occupational and social rehabilitation and on employment of persons with disabilities of Article 23a, a legal provision obligating employers to provide persons with disabilities with reasonable accommodation in the work process (paragraph 1) and considering refusal to provide such accommodation as a violation of the principle of equal treatment of persons with disabilities in employment within the meaning of Article 18^{3a} §§ 2-5 of the Labour Code (paragraph 3). This provision was introduced into the Act of 27 August 1997 by Article 27 of the Act of 3 December 2010 on implementation of certain EU laws on equal treatment.[10] A new concept of reasonable accommodation of workplaces to persons with disabilities adopted in Poland is based mainly on the following principles: (1) a positive obligation of each, public and private, employer to adapt a workplace to the requirements and needs of non-typical employee or candidate

10. Journal of Laws Dz.U.No. 254, item 1700. The Act entered into force on 1 January 2011.

employee. The above obligation is considered by the legislature as a significant element of anti-discrimination laws; (2) introduction in Article 23a(1) of the Act of 27 August 1997 of a justification (exception) excluding the possibility to consider positive actions undertaken by the employer to fulfil the above obligation as being contrary to the principle of non-discrimination; (3) using the criterion of reasonableness as an objective criterion for verification whether refusal to fulfil the above obligation was justified or not. Limits of positive actions undertaken in favour of persons with disabilities which could be considered as privileged treatment ('discrimination *à rebours*') by the critics of the policy of equalization of opportunities of persons with disabilities have not been clearly defined. Because of the natural, permanent constraints and barriers to participation in the social life, mainly to performance of any work to which they were trained, exclusion of the persons with disabilities was recognized by the UN Convention of 13 December 2006 as equivalent to violation of fundamental principles listed in Article 3 of that Treaty: the freedom to make one's own choices, (Article 3(a)), non-discrimination (Article 3(b)), right to full and effective participation and inclusion in society and social integration (Article 3(c)), the right to vocational guidance and vocational training (Article 3(d)), equality of opportunity (Article 3(e)), accessibility (Article 3(f)).

De lege lata, in the labour and employment relations in Poland Article 23a of the Act of 27 August 1997 is a source of an important obligation of the employer to guarantee to the persons with disabilities reasonable accommodation, enabling and facilitating work. A scope ratione personae of the above obligation includes employees, candidate employees, trainees and apprentices. A major mistake of the legislature is omission of other employed persons who perform work under non-employee legal relations (under civil-law contracts). Article 2 points 5 and 8 of the Act in question which includes definitions of several legal terms, uses expressions such as 'person with disabilities' or 'participation in social life' which imply that the legal protection is provided to all employed persons and not only to employees within the meaning of Article 2 of the Labour Code but also to juvenile persons who undergo vocational training or practice. The principle of equal treatment and non-discrimination expressed in Article 5 of the UN Convention applies to 'all persons equal before and under the law who are entitled without any exception to the equal protection and equal benefit of the law' (paragraph 1). A legal consequence of the above firm statement is an obligation of State Parties, expressed in paragraph 2 of Article 5 of the UN Convention, to prohibit 'all discrimination' and to guarantee to 'all persons with disabilities' equal and effective legal protection.

The limits of the employer's obligation to adapt workplaces to the needs and requirements of persons with disabilities are identified as 'necessary reasonable accommodation' for disabled persons within the employment relationship (Article 23a(1) first sentence of the Act of 27 August 1997). In Article 2(5) of the UN Convention the 'reasonable accommodation' is defined as a synonym of necessary and appropriate modification and adjustments of workplaces where persons with disabilities are to be employed. The modifications and adjustments should not impose disproportionate or undue burdens and should be limited to ensuring to persons with disabilities the 'enjoyment or exercise of all human rights and fundamental freedoms'. The limits of 'appropriate' modifications are defined as 'where needed' adaptation of a workplace to the needs and requirements of a particular person to be employed. Similar obligation of an employer to provide reasonable accommodation was expressed in Article 5 of Directive 2000/78/EC. The said provision obligates the employers who employ persons with disabilities to take 'appropriate measures' where needed in a particular case. The reasonable accommodation was specified with an emphasis put on its functional and economic aspect. On one hand it should allow a person with disabilities to have access to, participate in, or advance in employment, or to undergo training. On the other hand, such accommodation cannot impose disproportionate burden on the employer. This obligation was expressed identically in Article 23a(1) of the Act of 27 August 1997: 'Necessary reasonable accommodation means necessary, in a particular case, modifications and adjustments according to specific needs notified to the employer and resulting from disability of a person, unless such modifications impose a disproportionate burden on the employer'. Both the Act of 27 August 1997 (Article 23a(2)) and Directive 2000/78/EC (Article 5 *in fine*) *expressis verbis* provide that regardless of the costs, the financial burden associated with the necessity to adapt the workplace to the needs and requirements of a disabled employee may never be considered disproportionate within the meaning of applicable laws, if they are sufficiently remedied by measures existing within the framework of the policy of equal employment opportunities for disabled persons in the Member States. In the Polish labour law there are no examples which would illustrate the types and scope of adaptation of workplaces to the needs and requirements of persons with disabilities. It should be assumed that the determinants of the scope of accommodation are current regulations on health and safety at work and requirements of the production process.[11] The accommodation may involve not only giving the disabled employees an opportunity to efficiently and safely perform work. Depending on the specifics of work performed by a person with disabilities, the modification may relate to organization of work, order in which occupational tasks and related duties are to be performed and adaptation of working methods and tools and working environment to the needs and requirements of the disabled employee. In the Polish case law there are no rulings which would illustrate the determinants of the necessary, reasonable policy for adaptation of certain workplaces to the needs and requirements of a person able to work only in specific conditions. A dispute concerning reasonableness of accommodation and proportionality or lack of proportionality as regards expenditures for the accommodation that should be provided by the employer to a disabled employee to enable the latter efficient and safe performance of work most certainly can be subject to judicial recourse in matters relating to employment-based employee claims. Failure to provide necessary, reasonable accommodation prevents a disabled employee from performance of work. Therefore it is tantamount to denying provision to the employee

11. E. Górska, Projektowanie stanowisk pracy dla osób niepełnosprawnych [*Designing Workplaces for Persons with Disabilities*], Oficyna Wydawnicza Politechniki Warszawskiej [Warsaw Technical University Editorial House], Warszawa 2002, passim.

of work appropriate for the skills and abilities of the latter. By refusing to accommodate the work process, working methods and tools and/or the work environment, the employer violates a fundamental obligation expressed in Article 22 § 1 of the Labour Code. Despite entering into employment relationship the employer refuses to employ the employee under terms and conditions set out in a contract of employment concluded by the parties to the individual labour relationship. The legal status of a disabled employee, because of the specific conditions and requirements resulting from his objective (defined by disability) situation, is clear. Lack of reasonable adaptation of a workplace must be considered an obstacle to performance of an agreed work created by the employer. Article 81 § 1 of the Labour Code imposes on the employer an obligation to pay to the employee a part of the remuneration mentioned in the article in question. In the case of an employee whose remuneration is specified on the basis of a personal grading at hourly or monthly rate, an employer is obligated to pay the basic pay rate. If such element of the remuneration has not been specified in a contract of employment, then an employee should be entitled to 60% of the remuneration for standby duty. In no event the remuneration for work guaranteed by the legislator in the mentioned Article 81 § 1 of the Labour Code can be lower than the minimum wage specified each year on the basis of generally applicable provisions of the Act of 10 October 2002 on a minimum wage.[12]

In the case of disabled workers, the remuneration guaranteed to persons who remain on standby duty, not employed by the employer because of failure to adapt a workplace, a working process and working conditions to the needs of the employed person cannot be considered sufficient and satisfactory compensation for non-fulfilment of one of the fundamental duties of the employer specified in Article 23a(1) of the Act of 27 August 1997. In the case of persons with disabilities, depending on the type, cause and level of the injury causing the disability, work may be treated as a rehabilitation measure for the employed person. Therefore, a disabled employee has a claim for enabling him to perform work in compliance with the requirements determined by the disability. A disabled employee has a right to raise a claim for enabling him performance of work which he can perform without limitations and difficulties caused by his condition. The above indicates imposition by a court of law (labour court) on the employer employing a disabled worker, of an obligation to adapt a workplace to the needs and requirements of a person with disabilities.

Apart from the financial sanction mentioned in Article 23 of the Act of 27 August 1997 (payment to PFRON of an amount equivalent to fifteen times the average remuneration), an employer who terminates a contract of employment with a disabled employee because of a failure to adapt the workplace to the needs and requirements of the disabled employee violates the principle of equal treatment in employment and may be liable to a compensation amounting at least to the minimum wage (Article 18^{3d} of the Labour Code) and – depending on specific circumstances – may be liable to compensation for violation of personal rights. Employee's dignity and health are subject to legal protection.

12. Dz.U.Nr 200, poz. 1679.

§7.03 SPECIFIC RIGHTS AND OBLIGATION OF EMPLOYERS IN CONNECTION WITH EMPLOYMENT OF PERSONS WITH DISABILITIES

The 'appropriate measures' listed in Article 5 of Directive 2000/78/EC, which should be taken by the employers to enable persons with disabilities to have access to employment and to perform work in the conditions adapted to the needs and requirements of a disabled employee were formulated in the Act of 27 August 1997 in a legal form of obligations, legitimate expectations and rights of the employers and legal sanctions which should be imposed on them in the case of failure to fulfil the obligations to PFRON. A concept of general and equal access to the labour market by the persons with disabilities applied in the Act of 27 August 1997 was based on administrative obligations of employers employing at least twenty-five full-time equivalent (FTE) employees to make systematic, monthly payments to PFRON of an amount constituting a product of 40.65% of the average remuneration and a number of employees, corresponding to a difference between employment which ensures achievement of an employment rate of persons with disabilities at the level of 6% and the actual employment of persons with disabilities in the establishment operated by a respective employer (Article 21(1)).[13] Employers whose employment rate of persons with disabilities is at least 6% are by law exempt from the above obligation to make payments to PFRON (Article 21(2)). Such exemption applies also to non-profit public and private organizational units employing employees whose exclusive activity includes social and medical rehabilitation of persons with disabilities or care for people with disabilities (Article 21(2f)).[14]

The employers who employ at least twenty employees and who reached the employment rate of persons with disabilities at the level of 6% prescribed by the Act of 27 August 1997 are entitled to obtain from PFRON monthly wage subsidies for each disabled employee amounting to 180%, 100% or 40% of the lowest remuneration (Article 26a(1)). The amount of the subsidy depends on the level of disability (severe, moderate, mild) of an employee for whom the subsidy is granted to the employer. The

13. The above complicated elaboration should be accompanied by a hypothetical example: an employer employing 200 employees, each employed on a half-time basis, is obligated to make monthly payments to PFRON since, taking into account the necessary employment level conversion ratio, he employs 100 full-time equivalent (FTE) employees (200:1/2 = 100)), where four of the employees are persons with disabilities (which equals to 2 FTE employees, making 2% of the overall level of employment). Such monthly payments should amount to 4% (6%-2% = 4%) of 40.65% of the average monthly wage which presently amounts to PLN 4,002 i.e., PLN 984.50 per each disabled employee missing to reach the minimum limit established in Art. 21(1) of the Act of 27 August 1997.
14. Associations which run occupational therapy workshops for people with disabilities which support the process of their occupational and social rehabilitation are obliged to qualify for the workshops the persons holding certificates of disability with an indication to participate in the occupational therapy workshops. Organizers of the therapy are not entitled to evaluate and decide whether a person referred to the workshops is suitable for such therapy and whether such person actually can and should participate in the workshops. Judgment of the Polish Supreme Court of 16 April 2009, I CSK 397/08, OSNC Zbiór dodatkowy, 2010, No. 2, item 45, LEX no. 511973.

amounts of the subsidies are increased by 40% of the lowest remuneration in the case of employment of mentally ill or blind employees (Article 26a(4)). The maximum amount of the monthly wage subsidy in fact cannot exceed 90% of the monthly wage costs actually incurred by the employer. In the case of wage subsidies for persons with disabilities employed by an employer carrying out a business activity, the maximum wage subsidy should not exceed 75% of costs of wages of the disabled employees (Article 26a(4)).

An employer who employs persons with disabilities for a period of at least thirty-six months may obtain from PFRON reimbursement for the costs of: (1) adaptation of premises in the work establishment to the needs of persons with disabilities resulting from adaptation of the created or existing workplaces to such persons; (2) adaptation or purchase of equipment facilitating performance of work by a person with disabilities or functioning of such person in the establishment; (3) purchase and authorization of software for persons with disabilities and technological equipment supporting adaptation of persons with disabilities or adjusted to the needs of such persons resulting from their disability; (4) identification by the occupational health services of the needs of persons with disabilities which require adaptation of premises, equipment and work technology (Article 26(1)). It should be underlined that the reimbursement of the above-mentioned costs applies only to additional costs of an employer resulting from employment of the following categories of persons with disabilities: (1) persons unemployed or seeking employment who are not in employment relationship, referred to work by the local employment offices; (2) persons in employment relationship with an employer who applies for reimbursement of costs of adaptation of a workplace to the needs of persons with disabilities who lost, through no fault of their own and no fault of the employer, the full employability (Article 26(2)). Reimbursement of the costs may not exceed twenty times the average wage per each workplace adapted to the needs of a person with disabilities (Article 26(3)). Terms and conditions as well as the amount of reimbursement of the costs of adaptation of a workplace are specified in an agreement negotiated by the employer with a district governor (*Polish: starosta*).[15] The employer has only a right to negotiate with a representative of a public authority the terms and conditions and the amount of reimbursement of costs incurred. For that reason the reimbursement of the costs of adaptation of a workplace was classified in a category of a legitimate expectation and not a right of the employer employing persons with disabilities. The legitimate expectation of reimbursement of costs incurred by the employer for adaptation of premises, workplaces and processes to the needs and expectations of persons with disabilities arises upon conclusion of an agreement for refund. The applicable laws, Article 26e(2) of the Act of 27 August 1997, explicitly provide that the costs incurred by

15. A legal nature of the agreement between the unit running the occupational therapy workshops supporting the process of the occupational and social rehabilitation and a district governor (*starosta*) for financing a participation of entitled persons in the workshops has not been defined by the legislator. According to the Polish Supreme Court (judgment of 16 April 2009, I CSK 397/08), it is an agreement on behalf of a third party regulated in Art. 393 of the Civil Code.

the employer before conclusion of the agreement are not reimbursable. The reimbursement of funds used to organize or accommodate the workplace for a disabled employee is not granted automatically by law. The laws governing the legal status of employers employing disabled employees establish maximum limits for possible reimbursement of costs of adaptation of workplaces to the needs and requirements of persons with disabilities. Therefore, the refund does not have to cover all the costs incurred by the employer for that purpose. Detailed terms and conditions of the refund of partial costs of adaptation of the workplace to the needs of persons with disabilities are specified in agreements concluded by district governors with respective employers who undertake to employ disabled employees.[16]

A legitimate expectation of reimbursement of costs of equipment of a workplace in which a disabled employee is employed (previously registered with an employment office as an unemployed or a person seeking employment and not being in an employment relationship) for at least thirty-six months, is granted to an employer who negotiates with the district governor (*starosta*) an agreement setting out the terms and conditions and the amount of reimbursement of the incurred costs which cannot exceed fifteen times the amount of the average remuneration (Article 26e(1)).

A necessary condition for turning this legitimate expectancy into an entitlement is obtainment of a positive opinion of the Chief Labour Inspectorate *[Państwowa Inspekcja Pracy]* on adaptation of a workplace to the needs resulting from disability of an employed person or on fulfilment of standards of occupational health and safety (Article 26e(5)).

Moreover, the employers who employ disabled employees may apply for reimbursement of monthly costs of employment – not exceeding 20% of the number of working hours per month – of employees assisting the disabled employee in communication and fulfilment of tasks impossible or difficult for the disabled employee (Article 26d(1-3)).

In the case of failure to fulfil the obligation to make systematic payments to the State Fund for Rehabilitation of Persons with Disabilities (PFRON) resulting in minimum arrears to the Fund amounting to PLN 100, the President of the Management Board of PFRON must issue a decision on suspension of reimbursement of costs of a part of the remuneration of persons with disabilities and of adaptation of workplaces to the needs of such persons (Article 26a(8)). Employers who do not meet the conditions for reimbursement of costs of employment and adaptation of workplaces to the needs of persons with disabilities must repay to PFRON – through a competent district governor (*starosta*) – unused funds equal to 1/36 of the overall amount of reimbursement per each month until expiration of a minimum period of thirty-six months during which they must employ persons with disabilities, not less than 1/36 (Article 26(7)). The above obligation does not apply to employers who within three months following termination of employment with a disabled person employed other disabled person referred to work by a local employment office. The resulting interruption not exceeding

16. Judgment of the Polish Supreme Court of 5 September 2001, I CKN 395/00, LEX no. 736713.

three months is not included in the minimal, equal to thirty-six months, period of employment of persons with disabilities (Article 26(8)).

§7.04 A PRIVILEGED STATUS OF EMPLOYERS RUNNING SHELTERED WORKSHOPS (*ZAKŁADY PRACY CHRONIONEJ*) AND ESTABLISHMENTS OF PROFESSIONAL ACTIVITY (*ZAKŁADY AKTYWNOŚCI ZAWODOWEJ*)

An employer running a business activity for a period of at least twelve months, employing - in the workplaces meeting OHS requirements - at least twenty-five FTE employees and achieving - for a period of at least six months - a 50% rate of employment of persons with disabilities where at least 20% of the overall number of employed are persons classified as severely or moderately disabled, obtains a status of an entity running a sheltered workshop (Article 28(1)). At the same time, a status of an establishment of professional activity may be obtained by establishments created by local government organizational units, associations and social organizations employing severely or moderately disabled persons whose percentage in the overall number of persons employed in the establishment is at least 70%. The employment rate of persons classified as moderately disabled may not exceed 35% of the overall employment in a respective establishment (Article 29(1), (1a)). Another condition necessary for the obtainment of a status of establishment of professional activity is that an employer should designate the generated income to the establishment's activity fund (Article 29(1) point 3). A decision on the grant of a status of sheltered workshop or establishment of professional activity is issued by a voivode (*wojewoda*) as a government administration authority.

An employer running a sheltered workshop has a right to apply (legitimate expectation) for: (1) obtainment of a subsidy from PFRON amounting to 50% of interest rates of bank credits taken for the purposes relating to occupational and social rehabilitation of persons with disabilities; (2) reimbursement of additional costs incurred for construction or extension of premises and facilities in the establishment, transport and administration, resulting from employment of at least 50% of persons with disabilities (Article 32(1-2)). An employer running a sheltered workshop must create a fund for rehabilitation of persons with disabilities (Article 33(1)) and designate - among others - at least 15% of resources of such fund for individual rehabilitation programmes or at least 10% of resources of the fund for individual aid for disabled employees of the establishment (Article 33(3) points 4-5). An employer running a sheltered workshop has a right to provide aid to persons with disabilities who are not in active employment - former employees of such establishment - for medical and social rehabilitation (Article 33(10)).

Failure of the employer running a sheltered workshop to meet the conditions under which resources of rehabilitation fund specified in Article 33(4) of the Act of 27 August 1997 can be used, consisting in allocation of resources of the fund not in compliance with their intended use - financing of occupational, social and medical rehabilitation - constitutes grounds for an absolute obligation of the employer to return

100% of the amount of such resources to the rehabilitation fund and to make payment amounting to 30% of the amount of such resources to PFRON by the twentieth day of a month following the month in which illegitimate allocation of the funds was disclosed (Article 33(4a)).

§7.05 RIGHTS OF PERSONS WITH DISABILITIES

Apart from the above-mentioned right of an employee who became disabled (as a result of an accident at work or occupational disease) to continue work in a specially adapted workplace, persons with disabilities registered with a local employment office as unemployed persons or persons seeking work and not in employment relationship, have the right to benefit from services or instruments of the labour market on generally applicable rules specified in the Act of 20 April 2004 on the promotion of employment and labour market institutions.[17] They can also benefit, on equal terms with unemployed persons, from trainings, internships, intervention works, occupational training for adults, medical examinations or psychological tests, reimbursement of costs of transport to the trainings, internships, career counselling classes, costs of accommodation, costs of travel to medical examination and a one-off travel to a potential employer to whom the disabled person was referred by an employment office and back to a place of residence or costs of postgraduate studies (Article 11(1) of the Act of 27 August 1997).

Basically, the working time of a person with mild disability, employed under a contract of employment, cannot exceed eight hours per day and forty hours per week. Disabled employees with severe or moderate disability to whom a competent doctor issued a certificate of advised shorter working time cannot work more than seven hours per day and thirty-five hours per week (Article 15(1-2)). Except employees managing an establishment and selected organizational units on behalf on an employer,[18] disabled employees cannot work at night and during overtime (Article 15(3)). Disabled employees are entitled to an extra, fifteen minutes' break, included in the working time, for rehabilitation gymnastics or rest (Article 17). Application of the above, shortened working time does not result in reduction of the amount of remuneration paid to the disabled employee at a fixed monthly rate (Article 18(1)). However the hourly rates of the basic remuneration of a disabled employee are increased based on a relation between the previous working time and the above standards (Article 18(2)).

Disabled persons included in the category of severe or moderate disability are entitled to additional annual leave of ten working days in a calendar year. Such right cannot be exercised by the disabled employees who are entitled to the annual leave

17. Journal of Laws Dz.U. of 2008, No. 69, item 415 as amended.
18. Article 151[4] § 1 of the Labour Code cannot apply to a disabled employee managing an establishment since application of this provision would deprive such employee of his right to remuneration and allowance for the performed overtime work despite violation of specific and absolute legal norms prescribed by Art. 15(2-3) of the Act of 27 August 1997. Judgment of the Polish Supreme Court of 2 October 2008, I PK 64/08, OSNP 2010, No. 7-8, item 86, LEX no. 575178.

exceeding twenty-six working days per year or to additional leave granted under separate laws (Article 19(1-2)). In the case of concurrence of the rights to additional, separate leave amounting to less than ten working days, instead of such leave the disabled person is entitled to ten days' leave specified in Article 19(1) of the Act of 27 August 1997. Apart from additional leave, persons with disabilities are entitled to payable leave from work in order to participate once a year in rehabilitation holidays (twenty-one days) and to undergo medical examinations, medical or rehabilitation treatment and in order to obtain or repair orthopaedic equipment. The right to leave for the medical examinations, treatment and maintenance of the orthopaedic equipment may be exercised by the persons with disabilities only where the mentioned activities cannot be arranged outside the working hours (Article 20(1)). The aggregate additional leave cannot exceed twenty-one working days in a calendar year (Article 20(3)).

A disabled person with an assistance dog has a right to enter public facilities, public transport (Article 20a) and the work establishment.

§7.06 CONCLUSION

The legal measures presented in this study serving reasonable accommodation of an establishment, premises, workplaces, processes and working conditions as well as rights granted to disabled employees prove that the intentions of the European (EU) and international (UN) employers were implemented in Poland in accordance with applicable standards. The requirements specified in Directive 2000/78 and in the UN Convention of 13 December 2006 were to a large extent met by Poland before its EU accession. A legal integration of the employer's obligation to guarantee to persons with disabilities reasonable accommodation in workplaces and failure to make necessary adaptations treated as a breach of a principle of equal treatment of persons with disabilities in employment, effective from 1 January 2011, facilitates implementation of a policy (compliant with anti-discrimination laws) of privileged treatment of persons with disabilities in labour relations.

Relatively precisely defined obligations of employers benefiting from financial incentives granted by a public fund to support a policy of stimulation of processes of employment of persons with disabilities able to work in adapted conditions together with a quite well specified and controlled by public institutions rights to benefit from such incentives under terms and conditions specified in contracts with a representative of a local authority (*starosta*) seem sufficient to prevent abuse by the employers and the persons with disabilities of the financial stimulators and prevent fake occupational activity of people with disabilities.

Modification of a model applied in Poland in a period before EU accession, governed by the Act of 27 August 1997 on occupational and social rehabilitation and on employment of persons with disabilities, and previously by an Act of 9 May 1991 on employment and occupational rehabilitation of persons with disabilities,[19] adapted to the currently applicable model of convergence of the laws on the protection of rights of

19. Journal of Laws Dz.U. No. 46, item 201 as amended.

persons with disabilities with the European and international anti-discrimination standards, allows achievement of the key objectives specified in Directive 2000/78/EC and the UN Convention of 13 December 2006, including: promotion, legal protection and an opportunity of almost unlimited unemployment of persons with disabilities.

CHAPTER 8

The 'Integrative Function' of Labour Law in Ebb? Reasonable Accommodation for Religion or Belief and Company 'Neutrality Policies' in Belgium

*Katayoun Alidadi**

Human rights and anti-discrimination law have gone through substantial transformation in recent years, bringing religious discrimination in the private workplace under their respective purview. At the supranational European level, a number of momentous developments can be noted as precursors of a more religion or belief-accommodating European workplace. The European Court of Human Right (ECtHR) in its 2013 Eweida et al. case showed the potential of the European human rights framework for the protection of employee rights, while on the Court of Justice of the EU stands to make a contribution to the date when it decides two currently pending referrals for preliminary rulings related to religious discrimination (the headscarf) at work. These legal developments are significant for employees who want to wear religious dress on the job, seek time accommodation for religious reasons, or request some other form of exemption or accommodation from workplace tasks or social expectations.

However, lacking an explicit reference in the domestic (labour) law of most European Member States, reasonable workplace accommodations for religion or belief remain conditioned upon voluntarism and good practices often destined for a subterrain existence (so as to let sleeping dogs lie). Such is the case in Belgium, where

* This chapter was presented and discussed at the annual seminar of the International Association of Labour Law Journals on 24 June 2015 at the KU Leuven ('Reasonable Accommodation in the Modern Workplace: Potential and Limits of the Integrative Logics of Labour Law'). I want to thank the participants of that meeting, and Prof. Frank Hendrickx in particular, for the various useful comments, questions and suggestions for improvement.

social science studies and case law decisions illustrate a mixed reality on the ground; while various kinds of accommodations are in fact provided by employers, some companies pre-emptively reject religious accommodation requests by adopting company 'neutrality' policies, which Belgian labour courts in turn have legitimized.

In this contribution, I discuss the concept of reasonable accommodation – which fits within the integrative function of labour law – and compare it to the concept of indirect discrimination. I also consider whether we can speak of an 'accommodated workplace' in Belgium by analysing to what extent company neutrality policies are considered legitimate under the human rights and anti-discrimination law frameworks and offer a critique of the Belgian jurisprudence regarding private company neutrality policies.

§8.01 INTRODUCTION: THE INTEGRATIVE FUNCTION OF LABOUR LAW AND REASONABLE ACCOMMODATIONS

One of the most celebrated labour law and equality scholars of our time, Bob Hepple, discussed the new 'integrative' function of labour law as a central issue in the modernization of labour law.[1] Equality law as the 'fastest growing part of labour law'[2] certainly fits the integrative function, forming a crucial addition to a variety of other laws and policies (e.g., family accommodations) which aim to promote employment inclusion and fight social exclusion.[3]

The integrative function may seem like a far cry from labour law's original focus, which was focused on the need to find 'a balance of collective forces.'[4] Davies and Freedman note that 'the principal purpose of labour law… is to regulate, to support and to restrain the power of management and the power of organized labour.'[5] Upon closer consideration, however, it should be clear that the integrative function is essential to this paradigmatic role of classic labour law. Integration of newcomers or workers who do not fit the dominant expectations presents not only challenges for management but

1. Bob Hepple, *The Future of Labour Law*, Industrial Law Journal 322 (1995). This can be contrasted with Otto Kahn-Freund's concept of 'collective laisser-faire' in British labour law. The integrative function thus means convergence between the continental and the Anglo-Saksan approach to labour law regulation. To be sure, in fact 'this integrative task opens up an important field of expansion for labour law'. See Silvana Sciarra, *The "Making" of EU Labour Law and the "Future" of Labour Lawyers*, in *The Future of Labour Law: Liber Amicorum Bob Hepple QC* (Catherine Barnard et al., eds, Hart, 2004), pp. 201-210.
2. Marc De Vos, *Worden Europese arbeidsrelaties Amerikaans? Kritische rechtsvergelijkende perspectieven bij de discriminatieverboden in het arbeidsrecht, in* Gelijkheid in arbeidsrecht: gelijkheid zonder grenzen?. (Daniël Cuypers ed. 2003), p. 243.
3. For example in the area of care responsibilities, see Julie Wallbank & Jonathan Herring (eds), *Vulnerabilities, Care and Family Law* (Routledge, 2014).
4. Paul Davies & Mark Freedland, *Otto Kahn-Freund's Labour & the Law* (Stevens, third edition, 1983).
5. Paul Davies & Mark Freedman, *Otto Kahn-Freund's Labour & the Law* (Stevens, third edition, 1983), p. 15.

also for organized labour organizations.[6] When the first labour codes were adopted, the labour force was highly homogenous, the norm being the full-time working man who was employed for the length of his working life in a manufacturing company. It has been argued that this homogenous (image of) the workforce 'brought about the entrenchment, in unionized work environments, of a particular *formal* concept of equality.'[7] Indeed, insisting on formal equality made much sense since 'in order to put an end to employer practices that were arbitrary or marked by favouritism, trade unions at first demanded *identical treatment* for all employees without distinction.' Feminism, immigration and globalization, technological and societal developments have changed this. 'The gradual diversification of the labour force that began in the 1960s ... mass arrival of women and minorities on the labour market altered its make-up considerably.'[8] This has presented significant challenges for management and trade unions alike. The tensions between accommodation and the power of management/employers appears self-evidentiary. But the needs and requests of particular workers can also conflict with – real or perceived – interests of the collectivity of workers or trade union interests.[9]

The legal technique of 'reasonable accommodations' for particular characteristics of employees is a case in point. Such accommodations seek to remove obstacles or 'bottlenecks'[10] to participation in the workplace or generally promote equality and inclusion. Much like labour law accommodating developments in the area of care and family responsibilities, reasonable accommodation fits the integrative logic of labour law by allowing room for religious (or nonreligious) employees to combine and reconcile faith and employment. Indeed, employees (often women) seeking to combine work and care responsibilities may be in similar situations as religious employees who seek to combine religious duties with work in a secular context. Both of these

6. Christian Brunelle considers this to presents 'a formidable challenge to trade unions', pp. 145-146. See also Steve Jefferys & Nouria Ouali, *Trade Unions and Racism in London, Brussels and Paris Public Transport*, 38 Industrial Relations Journal 406 (2007). (distinguishing between four types of union approaches towards racism: (1) protectionist, (2) denial, (3) assimilationist or (4) equal opportunities).
7. Christian Brunelle, *The Growing Impact of Human Rights on Canadian Labour Law*, in *Human Rights at Work: Perspectives on Law and Regulation* (Colin Fenwick & Tonia Novitz eds, Hart, 2010), p. 134, referring to M-J Legault, 'Droits de la personne, relations du travail et défis pour les syndicats contemporains', 2005 *Relations industrielles/Industrial relations* 60 (4) 683, 696-698.
8. *Ibid.*, at p. 134-135.
9. Now, it has been said that '[a]s a power countervailing management the trade unions are much more effective than the law has ever been or can ever be.' See Otto-Kahn Freund, *Labour and the Law* (Stevens, 1977). Davies & Freedman, p. 14. 'This is not only true in this country [the UK], it also applies where the law has played a larger role in the development of labour relations than in Britain; in Continental countries such as France or Germany, in Australia and New Zealand, and in the United States and Canada. Elsewhere the effectiveness of the law depends on the unions far more than the unions depend on the effectiveness of the law.' In other words, labour union support may be a more effective means for an accommodation-seeking employee than a reliance on the 'the law'. The best results should be expected when both elements collide: union-backed negotiation in the shadow of the law stands as the ideal. While the law can be changed, change in the approach of labour unions may in fact be a greater challenge, especially when the approach is rooted in ideological stances and core values.
10. See Joseph Fishkin, *Bottlenecks: A New Theory of Equal Opportunity* (Oxford, 2014).

employees face conceptual divisions which impede their accommodation and full inclusion as there is affiliation between the 'traditional separation of "work" and "family" which has informed the development and provision of labour law'[11] and the perspective which sees a person's religion as an illegitimate element in professional settings. It should be clear that in both of these circumstances, securing trade union support has been challenging for these 'non-traditional workers' (i.e., white, male, able-bodied, religiously neutral). Litigation concerning reasonable accommodation cases in the US and Canada illustrate that individual employees can face a double uphill battle when they seek accommodations: they must face not only the employer or management but trade unions may also fight their individual claims as going against the represented interests of the collectivity of workers.[12]

If – collective – labour law is to operate fully in an integrative logic it has to give up any protectionist reflexes which disadvantage newcomers or those who in some ways diverge from the anachronistic dominant norm of the white, male full-time breadwinner employee.[13] All, including non-standard workers, should be provided 'an adequate floor of rights'.[14] However, this has to happen under conditions which reinvent and reposition collective notions of solidarity under a 'unity in diversity' motto. Thus, the challenge is to refocus the notions of 'adaptability' and 'employability' is not only directed towards the workers (who under market flexibility demands is required to adapt to new labour market circumstances), but also towards employers' and collective labour organizations (to adapt workplaces to worker's situation or needs).[15] We should bear this in mind when discussing the potentials and limits of reasonable accommodations within the labour law context.

In this contribution, I discuss the topic of reasonable accommodation on grounds of religion or belief from a European and Belgian perspective, comparing it to the concept of indirect discrimination. I also consider whether we can speak of an 'accommodated workplace' in Belgium by analysing to what extent private company neutrality policies are considered legitimate under the given anti-discrimination and human rights frameworks. I offer a critique of the Belgian jurisprudence regarding private company neutrality policies and argue that this provides an 'integrative opportunity' for labour unions (and other organizations) to push for a rectification of this case law.

---

11. Nicole Busby, *Labour Law, Family Law and Care: A Plea for Convergence*, in *Vulnerabilities, Care and Family Law* (Julie Wallbank & Jonathan Herring eds, Routledge, 2014) p. 194.
12. For example, Supreme Court of Canada, *Central Okanagan School District No. 23 v. Renaud*, [1992] 2 S.C.R. 970; US Supreme Court, *Trans World Airlines, Inc. v. Hardison*, 432 U.S. 63 (1977); US Supreme Court, *US Airways, Inc. v. Barnett*, 535 U. S. 391 (2002) (involving a cargo handler who wanted to keep his physically less demanding job in the mail room, which was considered impossible under a new seniority system).
13. See Brunelle, *supra*.
14. Hepple, *The Future of Labour Law*.
15. See also http://heimatkunde.boell.de/2013/09/10/racism-and-discrimination-work-challenge-european-trade-unions#3. 'Views of trade unions and employers in the European Union (Strengthening the fundamental rights architecture in the EU IV). (November 2010), p. 50. ('Trade unions may embrace "new" workers, but may at the same time come under pressure to appear to protect the interests of their existing "national" members.')

[A] Employment Discrimination Law as the Source of Reasonable Accommodation on the Basis of Religion or Belief in Europe and in Belgium

Reasonable accommodations, a concept first introduced in the United States, and later in Canada, in the context of *religious* employment discrimination, is now firmly established as a right for persons with disabilities under both international and EU law. Despite its origins, the concept has been most influential in the area of disability rights, having triggered a European and international 'revolution' in disability accommodations. In the EU, this starting in vanguard non-discrimination law countries like the UK and the Netherlands, and was later being included in Article 5 of the Employment Equality Directive of 2000.[16] The concept of reasonable accommodations, hardly restricted to employment, plays a central role in the Convention on the Rights of Persons with Disabilities (CRPD) of 2006.

Considering the lack of an explicit general duty of reasonable accommodations on the basis of religion or belief in EU law or in Belgian law (the Belgian Anti-discrimination law of 2007), the concept is most developed with regard to disability law. The question whether to extend a similar right for reasons of religion or belief has generated much debate and controversy, but legislative initiatives have remained absent.[17]

However, without a doubt, reasonable accommodation is related with other notions in employment law. The connection with indirect discrimination[18] is most prevalent. Both concepts seeking to realize a more substantive equality as opposed to formal equality. In his position as UN Special Rapporteur on the Freedom of Religion or Belief, Heiner Bielefeldt writes that:

> [a]gainst a widespread misunderstanding, the purpose of reasonable accommodation is not to 'privilege' members of religious minorities at the expense of the principle of equality. In fact, the opposite is true. What reasonable accommodation encourages is the implementation of substantive equality.[19]

While the two concepts – reasonable accommodations and indirect discrimination – are interconnected, they are not the same; some characteristics of the indirect discrimination concept – its group and provision/practice focus, its complexity – may

16. Article 5 of the Employment Equality Directive reads: 'In order to guarantee compliance with the principle of equal treatment in relation to persons with disabilities, reasonable accommodation shall be provided. This means that employers shall take appropriate measures, where needed in a particular case, to enable a person with a disability to have access to, participate in, or advance in employment, or to undergo training, unless such measures would impose a disproportionate burden on the employer. This burden shall not be disproportionate when it is sufficiently remedied by measures existing within the framework of the disability policy of the Member State concerned.'
17. Including at the EU level, where the –now stalled- Horizontal Anti-Discrimination Directive does not include a right to reasonable accommodations on the basis of religion or belief.
18. In the US, 'disparate impact' is the most frequently term, instead of indirect discrimination.
19. Interim report of the UN Special Rapporteur on the Freedom of Religion or Belief. Tackling religious intolerance and discrimination in the workplace. (2014), p. 16.

render reasonable accommodations an ideal complementary concept for more effective equality and inclusion on the shop floor level.

On the one hand, the notion of indirect discrimination appears promising in addressing structural inequalities that form de facto barriers for religious employees, similar to a duty to make reasonable accommodation, even if much will depend on the justification and proportionality test applied.[20] On the other hand, with positive action, reasonable accommodations may be 'particularly well suited for the promotion of social inclusion.'[21] Since certain barriers effectively result in labour market exclusion, there is a need to 'develop a concept of equality which requires adaptation and change,'[22] instead of conformist pressure and expectations being placed (solely) on the vulnerable employee involved. Both concepts seem to be able to play a role towards facilitating such equality standard which challenges the existing formal anti-discrimination model where 'sameness of treatment' is less controversial and justifiable under an economic rationality model.[23] Instead of considering irrelevant a certain personal characteristics, reasonable accommodations raises the awareness that 'ignoring, by failing to accommodate, the characteristic can result in denying an individual equal employment opportunities.'[24]

Meenan calls the development of the concept of indirect discrimination 'arguably the first major milestone in European anti-discrimination law.' In contrast to Wentholt who withholds judgment on the relationship between indirect discrimination and substantive equality, '[m]any notable commentators now view indirect discrimination as an important tool for dismantling systemic discrimination and credit it with attempting to achieve substantial equality.'[25]

The concept of indirect discrimination was developed through ECJ case law in the 1960s and 1970s with regard to two forerunner grounds of discrimination under EU law. In *Defrenne v. Sabena II* the ECJ distinguished between 'direct and overt discrimination' and 'indirect and disguised discrimination', the distinction which was maintained for a few years only.[26] For 'the real birth of indirect sex discrimination',

20. Religion and Belief Discrimination in Employment-the EU law. pt. 69 (2006), p. 4.
21. See Sandra Fredman, *Age as an Equality Issue* (Hart, 2003), p. 63.
22. Sandra Fredman, *Disability Equality: A Challenge to the Existing Anti-Discrimination Paradigm?*, in *Disability Rights in Europe. From Theory to Practice* (Anna Lawson & Caroline Gooding eds, Hart, 2005), p. 203.
23. See Charlotte O'Brien, *Equality's False Summits: New Varieties of Disability Discrimination, 'Excessive' Equal Treatment and Economically Constricted Horizons*, 36 European Law Review 26 (2011).
24. Lisa Waddington, *Chapter Six: Reasonable Accommodation*, in *Cases, Materials and Text on National, Supranational and International Non-discrimination Law* (Dagmar Schiek et al., eds, Hart, 2007), p. 632.
25. Helen Meenan, *Introduction*, in *Equality Law in an Enlarged European Union: Understanding the Article 13 Directives* (Helen Meenan ed., Cambridge UP, 2007), p. 18, referring to Craig and De Būrca, EU Law Text, p. 85; Ellis, EU antidiscrimination law, p. 188. This (over)reliance on indirect discrimination under EU law may have (unintended) consequences on other mechanism which also aim to promote substantive equality and social inclusion, such as positive action and reasonable accommodations i.e., the crowding-out effect of indirect discrimination.
26. The ECJ later acknowledged that direct discrimination can also be disguised. Case 69/80, *Worringham v. Lloyds Bank Ltd.*

Meenan refers to *Jenkins v. Kingsgate* (Clothing Productions) Ltd. [1981] ECR 911, while *Bilka-Kaufhaus* [1986] is credited with setting out the test for justifying indirect sex discrimination. These conditions are the existence of a 'real need on the part of the undertaking', being 'appropriate' and being 'necessary' to achieve the set-out objectives. (paragraph 36 Bilka case) 'The language of objective justification for indirect discrimination in the Article 13 Directives (and objective justification of direct age discrimination under Article 6 Employment Directive) differs only in that a "real need" has been supplanted by a "legitimate aim."'[27]

'Indirect discrimination' refers to 'an apparently neutral provision, criterion or practice' which places persons because of certain protected characteristic at a particular disadvantage compared with other persons.[28] A claim for indirect discrimination entails assessing two elements: (1) the existence of a detrimental effect and (2) the objective justification for a measure.[29]

In 2014, the European Commission recognized the difficulties surrounding this concept in both the implementation as well as in the application stage, writing that:

> [t]he concept of indirect discrimination is complex and many Member States had initial difficulties in transposing it correctly. It is now enshrined in law, but its application in practice remains a challenge. To illustrate the problem, some Member States report that concerns have been expressed about the lack of clarity or lack of understanding of the concept of indirect discrimination in national courts. Other Member States point out that they do not yet have any case-law providing interpretation of indirect discrimination.[30]

When it comes to rules or concepts with a level of openness ('open norms') such as the prohibition of indirect discrimination, proportionality of a measure, legitimate aim, reasonableness, and so on, the legislature has effectively referred the important task of setting parameters to the courts. Griffith expresses it as follows:

> The legislator is often caught on the horns of a dilemma. Effective communication of legal information to the shop floor requires the use of rather general, socially well-understood concepts like 'equality' and 'discrimination', but if the legal information the public receives makes use of such concepts, the social meaning of

27. Meenan, *supra*, p. 19.
28. Differences in treatment directly based on religion or belief cannot be justified unless the conditions for a 'genuine occupational requirement' are met, and provided that 'the objective is legitimate and the requirement is proportionate.' When the link to religion or belief under a difference of treatment is indirect, however, there is an open justification regime, i.e., the measure can be justified by showing that there is a legitimate goal and the means of achieving this goal are appropriate and necessary.
29. Dagmar Schiek, *Indirect Discrimination (Chapter Three)*, in *Cases, Materials and Text on National, Supranational and International Non-discrimination Law* (Dagmar Schiek et al., eds, Hart, 2007), p. 372.
30. European Commission, Joint Report on the application of Council Directive 2000/43/EC of 29 June 2000 implementing the principle of equal treatment between persons irrespective of racial or ethnic origin ('Racial Equality Directive') and of Council Directive 2000/78/EC of 27 November 2000 establishing a general framework for equal treatment in employment and occupation ('Employment Equality Directive') from the Commission to the European Parliament and the Council, Brussels, 17 January 2014, COM(2014) 2 final (17 January 2014), p. 8.

a legal rule will not be what the legislator *intended* but what ordinary people on the shop floor *understand*.[31]

Thus in the case of indirect discrimination, for instance, courts will have considerable leeway to deciding what is a legitimate aim and whether the restrictive measure at stake is necessary and appropriate (proportional to the legitimate goal), explaining the different interpretations by domestic courts across Europe. For instance, in Belgian employment disputes involving a Muslim headscarf courts have found for the employer who sought to institute a 'neutrality policy' implying that employees (all or front-office only) is prohibited from manifesting their religion though dress or other visible signs. Dismissals based on the 'refusal' to abide by legitimate and proportionate dress codes were thus considered justified.[32] In contrast, in the Netherlands the neutrality argument raised by private employers has been rejected.[33] Some cases have received generous media coverage, thus transmitting the messaging of the court to the wider public. In this way, courts aided by the media – as conduits – play instrumental roles in the transmission process[34] that carries legal information from the law on the books to potential beneficiaries and actors on the shop floor of social life; judicial decisions thus feed into how a rule is interpreted at the shop floor level, sometimes transforming or misinforming its meaning.[35]

One reason for the lack of sufficient general effects may be that the concept of indirect discrimination under which many religion or belief issues are assessed is complex and knowledge of this legal concept is lacking on the shop floor, whereby it is either misapplied or it remains dead letter.

In 1999, Woldringh and others conducted socio-legal research on the effects of Dutch equal treatment laws such as the 1994 General Equal Treatment Act in the Dutch workplace. They contacted 1,309 employers (both public and private, large and small) and talked to the HR managers. One question was meant to test the familiarity with the concepts of direct and indirect discrimination ('distinction' in the Dutch jargon).[36] While the familiarity with equal treatment law in general was broad, when asked about the difference between direct and indirect distinction, 90% of the respondents had never heard of the difference. The small group which indicated knowledge was then asked about the difference. Only a few were able to correctly state the difference; many respondents thought that direct distinction refers to 'clear and visible discrimination' while indirect distinction refers to concealed discrimination or discrimination via some

31. John Griffiths, *The Social Working of Anti-discrimination Law*, in *Non-discrimination Law: Comparative Perspectives* (M. L. P. Loenen & Peter R. Rodrigues eds, Brill, 1999), p. 318.
32. *Infra.*
33. *Infra.*
34. 'The transmission process is in fact a "transformation" process in which the original legislative message gets distorted and truncated....' Griffiths, p. 317.
35. Griffiths distinguishes between 'general effects' and 'specific effects'. The former is the effect of the rule at the shop floor in general, while the latter refers to cases of enforcement by the courts. However, in our specific cases, generous coverage of cases bridges both effects.
36. Claartje Woldringh, 'Arbeidsorganisaties en gelijke-behandelingswetgeving' in Gelijke behandeling: regels en realiteit (Asscher-Vonk and Groenendijk, eds, Sdu, 1999), p. 341 et seq.

backdoor.[37] Woldringh and others note that knowledge in this area had not improved since 1994, when another researcher[38] looked into the same issue.

One way of addressing the potential of the concept of reasonable accommodations is to assess its added value in comparison with indirect discrimination. Perhaps a system that combines the strengths of both concepts can overcome some of the shortfalls and limitations of both and reinforce the effectiveness of equality law on the ground.

But what are some of these differences? Do these two affiliated concepts form different sides of the same coin? Which interpretation of the concept of indirect discrimination could confront structural inequalities in the access to employment, best contributing to the aim of optimal participation in the workforce? What are the limitations of this concept, and where could reasonable accommodations come in? And, finally, what are some of the caveats which can be anticipated in the case of reasonable accommodations being applied at the shop floor of the workplace?

The concepts of reasonable accommodations and indirect discrimination are related, and may even be seen as functional equivalents, but there are differences.[39] By some accounts, the concept of indirect discrimination can be regarded as more encompassing and implying a much higher burden/duty on employers in comparison with a duty to reasonably accommodate.[40] When a measure or situation is considered to disadvantage a certain group by its very design, it should be corrected so it does not hurt potential and future employees. A simple accommodation for a current/individual employee would not seem to suffice.[41] Also, if there is talk of discrimination, economic cost arguments seem unlikely to succeed under the justification test:

> [T]he defence to a failure to provide reasonable accommodation is that it would result in a disproportionate burden, which explicitly allows for factors such as cost to be considered. The defense to a complaint of indirect discrimination is that the challenged measure was objectively justified, and issues of cost are less likely to be regarded as meeting this test.[42]

In this sense, depending on the standard adopted for assessing reasonable accommodations, indirect discrimination could be considered a stronger tool for employees than reasonable accommodations.[43] What's more, reasonable

37. Ibid., at p. 351.
38. Judith A.H. Blom, De effectiviteit van de Wet gelijke behandeling m/v: tweede deelonderzoek (Vuga, 1995).
39. On the relation between the two concepts, See Vickers; Kristin Henrard, *De Verhouding tussen de concepten redelijke aanpassing, indirect discriminatie en proportionaliteit, in* Les Nouvelles Lois luttant contre la discrimination/De Nieuwe Federale Antidiscriminatiewetten (Christian Bayart et al., eds, Die Keure 2008), pp. 257-295.
40. Marc De Vos, *De bouwstenen van het discriminatierecht in de arbeidsverhoudingen, in* De Wet Bestrijding Discriminatie in de praktijk (Marc De Vos & Eva Brems eds, 2004), p. 81 (arguing that requirements under indirect discrimination are more stringent than under reasonable accommodations, related to the ground of disability but also in a general conceptual way).
41. *Ibid.*, at p. 81.
42. Waddington, *supra*, p. 644.
43. For the U.S. (where *de minimis* is the standard for assessing whether there was an undue hardship freeing the employer from his duty to accommodate): Roberto Corrada, 'The Supreme Court and title VII', Liberty Magazine January / February 2003, http://www.libertymagazine.

accommodations could also be seen as *limiting* a duty not to indirectly discriminate if the employer can use it as a shield to show he met his obligations under anti-discrimination law.[44]

On the contrary, indirect – as well as direct – discrimination requires a group disadvantage and going through a comparison exercise, since the claimant must show that a requirement would put *persons of a particular religion or belief at a particular disadvantage compared with others*. Thus, although a successful claim of indirect discrimination does not require an *actual* comparator (a hypothetical comparator is accepted), a *group* disadvantage is still required. Because of this legal-technical group disadvantage requirement, certain claims have been blocked from receiving appropriate consideration under the equality framework. In contrast, assessing a claim for reasonable accommodations requires no such showing of *group* disadvantage, since the concept aims for tailored measures that meet individual needs and situations. This is significant because:

> [D]isadvantage is not necessarily experienced by all or most members of a particular group, but is ... experienced on the individual level depending on both individual and environmental factors. Such individual forms of disadvantage can only rarely be revealed by making of group comparison, which is characteristic for both direct and indirect discrimination standards. Reasonable accommodation discrimination therefore requires a different approach to do justice to the particularities of an individual in a given situation.[45]

In its individual-personalizing effect, the reasonable accommodations approach can be said to form an antidote to generalization about 'Muslims', 'Hindus' or indeed the 'standard/ideal employee', thus having decommodification effect aimed at under social policies generally. Instead of generalizing, the concept of reasonable accommodations forces the employer to engage into an interactive dialogue with his or her employees and see the person and the particular needs, struggles and potentials. Also, the fact that accommodations do not require group disadvantage implies that it is a symmetrical instrument that is not only aimed at empowering minorities but also benefits members of the majority in certain circumstances. This is illustrated by the four Christian cases in the UK. The *Eweida* case[46] illustrates how the *group* disadvantage requirement[47] under the prohibition of indirect discrimination can be paralyzing for (true or alleged) 'sole believers'. The UK Court of Appeal dismissed Eweida's claim

org/index.php?id=1273 (describing a case involving an air traffic controller (Don Reed) winning USD 2.25 million verdict in a Denver district court: 'but he won because the jury found disparate treatment, that Reed's employer had treated him differently because of his religion ... If Reed had been left to argue only that his employer refused a reasonable accommodation, Reed might not have prevailed.')

44. Shelagh Day & Gwen Brodsky, *The Duty to Accommodate: Who Will Benefit?*, 75 La Revue du Barreau Canadien 433 (1996) (criticizing the Canadian reasonable accommodations jurisprudence).
45. Waddington, *supra*, p. 745.
46. *Eweida v. British Airways* [2010] EWCA Civ 80. The claimant went on to win her case before the European Court of Human Rights.
47. Mark Bell, *Anti-discrimination Law and the European Union* (Oxford UP, 2002), p. 190 (speaking of statistical evidence and 'the group-based disparate impact analysis' as 'typical within indirect discrimination.')

of indirect discrimination, qualifying the request to visibly wear a crucifix as an idiosyncratic wish of the employee. In fact, the Court never reached the justification stage of indirect discrimination.

A second technical difference, besides the group requirement, consists of the formulation of indirect discrimination which is intended to tackle discriminatory '*provisions, criterions or practices*.' Therefore, Pitt argues 'it would be stretching the meaning of "provision, criterion or practice"[48] too far to include in it a one-off decision' such as refusing an employee a day off to celebrate a religious holiday or observe a religious obligation.[49] Pitt accordingly views this as 'an unfortunate gap in protection for workers, contrasting unfavourably with the position in the US and some Canadian provinces where employers are under a duty to reasonably accommodate the religious needs of their employees.'[50] Reasonable accommodations are under this perspective seen as an extension or addition to, rather than a limitation to the duty of reasonable accommodation.[51]

Finally, a subtle yet important difference between discrimination and accommodation lies in the more intuitive nature of accommodation. As any lecturer on discrimination law can attest, the concept of indirect discrimination can be quite difficult to grasp, even for those legally trained. Woldringh's socio-legal study with HR managers strikingly demonstrated the lack of understanding about indirect discrimination amongst those who form the first line in applying the anti-discrimination norms.[52] The opacity of indirect discrimination renders it mal-fitted to bring about socio-economic change. There is a need to demystify the importance of (and the idea behind) indirect discrimination on a continuous basis, e.g., through information campaigns or other resources directed at employers and employees.[53] In contrast, the language and framing of issues in terms of accommodations is much more intuitive

48. In Dutch (both under the Belgian ADL and the Dutch ETA) this is: 'ogenschijnlijk neutrale bepaling, maatstaf of handelwijze'; 'handelwijze' could be seen as way of handling a matter, in which case a single-off decision could without much stretching be seen as falling under this.
49. Gwyneth Pitt, *Religion or Belief: Aiming at the Right Target?*, in *Equality Law in an Enlarged European Union: Understanding the Article 13 Directives* (Helen Meenan ed. 2007), p. 219 ('what if an employer is asked by a single employee for time off for a day of religious obligation and refuses, simply because the employee's absence would cause a mind inconvenience to the business? It could be argued that the employer's decision is a "provision" or could be extrapolated as a "practice" of not allowing leave where this would cause mild inconvenience and would thus constitute prima facie indirect discrimination. However, the alternative and, it is submitted, better view is that it would be stretching the meaning of "provision, criterion or practice" too far....').
50. *Ibid.*, at p. 219 (references omitted).
51. *Ibid.*, at p. 220. In the case of disability, this implies more protection, not less: 'the express inclusion of reasonable accommodations for disability implies that it was not intended to be covered by the general concept of indirect discrimination in the Directive.'
52. Claartje Woldringh, 'Arbeidsorganisaties en gelijke-behandelingswetgeving' in *Gelijke behandeling: regels en realiteit* (Asscher-Vonk & Groenendijk, eds, Sdu, 1999) p. 351.
53. See Katayoun Alidadi/RELIGARE project, A comparative legal study addressing religious or belief discrimination in employment and reasonable accommodations for employees' religious or philosophical beliefs or practice, RELIGARE policy brief (2012) http://www.religareproject.eu/content/comparative-legal-study-addressing-religious-or-belief-discrimination-employment-and, p. 8 (recommending the demystification of the concept of indirect discrimination by using information campaigns and informational resources directed at employers and employees.)

and straightforward,[54] even if applying the various elements (reasonable, disproportionate/hardship) raises particular legal issues. 'Directness' of the language of reasonable accommodations refers to the fact that the specific goal is to advance solutions in terms of accommodations that meet individual needs in a given context. More 'indirect' provisions appear less reliable at securing this type of thinking.

Griffith's social working approach points to certain 'regulatory strategies' to improve the effectiveness of anti-discrimination in practice, i.e., influencing behaviour on the shop floor:

> Rules ... should be designed primarily with their *general* effects in mind, that is, their influence on behaviour in cases in which official institutions are not mobilized....At a minimum the rules must be known to the relevant non-official actors. This means they must be clear and simple, even if this involves a considerable sacrifice of regulatory refinement. Equal pay rules that depend on highly sophisticated functional classifications, for example, whatever their moral virtue, are unlikely to be used on the shop floor.[55]

Reasonable accommodations may be such 'less than perfect rule that works is better than a perfect one[indirect discrimination] that does not.'[56] The importance of language cannot be ignored; the duty to reasonably accommodate achieves in a more direct and – arguably – more effective fashion what the prohibition of indirect discrimination aims to achieve by way of a legal fiction and thought-exercise. When the addressees of a legal rule do not know or *understand* a rule, that rule is bound to be ineffective *in practice* despite legal rhetoric and aspiration.

Finally, a difference between indirect discrimination and reasonable accommodation is that the 'reasonableness rhetoric' resonates better in a conciliation mode of resolution than in the conflict-based discrimination framework and could produce better results in practice by avoiding the litigation route.[57] In this sense, it has the *general* effects of the law in mind. Being approached for failing to reasonably *accommodate*[58] or *discriminating against* an employee may mean the same thing in legal parlance but will be perceived differently by an employer. The first may trigger a far less defensive response that conserves space for negotiation.[59] It is arguable that a

54. Waddington, *supra*, p. 670.
55. Griffiths, *supra*, p. 327. 'Use on the shop floor depends on a number of factors which we have examined above, only some of which lend themselves to legislative manipulation.'
56. *Ibid.*, at p. 330.
57. On a good example of such defensive response by the employer hit by a discrimination claim: Socio-legal research on accommodation of religious diversity in family and labour law, in public space and state funding of religions in the Netherlands (Dutch sociological report RELIGARE project). (2012), p. 44 (regarding ETC opinion nr. 2006-215, 27 October 2006 (headscarf/call centre), a commissioner in his interview said: 'the employer was extremely offended that he was accused of discriminating against people because he was very conscious about providing people with equal opportunities. ... And to add insult to injury, an anti-discrimination agency got involved... Because of all the anger, the people in question weren't able to think creatively for themselves...)'.
58. Even though the failure to provide accommodations can fall under the definition of discrimination, the term does not necessarily by association acquire a pejorative connotation.
59. This pejorative connotation of the term 'discrimination' is a reason why the Dutch Equal Treatment Act avoided the term and used 'distinction' ('onderscheid') instead.

discrimination allegation could have a more disparaging effect on the employment relations as it carries an undeniably pejorative implication. As noted by Marie-Claire Foblets, 'labels ... exert extraordinary influence'[60] and this applies to the qualification of 'discrimination' as well. Once a *legal* claim has been presented (i.e., the *special effects* of the law), this difference in connotations can be considered less relevant, but while negotiations are pending it may be significant to the course of events on the shop floor level. The fact that the reasonable accommodations terminology allows a potential conflict situation to be framed in *positive* language makes it a potentially powerful instrument for employees. Therefore, the lack of a clear legal basis for religious accommodation in Europe has important consequences for Muslims, Jews, Sikhs, Christians and others who face issues related to their religious dress, time conflicts or other issues which have come up in litigation across Europe. In fact, the role of reasonable accommodation legislation is not unlike a right to collective bargaining. If collective bargaining has been key in developing effective responses for worker's need – and there are good indications this is indeed the case – we should see employment law as playing an ancillary role. A right to reasonable accommodations is much the same; it does not guarantee any given outcome or 'success'. What it does is *promote negotiation*.[61]

[B] Definition and Scope of Reasonable Accommodation

The fact that the duty to reasonably accommodate – unless this amounts to undue hardship or would be disproportionate – is more intuitive does not mean that there are questions concerning its definition, scope, limitations and case by case application; indeed, the existence of an explicit limitation (undue hardship; proportionality...) implies a case-by-case exercise which ultimately calls for an individualized approach.[62]

I have argued that a typology is useful when we look at reasonable accommodations for reasons of religion or belief,[63] i.e., adjustments of work rules or practices that

60. Marie-Claire Foblets, *Perspective 1: Legal Anthropology in Imperative Inheritance Law in the Late-Modern Society*, in *Imperative Inheritance Law in a Late-Modern Society: Five Perspectives* (Christoph Castelein et al., eds, 2009), p. 43.
61. See Paul Davies & Mark Freedland, *Otto Kahn-Freunds' Labour & the Law* (Stevens, third edition, 1983), see chapter on 'collective bargaining and the law: promoting negotiation' (In contrast, collective agreement law is to promote agreement).
62. For guidance on the criteria to assess the existence of undue hardship, we can best look to the Canadian experience. For example *Alberta Dairy Pool v. Alberta* (Human Rights Commission), [1990] 2 S.C.R. 489. (Criteria to assess hardship include: financial cost of the accommodation; a potential disruption of a collective agreement; problems of morale of other employees (the impact on the rights and freedoms of co-workers); interchangeability of the work force and facilities; size of the employer's operation; safety concerns.) Brunelle distinguishes between three types of factors (at times overlapping) which courts can take into account to determine undue hardship vel non: cost considerations; the rights of others; and employer's business operations. See Christian Brunelle, chapter, in *Human Rights at Work. Perspectives on Law and Regulation* (Tonia Novitz, Colin Fenwick, eds, Hart, 2010), pp. 136-137.
63. Since the kinds of accommodations made for religion or belief may very well be very similar to the ones requested on the basis of disability (e.g., dress accommodations or time accommodations) or other grounds, the notion 'religious accommodations' is misleading.

take away the conflict between work obligations and religious obligations of the employee.[64] I have proposed the following four working categories:

- *dress code* conflicts or tensions;[65]
- conflict or tension with regard to *time demands and constraints* coming from religious and workplace demands (religious holidays, flexible working);[66]
- conflict or tension related to certain *job duties*, including conscientious objections; and
- conflict or tension related to workplace socializing expectations or demands and *work conditions* (prayer facilities; dietary restrictions).[67]

Going by the increasing case law and (media) reports from a variety of EU Member States, it is clear that religious skin is not always necessarily shed when entering the workplace, so that religion *in* the workplace is an issue that will not go away. Certainly some may fail to understand or object to the role of religion in the workplace (e.g., adopting a one-way, assimilation mode of integration), but religion in various forms (beliefs, practices, symbols) is present and plays a role in various ways and at different moments in the labour relations cycle; in the selection and recruitment process, within the frame of an existing work relationship, and in the event of a termination of the employment relation by the employer or employee.[68] Considering the sheer number of hours an employee spends on the work floor, the issue of religious accommodation for religious dress,[69] observance or work-assignments[70] is bound to come up in even slightly diverse workplaces. The image of

64. This typology was initially developed within the frame of the European RELIGARE project which includes the of case law from the European Court of Human Rights and ten countries involved in the project (Belgium, Bulgaria, Denmark, France, Germany, Italy, the Netherlands, Spain, Turkey, and the UK). See Marie-Claire Foblets & Katayoun Alidadi, *The RELIGARE Report: Religion in the Context of the European Union: Engaging the Interplay between Religious Diversity and Secular Models*, in *Belief, Law and Politics. What Future for a Secular Europe?* (Marie-Claire Foblets et al., eds, Ashgate, 2014) This typology relates to secular workplaces, as opposed to FBO/religious-ethos employment where additional issues may arise (e.g., with the divorce or other private life aspects of employees). For an extensive list of illustrations from across 9 European Member States and Turkey, see Katayoun Alidadi, *Reasonable Accommodations for Religion and Belief: Adding Value to Article 9 ECHR and the European Union's Anti-Discrimination Approach to Employment?*, 37 European Law Review 693 (2012).
65. This most often relates to the Muslim headscarf. On the front-office/back-office distinction and the role it plays when it comes to the accepting of religiously distinct dress, see Katayoun Alidadi, *From Front-Office to Back-Office: Religious Dress Crossing the Public–Private Divide in the Workplace*, in *Religion in Public Spaces* (Silvio Ferrari & Sabrina Pastorelli eds, Ashgate, 2012), pp. 159-190.
66. For example, requests for time off to observe a day of rest/Sabbath, a religious holiday, an extended bereavement period, or daily and weekly prayer.
67. As we will discuss, the line between the latter two categories is somewhat fuzzy.
68. Lucy Vickers, *supra*.
69. Hege Skjeie, *Headscarves in Schools: European Comparisons*, in *Religious Pluralism and Human Rights in Europe: Where to Draw the Line?* (M. L. P. Loenen & J. E. Goldschmidt eds, 2007) (139-141 on hijab in the workplace).
70. Roger Cotterrell, *Conscientious Objection to Assigned Work Tasks: A Comment on Relations of Law and Culture*, 31 Comparative Labor Law & Policy Journal 511 (2010).

the religious/conviction-free (or deserting) or commitment-free employee is a reduction that simply does not correspond to reality.[71]

§8.02 AN ACCOMMODATED WORKPLACE FOR RELIGION OR BELIEF?

Considering that there is no explicit duty to reasonably accommodate in the European workplace, to what extent are employers obliged or allowed to adapt the workplace because of religious considerations? In particular, one question concerns the validity of company 'neutrality policies' under the anti-discrimination law framework. This refers to employers who pre-emptively declare that 'any religious, philosophical or political expressions' of employees is prohibited in the workplace.

Developments in Belgium are particularly relevant. Social science studies and case law decisions illustrate a mixed reality on the ground; while various kinds of accommodations are in fact provided by employers,[72] there has undeniably been a spill-over effect from the public sector[73] to the private sector and private 'neutrality policies' have mushroomed, often motivated by negative attitude of customers towards Muslims and/or a strategy of conflict avoidance.[74]

Routinely their main goal is to ban headscarves worn by female Muslim employees and there is little linkage of the need for such neutrality to any particular job function or work circumstances.

71. The idea that labour is not separated from the labourer is effectively expressed in the maxim of 'labour is not a commodity' (In the ILO context stated in the 1944 Philadelphia Declaration), which has historical roots going back to the Irish sociologist and economist Dr John Kells Ingram (1823-1907). Karl Marx and others also expressed the same idea. See Paul O'Higgins, *'Labour Is Not a Commodity' – an Irish Contribution to International Labour Law*, 26 Industrial Law Journal (1997). See however Stein Evju, *Labour Is Not a Commodity: Reappraising the Origins of the Maxim*, 4 European Labour Law Journal 222 (2013), pp. 222, 228-229 (arguing Ingram did not coin the maxim, he was only calling 'attention to labour being inseparable from the worker' thereby responding to the liberalist conception of the day that labour was a commodity like any other commodities as expressed by e.g., Adam Smith in his 'The Wealth of Nations' (1776); 'It seems that the first time the maxim appeared in positive terms was at the adoption of the US Clayton Antitrust Act 1914').
72. See Ilke Adam & Andrea Rea, Culturele diversiteit op de werkvloer: praktijken van redelijke aanpassing in België. pt. 149 (2010); Younous Lamghari, L'Islam en entreprise: La diversité culturelle en question (Editions L'Harmattan, 2012).
73. Even if the Belgian state recognizes and even finance some religions, so that a strict church-state relationship is absent, various municipalities have banned civil servants from displaying religious symbols or dress. Choice and Prejudice. Discrimination against Muslims in Europe. (2012), p. 34 ('The restrictions on wearing religious and cultural symbols and dress in the public sector are presented as being in compliance with the principle of neutrality. However, this principle is enshrined in the Belgian Constitution only in relation to education, in no way does it require civil servants and public officials to refrain from showing signs of religious affiliation in their appearance.') In 2013, the city of Ghent reversed its ban on religious symbols for civil servants. The city of Antwerp in 2007 banned the wearing of headscarves and all other religious or political symbols by all front-office city staff. The Brussels regional government and a few other Flemish cities issued a similar ban for their employees. At the federal level there are no specific directives on wearing religious symbols, with the notable exception of judges, police officers and other uniformed officials.
74. Amnesty International report, 'Choice and Prejudice: Discrimination against Muslims in Europe', (Amnesty International, 2012), p. 34.

Making things even more problematic, some Belgian Courts have legitimized such neutrality policies, failing to consider them direct discrimination (and thus invalid under the CJEU's *Feryn* reasoning) or considering them justified under the indirect discrimination framework and not violating the freedom of religion or belief (here, the ECtHR's *Eweida* et al. judgment) carries important ramifications.

In the remainder of this contribution, I will discuss an example of the Belgian jurisprudence[75] and offer a critique drawing from the case law of the CJEU, the ECtHR and the Belgian courts themselves.

The HEMA case involved the Dutch shopping street retailer, which had dismissed a young Muslim working as a cashier at one of its Belgian branches for wearing a headscarf on the job. The decision was motivated by several complaints made by customers who were unhappy or upset about seeing a saleswoman wearing a headscarf. Before the dismissal, the employee had worked front-office wearing her headscarf and was even given a scarf in the colours of the company (this headscarf came from the Netherlands, where this formed an accommodative practice at HEMA branches). Following the conflict and in the midst of close media scrutiny, HEMA adopted an explicit ban on all religious, ideological and political symbols, i.e., a company neutrality policy.[76] Also, when the case made headlines in Belgium, HEMA issued a rather peculiar but revealing press statement explaining that they saw themselves required to conform to 'local customs and preferences' and the fact that it was 'apparently' not customary to wear a headscarf at work in Belgium had triggered their decision to adopt a neutrality policy banning all religious symbols in the future.

In its judgment, the Tongeren Labour Tribunal on 2 January 2013 found in the employee's favour, with six months' pay being awarded as penalty under the Anti-discrimination Act of 2007.[77] However, its reasoning was problematic and meant the case can hardly be considered as a triumph in the struggle for equal opportunities for Muslim women and other visible religious minorities. The Labour Tribunal found there had been direct discrimination in the case at hand (and there was no talk of justification via a genuine and determining occupational requirement) because at the time of the dismissal HEMA had no clear, uniform policy banning religious dress. But the Tribunal also made explicit that the subsequent neutrality policy adopted by HEMA was legitimate and would block any similar claims from being successful in the future, indeed would prevent any Muslim women from being employed at HEMA in Belgium in a front-office position again.

Interestingly, the Labour Tribunal found inspiration in the decisions of the Dutch Equal Treatment Commission (now: College voor de Rechten van de Mens) and the way it distinguishes between two situations to be analysed respectively under the

75. For another example, which the Cour de Cassation has now referred to the CJEU, see Labour Tribunal Antwerp, 27 April 2010, case nr. AR/06/397639/A; confirmed by Labour Court of Appeals Antwerp, 23 December 2011, case nr. AR/2010/AA/453 and 2010/AA/467. In this case, while there was no pre-existing neutrality policy the Court interestingly found an 'unwritten rule' against religious dress in the workplace.
76. The company had also offered to hire the employee for a back-office position, which she rejected.
77. Labour Tribunal Tongeren, 2 January 2013, A.R. 11/2142/A, Or. 2013/4, 109 (HEMA).

direct and indirect discrimination (distinction) frameworks. However, its understanding of those decisions is considerably flawed. The Labour Tribunal considered the difference to lie in the fact of having a pre-existing dress policy at the time of the dismissal. If there was no such policy to start with, the analysis would involve assessing whether there was *direct* discrimination, only be justified in the case of a genuine occupational requirement. In the case at hand the Labour Tribunal could not possibly regard the non-wearing of a headscarf as such a genuine occupational requirement (it did state, *obita dicta*, that such could be considered 'at most desirable or appropriate'). In contrast, if there had been such neutrality policy in place, a dismissal or refusal to hire someone because of religious dress would have to be assessed under an *indirect* discrimination analysis. This implies that the measure can then more easily be justified, so long as a legitimate objective is pursued in a suitable and appropriate manner. And regarding this, the Tribunal foreshadowed that such neutrality policies generally meet the test and thus can justify indirect distinctions.

In order to decide whether it should assess the actions of an employer under direct or indirect distinction framework, the Dutch Equal Treatment Commission inquires whether the employer *referred to the employee's religion* when it prohibited her headscarf (or other religious dress): 'In case the [employer] directly referred to the religion of the [employee], there is talk of direct distinction on the basis of religion.'[78] Such direct distinction can only be justified by proving a genuine and determining occupational requirements, while indirect distinctions can more easily be justified under an open-justification system. A case is to be analysed under indirect discrimination when the dismissal or rejection of the candidate is based on a *neutral reason*. This implies the reason does not refer to the headscarf or other religious dress directly or even as pretext, not when a pre-existing private sector neutrality *policy* (which directly refers to religion or belief) is in place. Unlike the Tongeren Labour Tribunal, the Dutch Equal Treatment Commission considers neutrality policies which -directly and unequivocally - refer to religious symbols such as in the HEMA case as *direct discrimination*.[79] For instance, in 2010 the Dutch Equal Treatment Commission considered the ban on 'religious, political or philosophical dress, including headcovers' in the dress regulations of a private foundation operating care and nursing centres with some 1,400 staff members (90% of them female, less than 1% allochtoon) to violate the Dutch Equal Treatment Act. It considered the case one of *direct distinction* (stating that the 'neutrality provision' at hand was not even 'apparently neutral' so as to call for an assessment under the *in*direct distinction framework). It found the provision itself discriminatory, not just in its effects on certain groups. The motivation behind the policy - the perceived needs and wishes of elderly clients for a recognizable surrounding - was considered irrelevant, since no one - including elderly 'disoriented' nursing home dwellers - can be considered exempt from the collective aims of equality legislation. Thus, the subsequent adoption of the neutrality policy by HEMA should

78. '*Ingeval verweerster rechtstreeks heeft verwezen naar de godsdienst van verzoekster, is sprake van direct onderscheid op grond van godsdienst.*' (ETC nr. 2008-144, 3 December 2008, para. 3.9).
79. ETC nr. 2010-94, 28 June 2010.

change nothing to the legal situation of either employer or employee, on the contrary it would make proof of direct discrimination more straightforward.

Yet the message that a priori sweeping restrictions on religious dress founded on (a particular understanding of) the concept of neutrality were legitimate, and could avoid employment disputes, travelled fast through the media. This was all the more striking since HEMA's neutrality policy had been clearly adopted in response to discriminatory customer responses. In the face of such judicial backing for private company neutrality policy, any job applicant is also put on notice of his or her fragile position when it comes to religious requests and the fact of imminent and legitimated exclusion from a very wide array of employment opportunities. Effectively, the spill-over effect, the emulation of the same construction which has been utilized in the public sector/sphere by private profit-oriented companies not serving a public role but having a (local) customer base to please, is institutionalized and judicially approved. Arguably, the far-reaching effects of the endorsement of 'neutrality' policies means a significant blow to the fundamental rights of employees in the workplace, as contractual/unilateral policies (as long as adopted *a priori*) are set to trump fundamental employee rights without much ado.[80]

While the Tribunal explicitly addressed the claims under the anti-discrimination framework, it devoted only minimal attention to Article 9 ECHR arguments. It stated formulaically that 'on the basis of Article 9.2 ECHR and the jurisprudence of the European Court of Human Rights, the Belgian employer can prohibit the wearing of a headscarf during work hours by way of a neutrality policy.' This also is flawed, at least since the ECtHR issued its *Eweida* decision and thereby gave birth to Article 9 ECHR in voluntary employment settings.

[A] Legal Assessment of Private Neutrality Policies: Bias Hidden in Plain Sight

Here, I want to argue that the judicial legitimating of private sector neutrality policies (clauses banning religious, philosophical (and often also political) is legally flawed and must be reversed, sending the right – integrative – message out. I draw arguments from recent cases of Europe's two supranational courts,[81] the CJEU and the ECtHR, as well as reasoning of Belgian Courts in other matters. Despite recent judicial defeats, the Interfederal Centre for Equal Opportunity, NGO's and trade unions should push for a rectification of existing Belgian jurisprudence on private sector neutrality policies.[82]

First, *under anti-discrimination law* neutrality policies cannot be considered justified, rather they should be *framed as declaratory discriminations*, a form of direct discrimination. In the absence of special circumstances justifying it (e.g., health and

80. The issue of harassment, by customers who had made derogatory comments towards the Muslim saleswoman, was not addressed either.
81. See Sonia Morano-Foadi & Lucy Vickers (eds), *Fundamental Rights in the EU. A Matter for Two Courts* (Hart, 2015).
82. And since no actual victim is required (considering the dispersed effects of) declaratory discrimination, a company policy can in principle be challenged on its own.

safety concerns), general bans on religious dress in so-called neutrality policies – unduly and disproportionately restricting freedom to manifest religion – should not be accepted. Belgian jurisprudence is too willing to accept neutrality under an exclusive understanding as being possible, good, necessary and proportionate. Seeing neutrality policies as effective forms of *declaratory discrimination statements*, and thus *direct discrimination* on the basis of religion or belief, means only genuine and determining occupational requirements can offer justification. Since this can only be done on a case-by-case basis, *general policies* would thus by definition fail the test even if in particular cases restrictions could be seen as justified. In the CJEU's *Feryn* decision[83] there was direct discrimination under the terms of the Racial Equality Directive which involved discrimination on the basis of race or ethnicity. The CJEU accepted that employers can directly discriminate by declaration. The Centre for Equal Opportunities argued that even if there was no specific victim, the company had discriminated against a group based on their ethnicity; by stating as such Moroccans would not be hired, it was sure this group would not apply for the open posts at the company. The CJEU, responding to a number of prejudicial questions referred by the Brussels Labour Court of Appeals, agreed, thereby confirming the concept of 'discrimination by declaration' under Directive 2000/43 and confirming that (real of implied) discriminatory preferences of customers are no justification for discriminating (future) employees.

There is no reason the same cannot be argued with regard to the declaration that a company will not hire any persons who wear religious symbols such as the headscarf; the only difference is that this is being declared by reference to the notion of neutrality, under an aura of – unwarranted – legitimacy. The exclusion of a group, protected under anti-discrimination law, is no less the case. This is even more so when the 'neutrality' tool forms a sheer cloak for intolerant (under)currents in Belgian society. Effective anti-discrimination law in such circumstances can only be unsettling in both its special and general effects and to do so it must challenge such normalized instances of intolerance and discomfort with the presence of religious expressions. Indeed, 'fundamental rights ultimately exist to protect minorities, unpopular minorities in particular, against the tyranny of the majority.'[84]

Belgian cases in other areas of anti-discrimination law support this argument as well. In a 2013 decision, the Labour Tribunal in Bruges[85] held that the rejection of a job applicant because of his physical or genetic characteristic (ground covered under the Anti-discrimination law of 2007) or his alleged disability was unjustified. The case

83. ECJ, Case C-54/07, *Centrum voor gelijkheid van kansen en voor racismebestrijding v. NV Feryn*, 1 July 2008. NV Firma Feryn was a Belgian company specializing in the sale and installation of doors which had vacancies for employees to install garage doors in customers' houses. The CEO during an interview with a national Flemish newspaper (*De Standaard*, titled 'Customers don't want Moroccans') explained these vacancies were not being filled because he would not recruit persons of Moroccan origin. He confirmed on Belgian national television that he needed to take into account his customers' preferences and attitudes.
84. Jelle Flo & Jogchum Vrielink, *The Constitutionality of the Belgian Burqa Ban*, openDemocracy.net 14 January 2013.
85. Labour Tribunal Bruges, 10 December 2013, AR nrs. 12/25521/A en 12/2596/A, unpublished, https://www.law.kuleuven.be/arbeidsrecht/pdf_documenten/nieuwsbrieven2013/arbrbbrugge-10122013.pdf. The CEOOR was involved in this case, supporting the employee.

concerned an employee who had a condition known as congenital syndactyly, where some of his fingers were fused together. The employer had hired him as a temp agency in a computer business and was intent on offering him a permanent employment contract. But because some customers and co-workers saw the employee's hands as 'unpresentable' the employer had retracted its offer (which had appeared from a conversation between the employee's parents and the owner). The Labour Tribunal in Bruges did not accept this reason, finding a case of direct discrimination based on physical or genetic characteristic and disability. The court also referred to the *Feryn* case, expanding that decision to the protected ground of disability, saying that an employer cannot justify direct discrimination to meet (discriminatory) preferences of either customers or co-workers.[86] The need to have 'presentable hands' (not having congenital syndactyly) was also not considered to be a genuine and determining occupational requirement justifying direct discrimination (closed justification regime in case of disability) and such argument or policy also would not be in pursuance of a legitimate aim, a first step in being able to lead to a justification under an open-justification regime (such regime being applicable in the case of direct/indirect physical or genetic characteristic under the Anti-discrimination Act). The Tribunal held clearly that:

> [e]xcluding a person with congenital syndactyly does not correspond with any objective nor legitimate aim. The employer cannot justify direct discrimination on the basis of a physical or genetic characteristic and/or disability to meet the wishes of other employees and/or the wishes of its clientele.[87]

Consequently, the employee was awarded a lump sum of six months pay. The case also sends out a message against intolerant third party (co-workers and customers) attitudes and bolstering employment opportunities for the disabled employee. The employer – as distributive agent deciding over the distribution of scarce goods (jobs) – in a sense mediates between these parties and has certain fairness responsibilities expressed in non-discrimination law.

Another Belgian Labour Tribunal case, this time decided in Leuven, shows that employers choosing the 'way out' ('*vlucht vooruit heeft gekozen*') as an avoidance strategy in anticipation of difficult situations (and potential needs of accommodation and flexibility) is not a justified reason under anti-discrimination law. The case involved an employee dismissed after eight years on the job when he informed the employer (operating a fitness centre) that his newborn daughter had a serious and rare genetic disorder which would result in health complications and/or a disability;[88] the day after he had informed the employer he was called in for a personal conversation

86. Thus the Labour Tribunal expanded the Feryn holding to different discrimination grounds, but also added that preferences of co-workers (not at stake in the Feryn case) were no justification.
87. Labour Tribunal Bruges, 10 December 2013, AR nrs. 12/25521/A en 12/2596/A, unpublished, https://www.law.kuleuven.be/arbeidsrecht/pdf_documenten/nieuwsbrieven2013/arbrbbrugge-10122013.pdf, p. 15, nr. 4.3.2.1.7.
88. Labour Tribunal Leuven, 10 December 2013, AR nr. 12/1064/A, unpublished, https://www.law.kuleuven.be/arbeidsrecht/pdf_documenten/nieuwsbrieven2013/arbrbleuven-10122013.pdf. In this case the CEOOR, although it was not party to the case, also intervened on behalf of the employee.

and subsequently was given a six month dismissal notice, since apparently the employer feared that his family situation would soon lead to a lack of motivation on the job. The employee's dismissal form ('C4') listed as reason for his dismissal that 'he no longer met the required employee profile'. The Labour Tribunal confirmed that the Anti-discrimination law included protection against associative discrimination so that the employee's disadvantaged treatment based on his daughter's disability fell under the law.[89] Considering the motive for the dismissal to be established by a number of circumstances, including the timing of the decision right after conveying the news, and the employer's inability to provide alternative reasons, the court held for the employee, who was awarded six months pay under the Anti-discrimination act (amounting to over EUR 18,000). Employers should pursue non-discrimination policies and create an atmosphere of tolerance and respect instead of pre-emptively limiting employee rights (and excluding employees because of the strength of their convictions) based on stereotypical presumptions of the disruptive and conflict-ridden presence of certain people in the workplace. Even when tensions do arise in the workplace, this is no reason for exclusion of certain people, but rather a reason to step up on diversity and anti-harassment initiatives. Conflict/tension avoidance essentially reinforces assimilation, and in a sense is universal: the same avoidance strategy was used in the US when racial tensions were high in so-called whites-only policies. Here the exclusion is towards religious people or at least those with strong confessions: those are excluded unless they succumb to the pressure to assimilate. Even for those who pass the mark and get hired, it offers little good news in case tensions do arise in the end as the employer may be unwilling to address the concerns head-on but again look for an easy exit option.

Second, despite the summary consideration that Article 9 ECHR routinely receives in this context, *the human rights framework* too can bolster arguments against judicially legitimating private neutrality policies, in particular in the form of ramifications of the ECtHR's *Eweida* decision (2013).

Importantly, company policies cannot be considered to *automatically trump* Article 9 ECHR fundamental rights of employees any longer. There has to be an effective and genuine balancing of the various rights and interests at stake, including the fundamental right of the employee to express his or her religious beliefs and practices which must be given adequate weight in the exercise. It must be recognized that restrictive dress policies imply real restrictions on the employee's rights and critically impact the opportunities of (visible) minorities in the employment market. This does not mean restrictions on dress are no longer allowed in the workplace in any circumstance: a ban was, for instance, accepted (but not mandated) in the *Chaplin* case because of safety and security considerations. But in *Eweida*, the corporate image concerns of British Airways (even if legitimate) proved insufficient to warrant overstepping employee rights to manifest their freedom of religion in the workplace. It is

89. Labour Tribunal Leuven, 10 December 2013, AR nr. 12/1064/A, onuitg., https://www.law.kuleuven.be/arbeidsrecht/pdf_documenten/nieuwsbrieven2013/arbrbleuven-10122013.pdf, p. 4.

clear that after *Eweida*, where the European Court closely links pluralism, democracy, and the protection of religious freedom together, a more effective consideration of employee rights under Article 9 is due. What's more, while in *Eweida* the ECHR considered the corporate image argument of BA as legitimate, this need not be the case with neutrality which is motivated to meet discriminatory customer preferences.

Two additional arguments can bolster the anti-discrimination and human rights based arguments against the acceptance of neutrality policies in the private sector.

There is a textual argument which makes the parallel with the exception provided under Article 4(2) of the EED to the *religious-ethos companies*. Under the EED the provision which allows religious-ethos companies to select staff on the basis of religion or belief is an exception to the general rule protecting against religion or belief discrimination and must thus be interpreted (very) narrowly. A general requirement that all employees should be part of a certain church or of a certain faith is regarded as a clear violation of the limited exemption provided for FBO. Instead, whether a certain faith requirement is allowable depends on the job function in particular.[90] Thus, the so-called 'organic approach' (where the FBO requires adherence or practice from its entire staff) has been discredited in favour of a 'functional approach' (the requirement has to be justified in light of the context and job function in particular). This functional approach minimizes the exclusionary effects of FBO hiring policies while allowing for an organizational autonomy of key posts. One can argue that what is required of FBO (i.e., under the functional approach towards setting religious requirements) must also – at the very – least form a limitation for 'neutrality'-focused businesses. In other words, a *general* policy applying to all staff (organic approach) is unaccepted; only for staff where there is a 'specific need' considering the context and job functions and following a case-by-case analysis restrictions could be justified. If not, this would mean that private commercial companies – 'secular organizations' – are allowed more leeway than FBOs, by being allowed to require *all* their staff to abide by non-religious standards while FBOs can only make requirements when the context or the job function justifies such. Drawing a parallel between general 'neutrality policies' and religious requirements under Article 4(2) EED would mean that phrased generally both are to be regarded as illegitimate a priori exclusions and restrictions should be decided on a case-by-case basis (job function; actual conflicts or incidents) rather than set by general statements.

Finally, there is the issue of *spill-over effect* from the public to the private sector. The legitimacy of such policies even with regard to the public sector is up for debate[91]

90. See Yves Stox, Discriminatie en Identiteit. Identiteitsgebonden Werkgevers in het Belgisch en Europees Arbeidsrecht (Larcier. 2010); Lucy Vickers, *Religious Freedom, Religious Discrimination, and the Workplace* (Hart Pub., 2008).

91. For example, Hana M. A. E. van Ooijen, *Religious Symbols in Public Functions: Unveiling State Neutrality. A Comparative Analysis of Dutch, English and French Justifications for Limiting the Freedom of Public Officials to Display Religious Symbols* (Intersentia, 2012); Van Ooijen distinguishes 6 arguments offered in support of dress restrictions in the Netherlands and also offers compelling counter-arguments for each one. See p. 260 (the 6 'points of contention' being: equal treatment of the public official, personification of the state, public official's bias, risk of proselytism, image of the state, separation of church and state).

and the Belgian situation is not unambiguous with regard to the public sector.[92] But even in countries where the situation of public servants has been clear with formal bans, it does not mean the same approach can easily be accepted in the area of private employment. Thus in France it is established that public civil servants, without exception, need to respect the principle of laïcité, and in the interpretation of the Council of State, this implies withholding from showing religious affiliation through distinct dress or symbols in either back-office or front-office functions.[93] The debate more recent has concerned the extension of laïcité and religious symbol bans to the private sector, in particular to day care centres. On 19 March 2013 the French Cour de cassation found for a Muslim caretaker and co-director who had been dismissed for wearing a headscarf by the Baby-Loup day care centre, and held that laïcité could not be extended to the private sector by an employer which was not a faith-based organisation (*entreprise de conviction*).[94] However, in June 2014 – after the Paris Court of Appeals had found for the employer – the Grand Chamber of the Cour de cassation confirmed the appeals decision, while reiterating that laïcité only relates to the State and that an employee's freedom of religion can only be restricted to the extent that it is justified by the nature of the job duties and if proportionate to the objective sought.[95] It held that in the case at hand the Paris Court of Appeals could have interpreted the day care's internal policies not as a general restriction to the freedom to manifest one's religion, but as a 'precise' provision, justified by the nature of the job duties and proportionate to the objective sought.[96] Consequently, the extent to which the concept of laïcité – interpreted to require a formal ban on all public servants to manifest their

92. There has been (and still is) an elaborate and heated debate in Belgium concerning the headscarf (and other religious symbols) worn by teachers and students in public schools organized at Community level. Besides these public school teacher cases, a number of localities (Ghent (now reversed); Antwerp) have adopted explicit dress regulations banning religious, political and ideological symbols for their front-office staff, but there are no legal cases to be reported. See Katayoun Alidadi, *Approches comparatives du débat sur la 'neutralité': la liberté de culte des enseignants des écoles publiques et des fonctionnaires à travers l'Europe de porter des vêtements religieux in* Neutralité et faits religieux. Quelles interactions dans les services publics? (D. Cabiaux et al., eds, 2014).
93. In France, the principle of laïcité applies to civil servants and to agents, who have 'only' a fix termed contract – of public law – with the State or local public authorities. The French Law No 83/634 of 13 July 1983 Act on the rights and duties of civil servants is relevant here, and the Council of State has clearly set out what this and other legal provisions mean for public servants in a 2000 ruling (Council of State opinion, *Mlle M.*, 3 May 2000, n° 217077; Avis rendus par le Conseil d'Etat sur des questions de droit posées par un tribunal administratif ou une cour administrative d'appel). This advice of the Council of State, addressing three questions, has become a reference in this matter.
94. On this date, the French Cour de cassation issued its first Baby-Loup decision, holding that the internal regulations of the day care centre which prohibited staff from wearing the hijab and other religious symbols was unjustified. French Cour de cassation (social chamber), 19 March 2013, n° 11-286845, *Bull.* 2013, V, n. 75.
95. French Cour de cassation (grand chamber), *Mme A. c. Association Babyloup*, n° 612, 25 June 2014; Anne Jouan, 'Baby-Loup: la Cour de cassation confirme le licenciement de la salariée voilée,' *Le Figaro* 24 June 2014. Certainly, the French courts wanted to put the matter to rest.
96. Certainly, one can understand that the French courts wanted to put the matter to rest after six years of litigation and that the parties were so alienated that cooperation would be unfeasible but considering the general language used in the particular provision, this result is at the very least counterintuitive.

religious affiliation through symbols or dress – can apply to the private sector is limited even in France. The Belgian approach – under the concept of neutrality – effectively goes much further than the French approach when it comes to private sector employment.

A sign of the need for more and better guidance when it come to religion or belief discrimination are the two references for preliminary rulings currently pending before the CJEU. One was submitted by the Belgian Cour de cassation and another by the French Cour de cassation. Both relate to the question of the wearing of a Muslim headscarf in the workplace and whether a refusal to accommodate constitutes a direct discrimination on the basis of religion or belief.[97] These cases should be closely monitored as they may add significance to future legal developments and reshape the borders of an accommodated workplace.

§8.03 CONCLUSION

Labour law is an important tool in protecting the rights and freedoms of workers, irrespective of their religious commitments which can interact with and at times interfere with professional duties. The system of collective labour relations is a mechanism which seeks to use the numerical strength of employees to counterbalance the economic power of employers, and thus make the bargaining situation more balanced and fair.[98] But, as Brunelle notes, 'this system presumes that the community of interests of employees transcend their differences.'[99] In various ways, the interests of all employees do converge – e.g., interests of all workers are advanced with better salaries and work circumstances, and even in the abstract better protection for all freedoms and rights, but in some respects an employee or a group of employees can (seem to) stand apart. This is in particular so if the employee's characteristics, employment or other situation differs in some non-insignificant aspect from the majority or standard employee who is well-established in the trade union movement (in the membership and/or leadership). The cases of women and of ethnic minorities in the workplace have been most commonly discussed,[100] but the same applies to religious minorities in the workplace.

Despite the steady rise of EU non-discrimination law, its effectiveness in addressing instances of *religious or philosophical* disadvantage has been limited. Indeed, some have argued the religion strand under discrimination law is less worthy of protection than other human characteristics such as race/ethnicity, gender, disability, and sexual orientation.[101] The – perceived – lack of public support for reasonable accommodations for religion or belief in Europe affects the prospects for legislative actions. The lack of

97. See Belgian Cour de cassation 9 March 2015, AR S.12.0062.N; French Cour de cassation (social chamber), n° 630, 9 April 2015 (13-19.855),.
98. Brunelle, *supra*, p. 134.
99. *Ibid.*, at p. 134.
100. Jefferys & Ouali, *supra*, 2007.
101. Aileen McColgan, *Class Wars? Religion and (in)equality in the Workplace*, 38 Industrial Law Journal 1 (2009).

such explicit law effectively means a laissez-faire policy in the matter. Now, laissez-faire has its proponents and indeed such policy may allow for the empowerment of employees, who in isolated fashion lack the power-position the employer is typically considered to enjoy, if and when people can organize collectively in pursuance of shared interests and goals. Yet, this becomes much less viable when some workers are isolated in their needs and interests from the larger pool of workers. Indeed, one worker may be as such 'isolated' with regard to some issue, but share many interests with other workers, so that there is a system of overlap. Laissez-faire fails to meet this reality, and stands to disregard and marginalize those who remain 'isolated' to some extent. In contrast to Kahn-Freund's laissez-faire collectivism, the 'integrative function' of labour law as proposed by Bob Hepple recognizes and reinforces developments such as anti-discrimination law which are much more tailored towards the realities of today's diverse workforce. When employment and social exclusion ensue as a result of the status quo, laissez-faire will fail to alter this but instead becomes a conservative force[102] against the most vulnerable constituencies on the labour market.

Minority religious status (and needs) is a case in point. A minority Muslim or Sikh employee will have shared interests in decent work conditions, work time and pay, but may be willing to forfeit some demands in order to meet his or her more important needs of religious practice-professional compatibility. The will to forfeit may stretch quite far: e.g., the case of safety in return for wearing religiously mandated dress by Sikhs. Can this weaken the position of the collectivity of workers? It may well under certain conceptions, but we may need to reconstruct the idea of workers collectivity to keep collective organizing relevant under conditions of diversity. If labour is not a commodity, there is no sacristy regarding unity and collectivity of workers. The challenge for the minority worker is not (only) the employer, but (also) the threat can come from various corners, including the union, other workers or state policies.

In this contribution I consider whether we can speak of an 'accommodated workplace' in Belgium by analysing to what extent company neutrality policies are legitimate under the human rights and anti-discrimination law frameworks. The HEMA judgment discussed is an example of case law which – instead of combating – fortifies societal pressures on minorities to conform or to face far-reaching exclusion (limited employment opportunities and segregation). The judicial seal of approval de facto *promotes* broad and a priori restrictions on employment opportunities for Muslim women and other visible religious minorities. For Muslims and religious minorities in an already problematic Belgian labour market situation this constitutes an additional and hardly trivial barrier to participation. However, since there are a host of defendable arguments to support a reversal of case law legitimating private sector neutrality policies, there is an opportunity for trade unions and other organizations to play a key active role – without waiting for new legislation – in this regard and retain their relevance and effectiveness in promoting equality and inclusion in a quickly diversifying labour market. This requires the owning-up of religious accommodation as an issue of our time which relates to the new diverse workforce reality.

102. Historically, this was not the case; laissez-faire was able to divert legislative intervention in major disputes which would curtain collective organization and strike led by unions.

CHAPTER 9

Reasonable Accommodation for Religion, and Other Motives, in French Labour Law: Testing the Possibility of a Legal Transplant

Sophie Robin-Olivier

In France, recent case law made it clear that 'reasonable accommodation' is not the concept that serves to solve conflicts concerning religion in the workplace.[1] In the debate on religion at work that recently heated up, when new cases were brought to French superior courts, the notion of 'reasonable accommodation' for religious motives was nowhere to be found. Indeed, the very notion of 'reasonable accommodation' is only explicitly mentioned in the field of disability law: French implementation of Directive 2000/78[2] did not choose to extend the scope of the notion beyond what EU law specifically requires. Thus, in the famous recent cases, no duty to accommodate was opposed employers' decisions to dismiss women wearing an Islamic headscarf. Rather, the focus was on the French notion of '*laïcité*'.[3] Controversies have raged about

1. On this case law, see below. For a straightforward expression of the opinion that 'reasonable accommodation' for religion is not required in French law, see J.-G. Huglo, 'La Cour de cassation et le fait religieux dans l'entreprise: présentation des enjeux juridiques', Droit Social, n°9, September 2015, p. 682. For an in-depth study of religious accommodation at work, see K. Alidadi, 'Reasonable Accommodations for Religion and Belief: Adding Value to Article 9 ECHR and the European Union's Anti-Discrimination Approach to Employment?', European Law Review, Issue 6, 2012, p. 693. See also, for a comparative analysis with US law, M. Mercat-Bruns, 'Discriminations en droit du travail, Dialogue avec la doctrine américaine', Dalloz, 2013, p. 542 ff.
2. Directive 2000/78 of 27 November 2000 establishing a general framework for equal treatment in employment and occupation, *OJ L 303 of 2/12/2000, p. 16.*
3. On the conception of the notion of laïcité in the context of labour law, and in particular, the recent case law see, namely: S. Henette-Vauchez and V. Valentin, L'affaire Baby Loup ou la nouvelle

the need to revitalise this Constitutional reference and the possible extension of this notion to the private sphere, namely private childcare or education.[4]

Quite evidently, French labour law has not paved the way to an open conception of accommodation at the work place, when religion is at stake. Rather, what comes out of recent case law developments is a tendency to favour exclusion (from the workplace) for religious motives over more inclusive solutions. In other words, as the first part of this chapter demonstrates, 'negative accommodation', resulting in the dismissal of the worker concerned, tends to prevail, in important cases, over 'positive accommodation', in the form of adjustments to fit workers' religious needs. However, French labour law could lead to other outcomes. Indeed, workers' rights and freedoms at the workplace are protected by the law, and, under EU law umbrella, the prohibition of discriminations on the ground of religion implies a stricter review of employers' decisions than the one that has been applied until now. Thus, the absence of a concept of 'reasonable accommodation' in the legal vocabulary does not mean that there are no functional equivalents. Whether 'positive' accommodation of employees' requests for adjustments could be obtained in the current legal framework will be explored in the second part of this chapter. The third part turns to the larger context of French labour law to show that forms of accommodation have been welcomed, outside the field of religion. In many instances, accommodation, under other names, such as the duty to 'reclassify' workers, has been imposed upon employers. The objective is not only to evaluate the receptivity of the context in which the notion of 'reasonable accommodation' can be transplanted, but also to highlight the fact that resistance to accommodation for religion is rooted way beyond the frontiers of labour law.

§9.01 DEALING WITH RELIGION AT WORK IN THE FRENCH LEGAL CONTEXT: WHEN 'NEGATIVE ACCOMMODATION' PREVAILS

The protection of individual freedoms, at the workplace, has been a concern that the French legislator addressed, already, in 1992, in a very important statute, both symbolically and substantially. The 1992 legislation does not deal with religious freedom specifically but, as an umbrella law dealing with employees' rights and freedoms, it does include the protection of religious freedom. According to this statute,[5] no restriction to individual rights of persons or to individual or collective freedoms can apply if these restrictions are not justified by the nature of the task to be accomplished and proportionate to the objective pursued.[6] Ten years before, in 1982, the law had used the same language to prevent employees' handbooks or rules of procedure

laïcité, LGDJ, 2014; P. Adam, 'Les laïcités et l'entreprise privée, Représentation(s) dans un théâtre d'ombres', Droit Social, n°9, Sept. 2015, p. 708.

4. See the Bill on the extension of the obligation of neutrality to private childcare and ensure the respect of the principle of *laïcité:* the draft was adopted by the National Assembly in May 2015, and must now to be discussed by the Senate.
5. Article L1121-1 of the labour code.
6. 'Nul ne peut apporter aux droits des personnes et aux libertés individuelles et collectives de restrictions qui ne seraient pas justifiées par la nature de la tâche à accomplir ni proportionnées au but recherché'.

(*règlements intérieurs*) from including restrictions to employees' rights or freedoms when these restrictions were not justified and proportionate. Thus, in case religious freedom is at stake, the law requires that the employer's refusal to accommodate is justified by the nature of the task to be accomplished by the employee, and narrowly tailored. This leads, inevitably, to various solutions, depending not only on the precise elements of each concrete case, but also on the level of scrutiny applied by courts. For instance, the dismissal of an employee at a ladies' fashion retailer, when she decided to wear a burqa was considered justified because the situation was considered a genuine source of trouble for the employer's business.[7] Similarly, dismissing women wearing an Islamic veil was considered justified for security reasons[8] or when the employer contended it was a source of problems in the relationships with clients.[9] On the contrary, wearing an Islamic veil was not considered a just cause for termination when no trouble in the functioning of the business could be derived from it.[10]

In addition to the protection of workers' individual rights and freedoms, French labour law prohibits discriminations based on religion,[11] and a number of cases were decided on this ground. For instance, the Court of Appeal of Paris considered that dismissing an employee, who refused to take off her veil or wear it as a cap, was a case of discrimination when the employee had been wearing the veil since she was hired, without this creating any problem in her relationships with customers.[12]

However, decisions do not always rely on either of the seemingly appropriate labour code references. In a famous case concerning the 'butcher of Mayotte',[13] the highest court for civil matters (*Cour de cassation*) relied on the Constitution (Article 1, prohibiting discriminations based on race or religion) and the civil code (legal force of contractual obligations) to decide that a worker could not request reassignment to another department of the store, when, after two years at the meat counter, he realised that he was in contact with pork, a situation he considered incompatible with his religion. According to the Court, the obligation for the employer to respect his employees' beliefs does not mean that, except when the work contract mentions it, he has a duty to accommodate for religious motives. As a result, an employer does not violate any contractual obligation when he requires that the worker performs the tasks he has been hired for, as long as no public order provision is violated. Indeed, this solution falls short of accommodating the worker's beliefs. But it is not only on its merits that the case deserves strong criticism. Arguably, the court erred in its reasoning in the case: applying the legal regime concerning the protection of individual freedoms instead of contract law would have implied a proportionality test, that is to say, an assessment of the employer's decision, in the particular context of the case. This could have led to considering the refusal excessive, if possibilities of reassignment existed.

7. Court of Appeal, Saint-Denis de la Réunion, 9 September 1997 n° 97/703306.
8. For example Court of Appeal, Versailles 23 November 2006 n° 05-5149.
9. For example Court of Appeal, Paris 19 June 2003 n° 03-30212.
10. For example Conseil de Prud'hommes Paris, 17 December 2002 n°02-3547.
11. Article L1132-1 of the labour code.
12. Court of Appeal, Paris 19 June 2003 n° 03-30212.
13. Cour de cassation, chambre sociale, 24 March 1998.

A deliberation of the French independent body to combat discriminations[14] made it clear that another path should be followed in such cases. The deliberation concerned the refusal of an organisation to hire camp counsellors, when they did not accept to share the exact same meals as the children.[15] Such a solution, the French authority argued, is too strict to pass the proportionality test: in order to respect the law, the organisation should accommodate workers' needs.

However, this reasoning is still not a core and mainstream part of current law developments. On the contrary, the recent and highly-publicised Baby-Loup case has given a good illustration of tensions and resistance associated with accommodation for religion in French courts. The case concerned a Muslim woman, fired from her job at the Baby-Loup private crèche and nursery, for violating the organisation's rules of procedure, which prohibited the wearing the *hijab*. The employer claimed that the applicant purportedly breached the rule in the document that 'the principle of freedom of conscience and of religion of each staff member may not impede respect for the principle of *laïcité* and neutrality that apply in the exercise of developmental activities either on the premises of the crèche or during outside activities in which staff accompany children'.

In 2011, the Court of Appeal of Versailles confirmed that the decision of the first judges[16] was justified, and dismissal could not be annulled.[17] The *Cour de cassation* overturned that decision, based on the protection of employees' freedoms at the workplace, and in consideration of the fact that the employer had not justified the discrimination based on religion.[18]

However, when the case went back to another Court of Appeal (Paris), that court refused to apply the decision of the highest court, considering that the nursery was 'an ethos based organisation', and, as such, had a right to impose 'neutrality' towards religion on its employees.[19] To be sure, this line of reasoning, based on the particularity of 'ethos based' organisations, had been used in previous cases, where churches or religious schools were concerned.[20] And Article 4(2) of directive 2000/78 acknowledges that churches and other public or private organisations, the ethos of which is based on religion or belief, may 'require individuals working for them to act in good faith and with loyalty to the organisation's ethos'. But, in the Baby-Loup case, the

14. This independent body called HALDE has now merged into the 'Defenseur des droits'.
15. Delib. Halde n°2008-10, 14 January 2008.
16. Conseil de Prud'hommes, Mantes la Jolie, 13 December 2010 n° 10-00587.
17. Court of Appeal, Versailles, 27 October 2011 n° 10-05642.
18. Cour de cassation, Soc. 19 March 2013 n° 11-28.845. On this decision, see, namely: J.-Ph. Lhernould, 'Signes religieux au travail: arrêts Baby-Loup et CPAM 93', Jurisprudence sociale Lamy, Lamy, 2013, p. 8; B. Bossu, JCP S 2013 n° 1146; F. Rome, 'Baby Loup dans la bergerie', Recueil Dalloz, 2013, p. 761; G. Calvès, 'La chambre sociale de la Cour de Cassation face à l'affaire Baby Loup: Trois leçons de droit, et un silence assourdissant', Respublica, 21 March 2013; E. Dockès, 'Liberté, laïcité, Baby Loup: de la très modeste et très contestée résistance de la Cour de cassation face à la xénophobie montante', Droit social 2013, p. 388; R. Schwartz, 'La laïcité paradoxalement consacrée', Semaine sociale Lamy 2013, n° 1577, p. 8; I. Desbarats, 'Affaire Baby Loup: laïcité fragilisée ou liberté religieuse renforcée?', JCP S n° 29, 16 July 2013, p. 1297.
19. Court of Appeal, Paris, 27 November 2013 n° 13-02981.
20. See, for instance: Cour de cassation, Soc. 17 April 1991, n° 90-42636.

situation was different: the ethos, based on which the organisation claimed the benefit of a specific legal regime was not religious, but secular. The solution reached by the French Court of Appeal was strongly supported by those, among academics, who disapproved of the decision reached by the *Cour de cassation* in 2013.[21]

The rebellion of the Court of Appeal of Paris led to another claim brought to the *Cour de cassation*, which, this time, gathered as a full court (*Assemblée plénière*).[22] In this second decision, the capacity of the superior Court to resist the strong opposition that its previous case had faced in the legal and political sphere and in the public opinion was tested. The Court opposed weak resistance to this opposition, it came out. To be sure, the decision refused to consider that the nursery was an 'ethos based' organisation, but it nonetheless upheld the decision of the Court of Appeal of Paris. According to the *Cour de cassation*, the lower court had rightly considered that the restriction to the employee's freedom of religion was proportionate and justified by the nature of the tasks she had to accomplish. In the factual context of the case, which was for lower courts to examine, the right balance was struck, the highest court considered, between freedom of religion, and the employer's power to organise the workplace. Strange at it may seem, discrimination on ground of religion was not even mentioned.

An even more recent case confirmed the tension surrounding workplace conflicts concerning workers' religious practices.[23] The case concerns the dismissal of an IT consultant posted at clients' offices, after one of the client complained about her wearing an Islamic veil. Because other employees felt uncomfortable with her head-scarf, the client threatened to terminate the commercial relationship with the consultant's employer. The lower courts accepted that there was a just cause for dismissing the worker. In turn, the worker claimed, before the *Cour de cassation*, that her dismissal was discrimination based on religion, and should be annulled. Rather than deciding on the case on its own, the *Cour de cassation* decided, on 9 April 2015, to raise the question to the Court of justice. The European Court was asked whether the demand, by a client, that no IT consultant posted at its company's premises wears a veil can be considered a 'genuine and determining occupational requirement' related to the nature of the activity or conditions of its exercise, under Article 4(1) of directive 78/2000. Although the existence of a doubt in the interpretation of EU law is a condition for using the preliminary ruling procedure, it is, indeed, very hard to believe that such doubt exist, in the case. Indeed, the reference is explicitly citing to the *Feryn* case[24] and the conclusions of Advocate general Maduro in this case, according to whom a justification based on customers' preferences is 'wholly irrelevant'.[25] Since there is hardly any doubt on the interpretation of EU law, it is rather clear that the reference calls, above all, for external support in deciding a vexed question.

As this rapid overview of French most recent case law shows, 'reasonable accommodation' is not at play, when employees' religion and business activity

21. See F. Gaudu, L'entreprise de tendance laïque, Droit Social, 2011, p. 1186.
22. Cour de cassation (plenary court) 25 June 2014 n° 13-28.369.
23. Cour de cassation, Soc. 9 April 2015 n° 13-19.855.
24. ECJ, 10 July 2008, C-54/07.
25. Opinion delivered on 12 March 2008, § 18.

interfere with one another. If accommodation means taking appropriate measures, as article of Directive 2000/78 states, in order 'to enable a person to have access to, participate in, or advance in employment, or to undergo training', recent cases do not indicate that this is currently what French case law requires. Of course, these cases, which reached the superior Court, only give a limited idea of the general situation. They concern particularly tough conflicts, which could not be solved within the company. They touch on principles, both legal and moral, while employees' requests are solved, in most instances, through pragmatic compromises.[26] Nonetheless, it appears that, in these cases, 'negative accommodation' prevailed over 'positive accommodation'. By 'negative accommodation', I mean that religion is indeed taken into consideration, rather than simply ignored: a negative measure (such as dismissal) is based on religion. Thus, taking into account religion leads to the prohibition of religious practices and, potentially, the exclusion of the employee from the workplace. Business needs, consumers' preferences or other reasons tend to prevail over respect for religious freedom, without much scrutiny of the reasons invoked by employers being applied in French Courts. Whether these solutions are respectful of the law, and, in particular, of EU law obligations under Directive 2000/78, is highly uncertain. The question brought to the Court of justice by the *Cour de cassation* in 2015 is a good indication that, according to the Highest Court itself, accommodation should prevail, if anti-discrimination law was correctly applied.

§9.02 LEGAL BASIS FOR CLAIMING 'POSITIVE' ACCOMMODATION FOR RELIGION IN FRENCH LABOUR LAW

In the current legal framework, two lines of reasoning apply, in most cases of conflicts concerning workers' requests in relation with their religion: one of them is based on the general protection of workers' rights and freedoms, the other on anti-discrimination law. Whether accommodation takes place, functionally, or could take place, within these legal regimes can be questioned.

Under the general protection of workers' rights and freedoms, mentioned earlier, no restriction to individual rights or freedoms is allowed if these restrictions are not justified by the nature of the task to be accomplished and proportionate to the objective pursued. Arguably, the proportionality test required by this legal regime implies a certain degree of accommodation. However, this would restrict the concept of reasonable accommodation in an excessive manner. Reasonable accommodation requires, if we refer to the notion used for cases of disability by Directive 2000/78 (Article 5), that employers take appropriate measures, where needed in a particular case, to enable a person 'to have access to, participate in, or advance in employment, or to undergo training, unless such measures would impose a disproportionate burden on the employer'. Under the French proportionality test, as compared, if the tasks assigned to the worker cannot be fulfilled because they conflict with its religion, dismissal is

26. Recent studies have shown that most cases (80%) are handled by managers, and do not lead to conflicts. See, A. Crépin, Les entreprises privées face au fait religieux: entre fantsame et pragmatisme, Droit social n° 9, September 2015, p. 694.

deemed justified. Thus, the accomplishment of the tasks contractually accepted by the worker justifies that the employer limits its employee's religious freedom. As far as proportionality is concerned, the level of scrutiny applied to controversial measures is left to Courts. The doctrine of the *Cour de cassation*, in the last Baby-Loup case,[27] has been in favour of minimum scrutiny, rather than a rigorous control of employers' decisions. No strict scrutiny applied when the *Cour de cassation* considered that dismissing the employee was not overbroad since the employee was working in a small organisation (eighteen employees) and was 'in contact or potentially in contact with children and their parents'. The Court did not question the actual trouble to children and their parents, and did not envisage alternative, less restrictive, solutions.

Different conclusions can be drawn from anti-discrimination law. Under Article L 1132-1 of the labour code, direct and indirect discriminations, as defined by EU Directive 2000/78, are prohibited. In addition, according to Article 1132-4, all discriminatory decisions or measures are deemed null. Under this legal regime, distinguishing direct and indirect discriminations is indeed essential.

As far as direct discriminations are concerned, there is not much space for discussion. Such discriminations are not acceptable and hardly any justification is available.[28] The French superior Court was well aware of such limited possibilities, when it questioned the Court of justice on whether a client's demand not to be provided services by a woman wearing an Islamic headscarf could be considered a 'genuine and determining occupational requirement' according to Article 4 of directive 2000/78: no other legal basis could support the legality of the contested termination. As mentioned above, the expected outcome of the preliminary ruling procedure is that the European Court of justice will decide that the interpretation of the notion of 'genuine and determining requirement' does not stretch to include clients' preferences. As a result, termination should be annulled, which could lead to reinstatement of the employee. This means that accommodation would have to be granted. In terms of positive actions to be taken by the employer, it could imply, for instance, that the concerned employee is not posted at certain clients. The employee would have to be assigned to other clients and/or given other tasks. Reassignment of the employee to different job, which does not imply contacts with clients, is a possible option, even if it may not always be a simple solution to enforce, under French labour law, if the worker refuses to perform tasks for which he was not hired.

Cases of indirect justification, which are those in which a measure affects a higher proportion of workers because of their religion, require examination of the employer's reasons for adopting such measure, in order to assess whether it is 'objectively justified by a legitimate aim and the means of achieving that aim are appropriate and necessary'.[29] If no legitimate reason is given, the measure should be removed, which implies accommodation. When a legitimate objective is pursued (for

27. Decision of 25 June 2014, cited above.
28. See for instance, recently: ECJ, 16 Jul. 2015, *CHEZ RB*, C-83/14, § 76, indicating that direct discrimination (based on race) could only be justified by genuine and determining occupational requirement or positive action.
29. Article 2 (b) (i) of directive 2000/78 transposed into French law by Art. 1 of the Statute n° 2008-496 of 27 May 2008.

instance, to ensure workers' or clients' security, freedom of expression of co-workers, or – provided they can be considered legitimate aims – satisfying clients' preferences or ensuring the profitability of the business), proportionality may impose reframing the practice or measure, or even giving it up altogether and finding other means to reach the same objective.

It thus appears that, under French rules implementing EU anti-discrimination law, accommodation is already a requirement, even if the concept is not used. In cases of direct discrimination, accommodation, in French law, is not even qualified by the notion of 'reasonableness': the employer has to remove discriminatory measures and make sure that, if dismissed, the victim of a discrimination reintegrates the workforce (since dismissal is deemed null). No proportionality test applies. In other cases, appropriate measures must be taken to adjust the company's policies, in order either to remove the discriminatory measure which cannot be justified or limit the encroachment on workers' rights, to comply with the proportionality principle. Indeed, the notion of reasonableness is lacking in the general context of anti-discrimination law, but it can be derived from the proportionality test. In sum, there is a basis, in French law, on which claims for reasonable accommodation can be founded. But French law is much less receptive to this notion, if not totally unreceptive, when religious practices are at stake, than it would be in other fields.

§9.03 THE OPENNESS OF FRENCH LABOUR LAW TO ACCOMMODATION, OUTSIDE THE SPHERE OF RELIGION

'Reasonable accommodation' is not a familiar notion in French labour law. But this does not mean that there is no duty for employers to take into account their employees' private or personal life, or particular circumstances, which render employees unable to pursue the tasks assigned to them upon employment. On the contrary, French law requires accommodation, without using the word, in many instances.

Important developments in case law have made it clear, for example, that employers have to take into account workers' family lives, when applying mobility clauses of work contracts[30] or organising working time.[31] This is not unrelated to the notion of 'reasonable accommodation': as the European Court of justice explained, the organisation of working time, and, especially, a reduction in working hours, constitutes an accommodation measure according to Article 5 of Directive 2000/78.[32] The same could be said about the place of work, which is affected by mobility clauses: a change in the workplace may have an influence on the capacity for an employee to pursue its activity. Adjusting the place of work according to workers' needs, to allow them to carry on working, can be considered an accommodation measure. That conclusion finds support in the case law of Court of justice, which favours an broad interpretation of the notion of accommodation measure: that concept, the Court explained, 'must be understood as referring to the elimination of the various barriers

30. Cour de cassation, Soc. 9 May 2001 n° 99-40111.
31. Cour de cassation, Soc. 3 November 2011 n° 10-14702.
32. ECJ, 11 April 2013, *HK Danmark*, C-335/11 and C-337/11, § 48-53.

that hinder the full and effective participation' of workers in professional life on an equal basis with other workers.[33]

French case law does not, however, compel the employer to take positive actions, as accommodation does, according to the Directive, in order to, 'where needed in a particular case', enable a person 'to have access to, participate in, or advance in employment'. It only prevents employers from imposing changes on employees, when this can be considered an excessive encroachment on their family lives. This is quite different, of course, from truly and positively accommodating personal or family needs. However, this line of cases illustrates that French labour law is far from opposed to the idea that employers' power must be limited, and measures taken in the exercise of this power adjusted, in order to take into account legitimate constraints (family ones, in particular) that employees put forward.

Beside these cases in which workers' family life is taken into account, a central notion of French labour law is reclassification of workers. It does, of course, play an essential role in the field of economic redundancies, in which employers must strive to limit the number of workers affected through reclassification.[34] This obligation is also contained in Directive 98/59 on the approximation of the laws of the Member States relating to collective redundancies: redeploying or retraining workers must be considered by employers contemplating collective redundancies in order to avoid, reduce or mitigate the consequences of such redundancies, according to the Directive.[35]

But French law goes further. Both in collective and individual redundancies, case law made it a duty, for employers, based on contractual good faith, to adapt workers to the evolution of their activities, and, if necessary, reassign them to new positions, when their initial tasks disappear, in the wake of the evolution of the business or technological changes.[36] This means that training must be offered to the employee, if needed to occupy a new position or achieve new tasks.[37] Since 2002, a statute has incorporated the solution worked out in case law, and employers are now bound by the labour code to train and adapt workers and strive to ensure reassignment, before economic redundancy can take place.[38] The importance recognised by reclassification was confirmed and reinforced when the Constitutional court considered that reclassification was a constitutional right stemming directly from the 'right to work' protected by the French Constitution.[39]

Used in this context, however, reclassification does not have much in common with the notion of 'reasonable accommodation to protect workers' protection of fundamental rights or freedoms. Rather, it relies on the idea that companies must bear responsibility for changes in their activities or structures involving a transformation of jobs, and ensure the continuous employability of employees, as far as possible. Thus, even if accommodating and adapting workers to the transformation of the company

33. *Ibid.* §§ 53-54.
34. See Art. L 1233-4 of the labour code.
35. Article 2(2) of Directive 98/59 of 20 July 1998.
36. Cour de cassation Soc. 1 April 1992, 89-43.494.
37. Cour de cassation Soc. 25 February 1992 n° 89-41634.
38. Article 1233-4 of the labour code.
39. Conseil constitutionnel, DC 2004-509, 13 January 2005.

require similar actions by employers, the context, and justification for these actions, are hardly comparable.

Stepping out of the field of companies' restructuring, and turning to reclassification of workers who become ill or disabled, 'reasonable accommodation' and reclassification are brought closer together. In the field of health and disability at work, reclassification is indeed a central notion of French labour law. The labour code provides that employers have a duty to look for another position, as similar as possible to the one that the employee who is ill or disabled previously occupied.[40] Employers must strive to maintain employment, by looking for accommodation: based on the proposals of an occupational physician, reassignment, a modification of the tasks or changes in the organisation of working time must be offered. In addition, case law made it clear that reassignment had to be considered in the larger context of the group to which the company belongs.[41]

When a worker is unable to perform his job after an occupational accident or disease, French law includes a higher degree of protection, based on the objective of reclassification. When the employer does not fulfil his duty to try to reassign the worker to another job, a special protection is granted, corresponding to the payment of indemnity of at least twelve months of the workers' salary, in addition to the allowance benefiting to all workers, who are eventually dismissed after the employer has duly (but unsuccessfully) searched for reassignment. The employee can refuse reclassification. In such case, he is entitled to a special severance payment, unless refusal of reclassification is considered abusive. When inability has no occupational origin, reassignment of the worker is also imposed on the employer, but the legal regime is less favourable for employees. In case reassignment is impossible, no special allowance is due, only the legal or conventional severance payment. However, if the employer violates the obligation to search for reclassification, dismissal is considered without cause.

As this legal regime shows, French law does not ignore the duty for employers to accommodate in situations in which workers are unable to pursue their activity, because of health problems or disability. However, adjustments to be made for workers whose health justifies reassignment or changes in the definition or modalities of their work do not exactly correspond to 'reasonable accommodation'. For one thing, the notion of 'reasonable accommodation' explicitly includes a margin of appreciation, in the specific context of the case, which is not contained in the obligation to reclassify employees: other positions available must be offered and the position previously occupied by the worker must be adapted. Only when this is deemed 'impossible' can the employer dismiss the worker. Indeed, what is considered impossible may vary according to the level of scrutiny. And it could be considered that adjustments or reclassification are impossible when the burden it too heavy on the employer, in other words, when it is disproportionate and 'accommodation' is not 'reasonable'. But the concept of reasonableness is specific and that specificity justifies, at a minimum, that

40. See Arts L 1226-10 (concerning professional accidents and disease) and L 1226-2 (non professional accident or disease) of the labour code.
41. See, namely: Cour de cassation Soc. 18 April 2000.

some thought is given to the appropriate judicial review. In addition, reasonable accommodation does not only aim at avoiding dismissal, according to the definition used by Directive 2000/78. It is much more ambitious: its objective is to enable a person 'to have access to, participate in, or advance in employment, or to undergo training'. Neither access to employment, career opportunities or training (to pursue one's career plans) is concerned by the French obligation to reclassify employees. Thus, reasonable accommodation may imply more limited obligations than reclassification in terms of intensity of the efforts that are required on the part of the employer, but its scope is considerably broader.

Can anti-discrimination law bridge this gap? This cannot be excluded. Indeed, French law includes another legal ground on which accommodation for health reasons can be based: the prohibition of discriminations on ground of health. Although EU law does not cover this category of discrimination, the concepts of EU anti-discrimination law apply. Thus, just as for religion, French law does not only require that decisions explicitly based on ground of health are annulled, but the prohibition of indirect discriminations implies that measures affecting mostly workers, who suffer or have suffered health problems be suppressed, unless they are justified and proportionate. As mentioned about religion, this may imply reforms of companies' policies to avoid adverse impact on workers facing health problems. The *Cour de cassation* had no problem considering, for instance, that measures stigmatising workers taking leaves for health motives were to be removed because they constitute indirect discrimination on ground of health.[42]

As far a disability is concerned, the situation is different. French labour has implemented Directive 2000/78, and formally added 'reasonable accommodation' to the former legal regime,[43] which already contained measures to foster employment of disabled persons,[44] the prohibition of discriminations on the ground of disability,[45] and, as mentioned above, a duty for employers to reclassify disabled workers. The legal transplant of the concept of 'reasonable accommodation' takes place in a body of law that was culturally open to the idea of adjustments imposed upon employers to take into account health issues and disability.

42. Cour de cassation, Soc. 12 February 2013 n° 11-27689.
43. Statute n° 2005-102 of 11 February 2005. Article L 5213-6 of the labour code repeats the provisions of Art. 5 of the directive, with only limited adaptations, to take into account other related provisions of the code ('Afin de garantir le respect du principe d'égalité de traitement à l'égard des travailleurs handicapés, l'employeur prend, en fonction des besoins dans une situation concrète, les mesures appropriées pour permettre aux travailleurs mentionnés aux 1° à 4° et 9° à 11° de l'article L. 5212-13 d'accéder à un emploi ou de conserver un emploi correspondant à leur qualification, de l'exercer ou d'y progresser ou pour qu'une formation adaptée à leurs besoins leur soit dispensé. Ces mesures sont prises sous réserve que les charges consécutives à leur mise en oeuvre ne soient pas disproportionnées, compte tenu de l'aide prévue à l'article L. 5213-10 qui peuvent compenser en tout ou partie les dépenses supportées à ce titre par l'employeur. Le refus de prendre des mesures au sens du premier alinéa peut être constitutif d'une discrimination au sens de l'article L. 1133-3').
44. The labour code requires companies employing more than twenty workers to hire a certain proportion of disabled workers (6%). See Arts L5212-1 to L5212-17.
45. Article L1132-1 of the labour code.

To be sure, reasonable accommodation is a new concept, which will have to be absorbed by the legal system. This may take time, even when the notion has been formally incorporated in the law, as in the field of disability. The transformative capacity of this new concept must not be undermined. But, in a first step towards full integration, it can be used to reinforce pre-existing law, without forcing radical changes. This would also be true in the case of accommodation for health motives, where 'reasonable accommodation' could probably flourish just as well, even without formal integration in the law. As compared, accommodation for religion has to cope with a radically different pre-existing context. As a result, its problematic acclimatisation within French labour law, where it is conflicting with the central notion of *laïcité*, should come as no surprise.

CHAPTER 10

Reasonable Accommodation of Religion and Culture in South African Workplaces: Taken a Notch Too Far?

Karin Calitz

The South African Constitutional Court has developed the concept of reasonable accommodation in a diverse society with a history of discrimination to protect the religious and cultural rights of especially minority groups who were previously marginalised. Courts have followed this approach in respect of the employment relationship even outside the discrimination framework. The development of reasonable accommodation in South Africa has been criticised for taking the notion a notch too far and expecting too much of employers. However, the Constitutional Court has made it clear that in view of the country's past experience, the South African community will be expected to implement positive measures and possibly bear additional hardship to attain equality in the interests of transformative justice.

§10.01 INTRODUCTION

The decline in the importance of religion to individuals in many parts of the world can in part be explained by factors such as the secularisation of states;[1] the development of science;[2] individualism replacing a community-based ethos[3] and the reliance of

1. P. Norris and R. Ingelhart, 'Uneven Secularization in the United States and Western Europe', in Thomas Banchoff (ed.), *Democracy and the New Religious Pluralism*, New York: Oxford University Press, 2007, p. 32.
2. E.H. Ecklund and C.P. Scheitle, 'Religion among Academic Scientists, Distinctions, Disciplines and Demographics', *Social Problems*, vol. 54(2) (2007), 289-307 p. 290.
3. L. Halman and O. Riis, *Religion in Secularizing Society: The European's Religion at the End of the 20th Century*, Leiden, MA: Brill, 2003, p. 5.

citizens on social security instead of looking up to a deity to provide for their needs.[4] Regarding culture, the phenomena of internationalisation, globalisation and the rapid development of telecommunications seems to be having a conforming influence, doing away with or minimising cultural differences.[5] However, the presumption that religious and cultural differences would accordingly play a less prominent role in society[6] proved to be wrong, especially as far as the workplace is concerned. Since the 1990s employees have increasingly expected employers to accommodate their religious and cultural beliefs.[7]

The reasons for this can be sought in the dehumanising effects of technology; the lack of boundaries between work and personal time; and the need for employees to affirm their identity in a world in which they may feel that they are merely a number. Globalisation may further have had the effect that people feel less secure, they may be afraid of losing their jobs and status, and consequently may need to 'reaffirm a threatened self-identity'.[8] The greater emphasis on human rights such as freedom of speech, dignity and equality may also be conducive to employees exercising their religious rights in the workplace. What is clear is that many employees do not regard their religion as a private matter belonging to a sphere outside the workplace, but as an intrinsic part of their being, to be respected wherever they are, also at work.

The following dictum of the South African Constitutional Court captures the importance that religious freedom holds for the individual:

> [F]reedom of religion goes beyond protecting the inviolability of the individual conscience. For many believers, their relationship with God or creation is central to all their activities. It concerns their capacity to relate in an intensely meaningful fashion to the sense of themselves, their community and their universe ... religion provides support and nurture and a framework for individual and social stability and growth. Religious belief has the capacity to awaken concepts of self-worth and human dignity which form the cornerstone of human rights.[9]

One cannot but agree with the above, but do employers have to accommodate the expression of culture and religion at the workplace and, if so, what are the limits to that accommodation?

One way for employers to deal with the problem of accommodating different religions in the workplace is to adopt a neutral policy in order to avoid accusations of discrimination. But then questions arise as to what is neutral and who decides what

---

4. J.O. Baker, 'Perceptions of Science and American Secularism,' *Sociological Perspectives*, vol. 55(1) (2012), spx.sagepub.com, accessed on 24 August 2015.
5. J. Olivier, M. Thoenig and T. Verdier, 'Globalization and the Dynamics of Cultural Identity', April 2007, ecgi.ssrn.com accessed on 30 August 2015; J.J. Arnett, 'The Psychology of Globalization,' *American Psychologist*, (October 2002), 774-783 p. 781, http://isites.harvard.edu/, accessed 24 August 2015.
6. P. Norris and R. Ingelhart, *supra* n. 1, p. 32.
7. V. Bader, K Alidaadi and F. Vermeulen, 'Religious Diversity and Reasonable Accommodation in the Workplace in Six European Countries', *International Journal of Discrimination and the Law*, vol. 13(2-3) (2013), 54-82 p. 76.
8. C. Kinnvall, 'Globalization and Religious Nationalism: Self, Identity and the Search for Ontological Security', *Political Psychology*, vol. 25(5) (2004), 741-767 p. 742.
9. *Christian Education South Africa v. Minister of Education* 2000(10) 1051 (CC) para. 36.

constitutes neutrality. Bader et al. point out that so-called neutrality is often simply the norm of the majority.[10] There is merit in this view since, for example, in Europe neutral clothing for women would be seen as a dress or pants without a headdress, while in Middle East a robe and headscarf would be seen as neutral, because that is what the majority of women wear. Likewise the religious holidays of the majority may be regarded as the norm by employers, leading to an unwillingness to accommodate minorities.[11]

Indirect discrimination may be the result when policies which are on the face of it neutral and ostensibly do not differentiate have a disproportionate impact[12] especially on minority groups.[13]

In the following paragraph the legislative protection of employees' religious and cultural rights in South Africa will be discussed, followed by a discussion of jurisprudence on the reasonable accommodation of religion and culture in general and more specifically in the workplace.

§10.02 LEGISLATIVE PROTECTION OF RELIGIOUS AND CULTURAL RIGHTS OF EMPLOYEES

Section 9 of the South African Constitution[14] provides that neither the State nor any other person may unfairly discriminate directly or indirectly against anyone on one or more prohibited grounds. Sixteen grounds are listed, including religion and culture. Section 15(1) of the Constitution, focusing on the individual right to freedom of religion, provides that everyone has the right to freedom of conscience, religion, thought, belief and opinion. The right of communities to exercise cultural and religious rights is contained in section 31.

This discussion will focus on the individual right to freedom of religion, but it is evident from the Constitutional Court's judgments that the accommodation of an individual's right to religious and cultural freedom will also impact on the exercise of these rights by the religious community to which he or she belongs.[15]

Regarding labour legislation, section 187(1)(f) of the Labour Relations Act[16] (LRA) protects employees from dismissal based on discrimination. The Act provides

10. Bader et al., *supra* n. 7, p. 57.
11. E. Bribosia and I. Rorive, 'Reasonable Accommodation beyond Disability in Europe?', *European Commission*, (2013) p. 23, e.c.europa.eu/justice/discrimination, accessed on 30 August 2015.
12. In the USA the term 'disparate impact' has been used and in Canada 'adverse effect discrimination'. See R.C. Hunter and E.W. Shoben, 'Disparate Impact Discrimination: American Oddity or Internationally Accepted Concept?', *Berkeley Journal of Employment and Labor Law*, vol. 19(1) (2014) pp. 108-153.
13. The notion of indirect discrimination originated in the USA and was imported into the South African Constitution and labour legislation. See O. Dupper, 'Proving Indirect Discrimination in Employment: A South African Perspective,' (2000) 21 *Industrial Law Journal* 747 p. 747.
14. Constitution of the Republic of South Africa, 1996.
15. *Prince v. President of the Law Society of the Cape of Good Hope* 2002(2) SA 794 (CC) para. 146.
16. Act 66 of 1995.

that a dismissal is automatically unfair[17] if the employer unfairly discriminated against an employee, directly or indirectly, on any arbitrary ground. The listed grounds include culture and religion.

Two justification grounds are provided to employers in section 187(2), namely if the reason for the dismissal is based on an inherent requirement[18] of the particular job, and if the employer dismissed someone who reached the normal or agreed retirement age for employees.

The Employment Equity Act[19] (EEA) was specifically enacted to give effect to section 9 (the equality clause) of the Constitution in the workplace, excluding discriminatory dismissals, which are dealt with in the LRA as discussed above. Section 6 of the EEA provides that no person may unfairly discriminate directly or indirectly against an employee, in any employment policy or practice, on one or more grounds, including religion and culture. Similarly to the LRA, the Act provides that it is not unfair discrimination to distinguish, exclude or prefer any person on the basis of an inherent requirement of the job. The EEA further provides that it will not be regarded as unfair discrimination to take affirmative action measures consistent with the purpose of the EEA.

To date all cases on a failure to accommodate an employee's religious and cultural rights were brought in terms of the LRA, since all complainants have been dismissed. Referrals in terms of the EEA which does not deal with dismissal were thus not appropriate.

Although the term reasonable accommodation is not found in the Constitution or the LRA, it is mentioned in the EEA, but only in respect of designated groups (black people, women and people with disabilities) who are the beneficiaries of affirmative action measures.[20] In terms of section 15(2)(c) designated employers[21] are required to make:

> reasonable accommodation for people from designated groups in order to ensure that they enjoy equal opportunities and are equitably represented in the workforce of a designated employer.[22]

Reasonable accommodation is defined in section 1 as:

> Any modification or adjustment to a job or to the working environment that will enable a person from a designated group to have access to or participate or advance in employment.

17. This means that if it is proven that the employee was dismissed on one of these grounds infringing constitutional rights, no justification except the narrow grounds of s. 187(2) is available.
18. The meaning of inherent requirement of a job will be discussed in para. 4.1. *infra*.
19. Act 58 of 1997.
20. These measures are defined in s. 15(1) as 'measures designed to ensure that suitably qualified people from designated groups have equal employment opportunities and are equitably represented in all occupational levels in the workforce of a designated employer.'
21. Section 1 of the EEA. Employers employing more than fifty employees, municipalities and state organs are among designated employers.
22. Section 15(2)(c).

The legislator has thus paid scant attention to the concept of reasonable accommodation in the workplace and technically employers only have to reasonably accommodate persons belonging to groups who were previously disadvantaged on account of their race, sex and disability. The above definition of reasonable accommodation is also not entirely appropriate for accommodating religious and cultural rights.

In contrast, the Act on the Promotion of Equality and Prevention of Unfair Discrimination (PEPUDA),[23] also referred to as the Equality Act, deals with equality outside of the employment relationship and contains important provisions regarding reasonable accommodation, going much further than the EEA. This Act provides that in certain circumstances the absence of reasonable accommodation will constitute unfair discrimination.[24] In *MEC for Education Kwazulu-Natal v. Pillay*,[25] which dealt with religious discrimination in a school, the Constitutional Court analysed the Equality Act and laid down principles that influenced subsequent jurisprudence on religious discrimination in employment.

The next two sections will discuss the common law development of the concept of reasonable accommodation by the courts.

§10.03 DEVELOPMENT OF THE CONCEPT OF REASONABLE ACCOMMODATION BY THE CONSTITUTIONAL COURT

Although the cases discussed below do not deal with the employment relationship per se, subsequent judgments in employment disputes about religion and culture were based on the principles and ethos related to accommodation as developed by the Constitutional Court.

In *Christian Education South Africa v. Minister of Education*[26] parents who believed that corporal punishment for children is part of biblical prescriptions argued that their right to religious freedom was infringed by section 10 of the South African Schools Act[27] (Schools Act). This act prohibited corporal punishment of children by teachers in both public and private schools.

The court acknowledged the importance of freedom of religion, but posed the question asking:

> how far ... democracy can and must go in allowing members of religious communities to define for themselves which laws they will obey and which not. Such a society can cohere only if all its participants accept that certain basic norms and standards are binding. Accordingly, believers cannot claim an automatic right to be exempted by their beliefs from the laws of the land. At the same time, the state should, wherever reasonably possible, seek to avoid putting believers to extremely painful and intensely burdensome choices of either being true to their faith or else respectful of the law.[28]

23. Act 4 of 2000.
24. Section 14(i).
25. 2008 (1) SA 474 (CC).
26. 2000(4) SA 757.
27. Act 84 of 1996.
28. *Christian Education* para. 35.

The court undertook a proportionality exercise in terms of the limitations clause, section 36 of the Constitution, which it regarded as a nuanced and contextual approach. The court preferred this test for evaluating the fairness of a limitation to the controversial strict scrutiny test (which the appellants invited the court to follow) applied in American jurisprudence.[29] In terms of the strict scrutiny test a compelling state interest would be required for a limitation of the right to freedom of religion. This test was later rejected by a majority of the US Supreme Court.[30]

Section 36 provides that a constitutional right may only be limited in terms of a law of general application if the limitation is reasonable and justifiable in an open and democratic society based on human dignity, equality and freedom. Relevant factors to be taken into account include the nature of the right; the importance of the purpose of the limitation; the nature and extent of the limitation; and less restrictive means to achieve the purpose.

The court weighed up the parents' right to freedom of religion against the constitutional imperative to act in the best interests of the child,[31] the constitutional rights of children to dignity,[32] freedom and security of the person, and to be free from all forms of violence.[33] The conclusion was that the constitutional rights of children outweighed the right of the parents to freedom of religion and that an exemption would undermine the 'symbolic, moral and pedagogical purpose of the measure'.[34] The prohibition on corporal punishment was seen in the context of breaking with the past, which 'permitted degrading treatment of persons.'[35]

In *Prince v. President of the Law Society of the Cape of Good Hope*[36] the complainant applied to be registered with the Law Society for community service, since this was a requirement to practice as an attorney. He had the necessary qualifications but could not be registered, as he had previously been sentenced on two counts of unlawful possession of cannabis (marijuana or dagga). The possession and use of cannabis is prohibited by section 4(b) of the Drug and Drug Trafficking Act.[37]

Prince was also open about the fact that he would in future also use marijuana for religious purposes as part of a practice of the Rastafari faith. The question was whether the Drug Act discriminated against Prince and the Rastafari religion by not allowing an exemption. Ngcobo J emphasised the importance of protecting minorities:

> [T]he appellant belongs to a minority group. The constitutional right asserted by the appellant goes beyond his own interest – it affects the Rastafari community.

29. *Christian Education* para. 29.
30. *Employment Division, Department of Human Resources of Oregon et al v. Smith et al* 494 US 872 (1990).
31. Section 29 of the Constitution.
32. Section 9 of the Constitution.
33. Section 12 of the Constitution.
34. *Christian Education* para. 52.
35. The court referred to these words of Mahomed DP in *S v. Makwanyane* 1995(3) SA 391 (CC) para. 262.
36. 2001 (2) SA 388 (CC) para. 26.
37. 140 of 1992.

> The Rastafari community is not a powerful one. It is a vulnerable group. It deserves the protection of the law precisely because it is a vulnerable community.[38]

The case was postponed to allow parties the opportunity to gather information about the use of marijuana by the Rastafari. In the second *Prince* case[39] Ngcobo J remarked similarly to the court in *Christian Education* that the courts could best secure reasonable accommodation by processes of balancing and proportionality in terms of section 36 of the Constitution. The judge pointed out that the Constitutional Court has 'rejected the view of the majority in the United States Supreme Court that it is an inevitable outcome of democracy that in a multi-faith society minority religions may find themselves without remedy against burdens imposed upon them by formally neutral laws.'[40]

Regarding the importance of a certain religious practice for an individual, Ngcobo J stated that although the religious beliefs of persons may be regarded by others as 'bizarre, illogical and irrational', believers should generally not be required by courts to prove that a certain practice is central to their faith.[41] This approach is similar to the Canadian approach requiring 'sincere individual belief' for a practice to be protected.[42] The judge remarked that in this case there was no doubt about the centrality of Prince's religious belief, since he was prepared to sacrifice his career for his belief.[43]

Sachs J emphasised that reasonable accommodation is not a matter of a formula that can be applied by 'jurisprudential technique which facilitates settlement of disputes, but as a question of principle central to the whole constitutional enterprise'.[44] He further explained why the particular case illustrated the importance of reasonable accommodation for the South African community:

> The appellant has shown himself to be a person of principle, willing to sacrifice his career and material interests in pursuance of his beliefs. An inflexible application of the law that compels him to choose between his conscience and his career threatens to impoverish not only himself but all of South Africa and to dilute its burgeoning vision of an open democracy. Given our dictatorial past in which those in power sought incessantly to command the behaviour, beliefs and taste of all in society, it is no accident that the right to be different has emerged as one of the most treasured aspects of our new constitutional order ... Religious tolerance is accordingly not only important to those individuals who are saved from having to make excruciating choices between their beliefs and the law. It is deeply meaningful to all of us because religion and belief matter, and because living in an open society matters.[45]

38. *Prince v. President of the Cape Law Society* 2000(3) SA 845 (SCA) para. 26.
39. *Prince v. President of the Western Cape Law Society* 2002(2) SA 794.
40. *Prince* para. 155 in which Ngcobo J referred to *Employment Division, Department of Human Resources of Oregon v. Smith* 494 US 872 (1990) p. 890. This case dealt with the use of '*peyote*', a 'controlled substance' by indigenous minorities for religious purposes.
41. *Prince* para. 42.
42. *Syndicat Northcrest v. Amselem*, [2004] 2 SCR 551, 2004 SCC 47, which dealt with persons of the Jewish faith who wanted to erect religious structures on their balconies which formed part of communal property.
43. *Prince* para. 43.
44. *Prince* para. 146.
45. *Prince* para. 170.

All nine judges in *Prince* were in agreement that the prohibition on the use or possession of marijuana manifestly limited the rights of the Rastafari as a minority group to practice their religion and that it had to be considered whether this limitation is justifiable in terms of the limitation clause.[46]

However, the court split on the outcome of the application of section 36. A minority of four judges held that the fact that no exemption was made for Rastafari to use cannabis as part of a religious exercise was discriminatory, since a narrow exemption for religious purposes should be made. The majority held that it is reasonable and justifiable to withhold an exemption in the light of the difficulties of the state to enforce the Drug Act in the interests of the public and to honour the international obligations of the state in this regard.[47]

Although Prince lost his case, the support of four constitutional court judges (and serious consideration by the majority) for an exemption for the Rastafari, who are a small minority and stigmatised because of their practice of using marijuana, signifies the importance attached to accommodation of religion in a transformed South African society.

The value that the Constitutional Court places on the protection of the religious and cultural beliefs of the marginalised was again evident in *MEC for Education: KwaZulu-Natal and Others v. Pillay,*[48] which concerned a schoolgirl who, like Prince, belonged to a minority, in this case the South Indian Tamil Hindu group. The girl insisted on wearing a nose stud to school in defiance of the school's dress code, which prohibited the wearing of jewellery.[49] The school's arguments were *inter alia* that there was no discrimination, since all religions were treated equally[50] and, furthermore, that wearing uniforms at school are essential to maintain discipline.[51]

Regarding whether wearing the stud was a cultural or religious practice, Langa J remarked that it is often difficult to draw the line, since religion and culture may overlap and a practice may be both religious as well as cultural.[52] The court emphasised that freedom of culture is as worthy of protection as freedom of religion:

> Cultural identity is one of the most important parts of a person's identity precisely because it flows from belonging to a community and not from personal choice or achievement. And belonging involves more than simple association; it includes participation and expression of the community's practices and traditions.[53]

A practice, furthermore, does not need to be compulsory for it to be worthy of reasonable accommodation, if the voluntary adherence is central to a person's religious

46. Section 36 of the Constitution.
47. *Prince* para. 139.
48. 2008 (1) SA 474 (CC).
49. See *R. Watkins-Singh v. Governing Body of Aberdare Girls' School* [2008] EWHC 1865 (Admin), an English case in which it was found that the governing body of the school indirectly discriminated against a girl who was not allowed to wear a *kara* (thin bangle) as a token of the Sikh faith.
50. *Pillay* para. 25.
51. *Pillay* para. 26.
52. *Pillay* para. 47.
53. *Pillay* para. 53.

or cultural identity. Centrality must be judged with reference only to how important the 'belief or practice is to the person's religious or cultural identity.'[54] Thus, 'if Sunali states that the nose stud is central to her as a South Indian Tamil Hindu, it is not for the Court to tell her that she is wrong because others do not relate to that religion or culture in the same way'.[55]

Langa J agreed with the dictum in *Christian Education* followed by *Prince* in terms of which the State should, 'wherever reasonably possible, seek to avoid putting believers to extremely painful and intensely burdensome choices of either being true to their faith or else respectful of the law.'[56] He added that '[o]ur society which values dignity, equality and freedom must therefore require people to act positively to accommodate diversity'.[57] Here is a clear message that simply abstaining from discriminating is not sufficient and that the positive duty to accommodate is not that of the state alone, but a duty of the wider community.

Regarding the question of how far the community must go to accommodate minorities the court, in referring to the term 'undue hardship', pointed out that the South African approach is more in line with the Canadian than the US approach. This is because the US approach only entails a narrowly construed duty of reasonable accommodation requiring a '*de minimis*' cost[58] to the employer, while the Canadian approach requires 'more than mere negligible effort to satisfy the duty to accommodate'.[59] The court found these phrases of limited value and said that reasonable accommodation is an exercise in proportionality based on constitutional principles and not on a 'judicially created slogan'.[60]

Langa J held that the concept of reasonable accommodation is most valuable when dealing with a practice which is apparently neutral but has a marginalising effect on some groups, especially in a localised context such as schools and workplaces where a balance of conflicting interests can be more easily attained.[61] It is significant that the court mentioned workplaces, again indicating that the principles laid down in the case were also meant to be applicable in the employment context.

Ultimately the court held that the question of whether Sunali should be reasonably accommodated depended on the question of what the importance of wearing the stud was for the girl and the hardship to the school if she should be allowed to wear the nose stud.[62] Regarding the hardship to the school, the court held that 'If allowing

54. *Pillay* para. 88.
55. *Pillay* para. 87.
56. *Pillay* para. 73 referring to *Christian Education* para. 35.
57. *Pillay* para. 73.
58. See *Trans World Airlines v. Hardison* 432 US 63 (1977) in which an employee sought to have Saturdays off for religious reasons. See also *Tagore v. United States of America* No 12-2014 (5th Cir. 13 November 2013) in which an employee insisted on wearing a Sikh ceremonial *kirpan* to work.
59. See *Central Okanagan School District No 23 v. Renaud* [1992] 2 SCR 970 in which the union opposed accommodation of an employee who refused to work a shift on Friday evenings for religious reasons.
60. *Pillay* para. 76.
61. *Pillay* para. 78.
62. *Pillay* para. 79.

the stud would cause indiscipline and a drop in academic standards, that might indeed be an undue burden to impose on the School.'[63] In this case there was no evidence that the exemption would have this effect. The court did not agree with the school's arguments that since the dress code was the outcome of negotiation, it cannot be disregarded, or that the complainant could go to another school which would allow the wearing of a nose stud.[64]

Regarding duties arising from reasonable accommodation, the court stated that:

> At its core is the notion that sometimes the community, whether it is the State, an employer or a school, must take positive measures and possibly incur additional hardship or expense in order to allow all people to participate and enjoy all their rights equally. It ensures that we do not relegate people to the margins of society because they do not or cannot conform to certain social norms.[65]

The Constitutional Court held that the school's failure to reasonably accommodate the complainant by granting an exemption constituted unfair discrimination.[66]

It is significant that the court again specifically referred to the workplace. Thus, suffering additional hardship would in certain circumstances not provide a defence to employers for not accommodating the religious practices of their employees. Moreover, in certain instances the employer may be required to take positive measures to accommodate.

§10.04 JURISPRUDENCE ON ACCOMMODATING RELIGION AND CULTURE IN THE WORKPLACE

Recurring themes in South African judgments on reasonable accommodation of religion and culture in the workplace are conflict with the employer's dress code and the issue of time off for religious and cultural purposes.

[A] Dress Code

In *Dlamini v. Green Four Security*[67] the Labour Court had to decide whether a security firm unfairly discriminated against employees belonging to the Baptized Nazareth Group, who were dismissed when they refused to shave or trim their beards. This case was decided before the *Pillay* decision and the court thus did not have the advantage of the guidance of the Constitutional Court on the issue of reasonable accommodation as developed in that case.

63. *Pillay* para. 97.
64. *Pillay* para. 81. These arguments by a school were taken into account by the House of Lords in ruling that a schoolgirl's right to freedom of religion had not been infringed when she was prohibited from wearing a *jilbab*. See *R (on the application of Begum) v. Denbigh High School*, [2006] UKHL 15.
65. *Pillay* para. 73.
66. *Pillay* para. 112.
67. [2006] ZALC 4.

In order to establish that the employer discriminated against them, the court required the complainants to prove that abstaining from shaving or trimming their beards was a central tenet of their faith. The complainants called a priest as an expert witness, but he was unfortunately cross-examined about the centrality of non-trimming of beards to the religion. The court in effect examined the validity of the belief system of the employees, while the Constitutional Court has held that the centrality of the belief turns on the subjective value that the believer places on the practice.[68] The evidence of the priest was rejected, since he could not explain the origin of the rule, and also not why certain practices in the scriptures that he referred to were prohibited by the Nazareth Group while other practices (such as working on Sundays) were allowed. The court found that since the employees could not prove that the practice was central to the belief, there was no discrimination.[69]

On whether the shaving or trimming of a beard was an inherent requirement of the job as alleged by the employer, the court explained this term as 'a permanent attribute or quality... something intrinsic or essential ...[or] an indispensable attribute which must relate in an inescapable way to the performing of the job.'[70] The court found that trimming or shaving of beards was indeed an inherent requirement since:

> [c]ompliance with a dress code can be compulsory ... for purposes of promoting an image or brand. In this case the rule against wearing beards was driven by the practical and inherent need to look like security guards and to project the respondent as a security company with a distinctive image.[71]

This line of reasoning was also put forward by the employer (British Airways) in *Ewieda v. the United Kingdom*[72] to justify a prohibition on an employee wearing a small cross to work. The European Court of Human Rights held that in the proportionality exercise the UK court placed too much emphasis on corporate image.[73]

The *Dlamini* case was not followed in *Department of Correctional Services v. POPCRU,*[74] which involved a new commissioner at Pollsmoor prison who decided that, to improve discipline, a stricter dress code for warders would be implemented. The dress code entailed *inter alia* that no male Rasta locks would in future be allowed. Female warders were not affected by the new policy and up until then male Rasta locks were also allowed.[75]

Five employees refused to cut their locks. Three of these who belonged to the Rastafarian faith alleged that their faith required them to wear locks.[76] Two employees belonging to the Xhosa ethnic group refused the order on cultural grounds. According to them, they had a call from their ancestors to be trained as *sangomas* (traditional

68. *Prince* para. 42; *Pillay* para. 87.
69. *Dalmini* para. 19.
70. *Dlamini* para. 40.
71. *Dlamini* para. 66.
72. European Court of Human Rights (4th chamber) 27/May 2013 para. 94.
73. *Eweida* para. 94.
74. [2013] ZASCA 40 28 March 2013.
75. *POPCRU* paras 3-5.
76. *POPCRU* para. 6.

healers) and this required them to abstain from cutting their locks.[77] All five employees were dismissed for disobedience.[78]

In court the employees argued that their dismissals were automatically unfair in terms of section 187(1)(f) of the LRA, which prohibits discrimination on the grounds of *inter alia* religion and culture. The employer argued firstly that there was no discrimination, since the uniform dress code was a neutral policy that applied to all employees.[79] Second, even if there was discrimination, it could be justified in terms of section 187(2) of the LRA, since short hair was an inherent requirement of the job. The employer argued that hair locks were a safety risk, since they could be grabbed by inmates. A later argument added by the employer was that, since it is a well-known fact that Rastafarians smoke marijuana as part of their religion, they would be open to corruption and manipulation by prisoners.[80]

The Supreme Court of Appeal (SCA) held that there was direct discrimination on the basis of sex, since women were allowed to keep their locks and further also indirect discrimination based on religion and culture because of disparate treatment.[81] The court proceeded to establish whether the discrimination was unfair in terms of a test developed in *Harksen v. Lane NO:*[82]

> Once discrimination has been established on a listed ground, unfairness is presumed, and the employer must prove the contrary. Relevant considerations in this regard include the position of the victim of the discrimination in society, the purpose sought to be achieved by the discrimination, the extent to which rights or interests of the victim of the discrimination have been affected, whether the discrimination has impaired the human dignity of the victim, and whether less restrictive means are available to achieve the purpose of the discrimination.[83]

The court remarked that: 'A policy that effectively punishes the practice of a religion and culture devalues the followers of that religion and culture in society [and] it is a palpable invasion of their dignity.'[84] The measure further had a profound impact, since the employees were dismissed for adhering to their faith and culture.[85]

The SCA did not agree with the employer's argument that short hair was an inherent requirement of the job,[86] since female warders were allowed to keep their locks. There was also no evidence that the Rasta locks detracted from the performance of the employees' duties.[87] The court saw the argument of the employer concerning the corruption and manipulation based on the smoking of marijuana as a belated attempt to strengthen its arguments and did not take it into account.[88] Had this argument been

77. *POPCRU* para. 7.
78. *POPCRU* para. 9.
79. *POPCRU* para. 12.
80. *POPCRU* para. 20.
81. *POPCRU* para. 18.
82. 1998(1) SA 300(CC) para. 48.
83. *POPCRU* para. 21.
84. *POPCRU* para. 22.
85. *POPCRU* para. 22.
86. The court referred to the meaning ascribed to the phrase in *Dlamini.*
87. *POPCRU* para. 25.
88. *POPCRU* para. 24.

raised earlier, it could possibly have been regarded as an inherent requirement, since drug smuggling and trading in drugs by prison guards is a serious concern in South African prisons.[89]

The court stated that a policy that limits religious or cultural belief and which does not impact on the employees' capability to perform their jobs, nor compromises public safety nor causes 'undue hardship in a practical sense to the employer' cannot be justified. Finally, the court held that 'no rational connection was established between the purported purpose of the discrimination and the measure taken. Neither was it shown that the department would suffer an unreasonable burden if it had exempted the respondents'.[90] This formulation was based partly on the test in *Bhinder v. Canadian National Railway Co*,[91] in which the court held that the employer did not have to accommodate an employee belonging to the Sikh faith who refused to wear a hard hat on a construction site since wearing the hard hat was a bona fide occupational requirement.[92]

What can be distilled from *POPCRU* is that while it is undoubtedly within an employer's managerial prerogative to expect employees to comply with its dress code, the courts will interpret inherent requirements of the job restrictively. This is in line with South African jurisprudence such as *Hoffman v. South African Airways*[93] in which the Constitutional Court held that it is not an inherent requirement of the job of a cabin attendant on an airline to be HIV negative, since he did not yet suffer from AIDS and thus posed no medical or safety risk. The Labour Court further held in *IMATU and another v. City of Cape Town*[94] that it is not an inherent requirement that an employee working for the fire brigade should not suffer from diabetes, since his condition was under control. Regarding sexual orientation, the court held in *Strydom v. Nederduitse Gereformeerde Gemeente Moreleta Park*[95] that it was no inherent requirement for a teacher at a music academy attached to a church to abstain from a homosexual relationship, since the complainant did not hold a position of religious leadership. It is clear that the courts will not tolerate blanket exclusions and will require a rational connection between the rule and the object that the employer wishes to attain as clearly illustrated in *POPCRU.*

[B] Time Off for Religious Reasons

In *SACTWU v. Berg River Textiles*[96] the employer concluded a collective agreement with the trade union that changed shift systems would be worked to meet operational needs.

89. R.P. Maiden, *Employee Assistance Services in the New South Africa*, Binghamton, New York: Haworth Press, 1999, p. 47.
90. *POPCRU* para. 25.
91. [1985] 2 SCR 651.
92. *Bhinder* para. 29.
93. 2001 (1) SA 1.
94. [2005] 11 BLLR 1084 (LC).
95. (2009) 30 *ILJ* 868.
96. (2012) 33 *ILJ* 972(LC).

One of the consequences was that employees had to work on Sundays.[97] Williams, a lay preacher in a Christian church, refused to work on Sundays since this was against his religious principles. The employer dismissed him for not carrying out a lawful instruction. Williams alleged that his was an automatically unfair dismissal in terms of section 187(1)(f) of the LRA, since the dismissal constituted discrimination on the ground of religion.[98] In following the principles laid down in the *POPCRU* case[99] the court held that the employee had proved that abstaining from work on a Sunday was a central tenet of his religion, since he had previously turned down lucrative work and promotion in order to be free on Sundays to worship and preach.[100] The court found that the policy, although applied to all employees, discriminated against Williams and the fact that the employer did not accommodate him (in a fairly large business) rendered the dismissal automatically unfair.[101]

Kievit's Kroon Country Estate v. Mmoledi[102] was a controversial decision dealing with absence from work for cultural reasons in which the principles of reasonable accommodation was applied outside the discrimination context. An employee who had been working for the employer for two years applied for unpaid leave for a period of almost five weeks to complete her training as a traditional healer (*sangoma*). The employer had previously adjusted the shift system after consultation with other staff members to accommodate her training in the afternoons.[103] Now the employer offered only one week's leave, since it was a busy time of the year and they were experiencing a staff shortage.[104]

The employee nevertheless absented herself after leaving a letter, written by the *sangoma* who would train her, on the human resources manager's desk. The letter explained that the employee suffered from 'perminisions' from ancestors and that she could become seriously ill if she would disobey and not complete her training as a traditional healer.[105] When she returned, a disciplinary hearing was held, she was found guilty of misconduct on account of being absent without the employer's permission and dismissed.[106]

The employee alleged that she was unfairly dismissed and referred the dispute to the Commission for Conciliation, Mediation and Arbitration (CCMA). Surprisingly, she did not allege that the dismissal was automatically unfair in terms of section 187(1)(f), which deals with discriminatory dismissals. The reason for her choice could be that automatically unfair dismissals have to be referred to the Labour Court and not the CCMA,[107] which can involve higher costs and a longer process.

97. *Berg River* para. 4.
98. *Berg River* para. 39.
99. *Supra* s. §10.04[A].
100. *Berg River* para. 41.
101. *Berg River* para. 48.
102. [2013] ZASCA 189 (29 November 2013).
103. *Kievit's Kroon* para. 4.
104. *Kievit's Kroon* para. 6.
105. *Kievit's Kroon* para. 8.
106. *Kievit's Kroon* para. 12.
107. LRA s. 191(5)(b).

The commissioner at the CCMA found that there was a cultural chasm between the employer and the employee, since the employer did not understand that the employee genuinely believed that she could die if she did not go for training. Had the representative of the employer understood this, he would have granted sick leave to the employee. She had no option but to absent herself from her job due to circumstances beyond her control.[108] Her dismissal was thus found to be substantively unfair.

The case was referred for review, wound its way through the courts and was eventually heard by the SCA. The employer argued that in the absence of expert evidence on the meaning of 'perminisions' the commissioner should not have taken judicial cognisance thereof. A further argument was that the employer could not be expected to plan for perceptions of the supernatural in the running of its business and that, if the commissioner had taken into account the operational requirements of the business and the fact that the employer did endeavour to accommodate her by granting one week's leave, he would have found that the dismissal was fair.[109]

Both the Labour Court and the Labour Appeal Court[110] confirmed the decision of the CCMA. Although the case was not based on discrimination, the Labour Appeal Court (LAC) said the following:

> What is required is reasonable accommodation of each other to ensure harmony and to achieve a united society ... The fact that the appellant's attorney does not believe in the authenticity of the culture and that no credible and expert evidence was presented to prove that the respondent was ill is, in my view, subjective and irrelevant. A paradigm shift is necessary and one must appreciate the kind of society we live in. Accommodating one another is nothing else but 'botho' or 'Ubuntu' which is part of our heritage as a society.[111]

The concept of *ubuntu* is often referred to in South African jurisprudence and can be described as:

> the principle of caring for each other's well-being and as a spirit of mutual support. Each individual's humanity is ideally expressed through his or her relationship with others and theirs in turn through a recognition of the individual's humanity. Ubuntu means that people are people through other people.[112]

The LAC, with its reference to *ubuntu*, placed reasonable accommodation firmly within the context of African culture and South African society, clearly requiring a new way of thinking about accommodating different cultures in the interests of a united society.

Although there was no evidence before the SCA about the belief system of the employee, Cachalia J was prepared to accept that such belief systems did exist and that, according to the World Health Organisation, up to 80% of South Africans turn to

108. *Kievit's Kroon* para. 15.
109. *Kievit's Kroon* para. 18.
110. (2012) 33 *ILJ* 2812 (LAC).
111. *Kievit's Kroon* (LAC) para. 26.
112. The South African White Paper on Welfare *South African Government Gazette*, 2 February 1996, No. 1643 para. 18. See further C. Himonga, M. Taylor and A. Pope 'Reflections on Judicial Views of Ubuntu' [2013] *Potchefstroom Electronic Law Journal* 2013(16) 5.

traditional healers for their physical, spiritual and emotional wellbeing.[113] The court confirmed that courts should not evaluate belief systems, since a court should only be concerned with the sincerity of the belief[114] and thus followed the guidance of the Constitutional Court in *Pillay* and *Prince*. The court accepted that the employee believed that she would die and the sincerity of her belief was confirmed by her traditional healer. The court regarded it as well established that if an employee disregards an employer's lawful instruction, 'a court is entitled to grant relief to the employee if the failure to obey the order was justifiable or reasonable.'[115]

The SCA remarked that the employer conceded that leave would be granted if the employee had provided a medical certificate, (the employer argued that the legislator chose a 'Western model' requiring certificates from a medical practitioner) but apparently regarded the letter of the *sangoma* as meaningless. Had the employer understood the letter to be equivalent to a medical certificate, alternatives could have been explored, for example, granting leave during another time of the year.[116]

The fact that the court expected the employer to accept a sick certificate (which can only be issued by a registered medical practitioner in terms of the Basic Conditions of Employment Act[117]) from a *sangoma* was criticised, since the Interim Traditional Health Practitioner's Council has not yet given any information on registrations. This is required by the Health Professions Council, but no traditional healers have been registered yet.[118]

Another point of criticism against the judgment is that the justifiable refusal to carry out an instruction was previously only found where unsafe conditions justified the employee disobeying an instruction of the employer. This ground has now been widened by the court without much of a discussion of what type of conduct by an employee would be regarded as reasonable.[119]

Although the result of the judgment is in harmony with jurisprudence on reasonable accommodation, a more principled proportionality approach, balancing the interests of the employer and employee, would have provided guidance in future cases of this kind. This would have taken into consideration the business needs of the employer as well as the fact that it did accommodate the employee in the past and endeavoured to accommodate her again with a week's leave. It must be kept in mind, however, that the complainant did not allege discrimination and that the concept of reasonable accommodation is unfamiliar in the context of an 'ordinary' unfair dismissal. This could be solved if the requirement in the Code of Good Labour Practice: Dismissal,[120] namely that a fair dismissal for misconduct must be an 'appropriate

113. *Kievit's Kroon* para. 24.
114. *Kievit's Kroon* para. 27.
115. *Kievit's Kroon* para. 28.
116. *Kievit's Kroon* para. 30.
117. Act 75 0f 1997.
118. C.A. Moekoena, 'The Legality of Traditional Healers' Sick Notes in South Africa' *Ethno Med* 2014(8)(2) 111-117; A. Rycroft, 'Business Needs, Cultural Beliefs and Fairness: *Kievit's Kroon Country Estate (Pty) Ltd v. Mmoledi & Others* (2014) 35 *ILJ* 406 (SCA).'
119. Rycroft, pp. 915-916.
120. Schedule 8 of the LRA.

sanction for the contravention of the rule or standard',[121] is to be interpreted to include an examination of whether an employer reasonably accommodated the employee.

The limits as to how far the courts will go in accommodating employees' absence from the workplace for religious and cultural reasons are indicated in *NUM v. Samancor Ltd (Tsubatse Ferrochrome)*.[122] The employee also left work without permission to train as traditional healer, but gave no notice to the employer of the length of his absence or his whereabouts. Moreover, the traditional healer testified that there was no need to go on the training immediately. The court held that the employee had no justifiable reason for her unauthorised absence and that the dismissal was thus fair.[123]

§10.05 CONCLUSION

From the judgments above a number of principles have crystallised regarding the reasonable accommodation of religion and culture in the South African workplace.

The courts regard culture and religion as equally worthy of protection[124] and a religious or cultural practice will be protected even though it is not mandatory.[125] Furthermore, to establish whether a certain practice is a central tenet of a belief, it must be of great personal importance to the particular employee and courts should not require complainants to prove the validity of their religion.[126]

A practice that is prima facie neutral may constitute indirect discrimination if there is a disproportionate impact on the complainant.[127] If an employer alleges that the discrimination is justified by an inherent requirement of the job, the courts will require a rational relationship between the requirement and the ability to do the job.[128]

Regarding establishing the limits of reasonable accommodation, concepts such as undue hardship and legal formulas applied in other jurisdictions are of limited use in the South African context. The limitation clause, section 36 of the Constitution, was seen by the courts as providing for a nuanced balancing approach to proportionality based on constitutional principles.[129] Furthermore, the unique African concept of *ubuntu* should guide South Africans to accommodate each other.[130]

The practice of reasonable accommodation has had wider application than within the traditional discrimination context, as illustrated in *Kievit's Kroon*,[131] which dealt with an unfair dismissal in which discrimination was not alleged. The result of the judgment is in line with South African jurisprudence regarding reasonable accommodation, but it is recommended that a more principled approach based on a proportionality analysis should be followed.

121. Item 7(b)(iv)of the Good of Good Practice: Dismissal.
122. [2011]11 BLLR 1041 (SCA).
123. *Tsubatse* para. 12.
124. *Pillay* para. 53.
125. *Pillay* para. 88.
126. *Pillay* para. 7.3.
127. *Pillay* para. 78.
128. *POPCRU* para. 25.
129. *Pillay* para. 76; *Prince* para. 146.
130. *Kievit's Kroon* (LAC) para. 26.
131. [2013] ZASCA para. 189.

From the discussion it is evident that South African courts have expected more from employers regarding reasonable accommodation of the religion and culture of employees than in some other jurisdictions.[132] The emphasis on transformative justice[133] must be seen in the light of South Africa's past, when the majority of the population was excluded and marginalised. The message from our highest court is that diversity should not only be tolerated but celebrated.[134]

132. *Pillay* para. 73; *Kievit's Kroon* (LAC) para. 26.
133. L. du Plessis 'Affirmation and Celebration of the "Religious Other" in South Africa's Constitutional Jurisprudence on Religious and Related Rights; Memorial Constitutionalism in Action?' *African Human Rights Law Journal* vol. 8(2) (2008) http://www.ahrlj.up.ac.za/ accessed on 1 September 2015.
134. L. du Plessis, 'Religious Freedom and Equality as Celebration of Difference: A Significant Development in Recent South African Case Law' *Potchefstroom Electronic Law Journal* vol. 12(4) (2009) pp. 10-35.

CHAPTER 11
Reasonable Accommodation in the Modern Workplace: Russian Perspective

Nelly Diveeva, Mikhail Kharitonov & Fatima Nogajlieva

At first glance, the concept of reasonable accommodation might appear in the national legislation in three ways. The first way – the easiest one – through the adoption of the concept from a foreign legislation. This method is the least interesting in cognitive terms since it offers nothing to explain this phenomenon.

The second way – through the logical development of ways to counteract discrimination at work. Actually, the non-discrimination principles can englobe internal conflicts, which can be overcome either by limiting the validity of this principle, or by developing a reasonable accommodation institute. We are talking about the following.

The prohibition of discrimination is based on the idea that certain characteristics of the worker as a subject, should not affect his legal status as a subject of labor and employment. These characteristics may include both biological (e.g., skin color) and social (e.g., religion) features of the subject. However, even though some of these characteristics can really never influence the behavior of the person as a subject of labor and employment (considering skin color for instance); nothing can be said about the others. Thus, the religious beliefs of a person may require a certain behavior of him, which could conflict with the requirements of the employer to him as an employee. As a result, the employee may be faced with a choice: either stop doing what he thinks is right, or quit his job. However, it will be perceived by the employee as nothing else but discrimination on religious grounds. Accordingly, the law-making body (i.e., the legislature and/or the court – depending on which system of law is in force in the particular country) would have to somehow resolve this conflict: either admit that the principle of non-discrimination in the present case does not apply, or create the conditions under which the employee will not be put before the choice of either rejecting the form of behavior he chose or quitting his job / any other adverse consequence. Since preventing discrimination is essential for the civilizational achievement of modern society, the limitation of the principle is extremely undesirable: once a limitation is enforced on any humanistic principle, such a situation may arise where nothing is left of this principle. Consequently, there is a second way – the creation of conditions to eliminate the cause of the conflict. However, it is necessary to take into account the legitimate interests of the employer, because the protection of one subject cannot be applied while the other is denied recognition of his rights. Hence, we logically come to the idea of compromise, which is reasonable accommodation.

Third way – through the idea of ensuring the implementation of human rights. It can be applied jointly with the idea of non-discrimination, and independently of it. Its essence consists in the following.

In modern society, everyone has certain rights for protection which should be provided for by the state as it is its aim and justification for existence. Furthermore it is normal in this regard that the rights are not "mutually exclusive." In other words, the possibility of implementing a certain right should not, as a general rule, be due to the denial of other rights. In addition, the execution of right shall not be accompanied by encumbrances for the right owner, thus rendering this execution senseless, when in the end more harm is caused than good. At the same time, due to the nature of his labor and its effect on his life, the employee can always be faced with a choice: his job or something else (e.g., his family) or the execution of his right to work would be difficult or impossible for example, when no special working conditions are set for an invalid person). Because such situations are clearly incompatible with the idea of a complete and smooth implementation of human and civil rights, the state must take measures to eliminate or at least soften them (difficulties).

Of course, ascertaining the objective necessity of implementing the idea of reasonable accommodation to modern society in itself does not answer the other, equally important question that is: at whose expense should reasonable accommodation be applied: specific employers or the state (i.e., society as a whole)? This issue will not be considered by us in this article, since a separate study should be devoted to it, considering its size and complexity. We confine ourselves to a description of which mechanisms of reasonable accommodation are present in the Russian labor legislation.

Through which of the above-mentioned three ways is reasonable accommodation present in the Russian legal system?

Obviously, we are not considering borrowing at the moment the modern institute of reasonable accommodation as understood in the West as it is not well known in Russia (which does not mean that its peers are absent – more on that below). This terminology is not used in the legislation and legal practice, and the development of its main ideas is not a major field in scientific recommendations devoted to improve the legal management of labor and employment.

In order to assess whether it is possible to implement the principle of reasonable accommodation using the development of the principle of prevention of discrimination, it is essential to consider how this principle is represented in the modern Russian legal system.

In accordance with Part 2 of Article 6 of the Constitution of the Russian Federation, "every citizen of the Russian Federation shall enjoy in its territory all rights and freedoms and bear equal duties as stipulated in the Constitution". Part 1 of Article 19 provides that "all are equal before the law." Article 19 provides that "the state guarantees equality of rights and freedom of man and citizen, regardless of gender, race, nationality, language, origin, property and official status, place of residence, religious belief, convictions, membership of public associations or other circumstances. Any restriction of the rights of citizens on social, racial, national, linguistic or religious identity is prohibited".

The Constitution provides that generally recognized principles and norms of international law and international treaties of the Russian Federation are an integral part of its legal system. Therefore, acts to ensure protection against discrimination as provisions of the Universal Declaration of Human Rights, the International Covenant on Civil and Political Rights, the International Covenant on Economic, Social and Cultural Rights, the European Convention on Human Rights, and Convention number 111 of the ILO "Concerning Discrimination in Respect of Employment and Occupation" and other international acts are fully applicable in Russia.

In addition, Russian legislation has its own definitions of discrimination based on various statutory acts, which are not always identical textually.

Thus, in accordance with Article 5.62. of the Code of Administrative Offences, discrimination is a violation of the rights, freedoms and legitimate interests of citizens, depending on their sex, race, color, nationality, language, origin, property, family, social or employment status, age, place of residence, attitude to religion, beliefs, membership or non-governmental associations or any social groups.

Article 136 of the Criminal Code explains discrimination in almost the same way, defining it as a violation of rights, freedoms and legitimate interests of citizens, depending on their sex, race, nationality, language, origin, property and official status, place of residence, attitude to religion, beliefs, membership of public associations or any social groups, committed by a person using his official position.

In labor law the concept of discrimination covered by Article 3 of the Labour Code of the Russian Federation, according to which:

> Everyone has an equal opportunity to exercise their labor rights.
>
> No one may be restricted in his labor rights and freedoms or receive any advantages based on gender, race, color, nationality, language, origin, property, family, social or employment status, age, place of residence, attitude to religion, beliefs, membership or non-governmental associations or any social groups, as well as from circumstances not related to professional qualities.
>
> Distinctions, exceptions, preferences, as well as the restriction of workers' rights, which are determined by requirements inherent to the job and established by federal law or special care of the State to people requiring enhanced social and legal protection, or established by the LC or in cases and in the order that they are provided to ensure national security, maintain an optimal balance of labor resources, the promotion of priority employment of citizens of the Russian Federation in order to solve other problems of internal and foreign policy is not to be considered as discrimination.
>
> People who believe they have been discriminated against at work, have the right to apply to the court for redress, compensation for material damage and compensation for moral damages.

It is difficult to call this definition of discrimination satisfactory. On the one hand, it does not determine the precise boundaries of the concept of discrimination, formally attributing to it any restrictions or benefits that are not related to the qualifications of the employees (except as required by law), which gives reason to understand any illegal action by an employer against an employee as a discrimination if his motive is not related to the qualifications of the employee, which is clearly wrong because it contradicts the nature of discrimination and objectives of the Institute against discrimination, as well as part of the dissonance of the other provisions of the Labour Code (LC) (Article 252), which states that specific labor regulations due to the nature and conditions labor, psycho-physiological characteristics of the organism, climatic conditions, availability of family responsibilities, as well as other grounds established by the labor legislation and other regulatory legal acts containing norms of labor law, collective agreements, contracts, local normative acts (the features of the regulation of labor, entailing a decrease in the level of guarantees to workers, limiting their rights, increasing their disciplinary and (or) the liability may be established solely by the LC, or in the cases and manner provided by it).

On the other hand, "linking" discrimination to direct limitation of rights, or provision of benefits pulls cases of de facto discrimination away from the field of vision of many jurisdictional authorities, especially if they are formally based on the discretionary power of the employer.

For example, if the head is a man, who runs a roughly equal number of men and women in identical positions at the expense of the company and sends them on an annual two-week business trip to Las Vegas to participate in negotiations with foreign partners (the actual negotiations usually don't last more than three to five days) with a high business trip allowance and only sends men, despite the fact that the female employees have expressed their outrage on the matter and objectively can cope with the service objectives within the framework of this trip as well as their male counterparts, in terms of the current legislation of the Russian Federation, this will not be regarded as gender discrimination, because the employee does not have the subjective right "to be sent on a particular trip," and the business trip itself is not an advantage. The law does not provide to take into account the individual features of this particular case (where the trip, is in fact, a disguised form of additional paid leave).

A more common example: if men and women hold the position of lawyer in a law firm and are responsible for both "technical" and "creative" work, the employer may, without any risk for himself, "redistribute" duties in accordance to gender - for example, by only handing technical duties to women, and creative work only to men. It will also formally not be considered as discrimination (though in fact it actually is), as, according to law, the employer distributed jobs to the employees within their job description and entirely depends on the employer and is not considered as a violation of the rights of the employees.

Standards dedicated to equality and protection from discrimination are also contained in a number of other articles of the LC (2, 4, 22, 64, 132, 179), but nothing fundamentally new to the concept of "discrimination" has been added.

In addition, we may note such a rule as paragraph 6 of Article 25 of the Law of the RF dated April 19, 1991 No. 1032-1 "On employment", which prohibits the dissemination of information about vacant work places or vacancies containing discriminatory information under threat of administrative responsibility.

The rest of the Russian legislation does not establish special forms of discrimination for its effective counter (such as indirect discrimination, although this concept is well known and used in the science of labor law).

As a whole, we can affirm that, the legislation and its application consider discrimination as a rule as far as protection of the employee from the employer is concerned, in the model of "unlawful conduct with an additional discriminatory motive of optional nature" (there are exceptions, but they do not play a serious role in law enforcement). This model implies that the finding of a violation to the rights of the employee necessarily proves that there has been a discrimination.

For example, the LC, as a general rule, provides a closed list of grounds on which an employer can dismiss an employee. Therefore, if the employee can prove that there was no ground in his case, then it does not matter, whether there was discrimination or not (e.g., the employer simply wrongly qualified an employee's lateness as absenteeism - firing the employee on these grounds would be illegal, but not discriminatory) in any case it is necessary to reinstate the employee, to compensate for lost earnings and non-pecuniary damage.

Discrimination in such cases, in fact, is an additional motive for unlawful wrongful conduct of the employer, the establishment of which, however, does not bring any additional benefits to the employee.

As a result, citing regulations prohibiting discrimination in judicial decisions of Russian courts into a "beautiful wrapper" does not fundamentally affect the essence of the case.

Protection against discrimination from the employer as a formal part of his discretionary power (see examples above), is actually nearly impossible for the employee.

This allows us to state that the spread of the concept of reasonable accommodation through the development of discrimination prevention in the legal system of Russia is highly unlikely. The law draws a clear line against discrimination - limiting labor rights and freedoms or receives benefits based on discriminatory criteria. If the situation of the employee cannot be corrected directly such that he doesn't find himself in a worse position as compared to other employees, and the employer has not violated the formal requirements of the law governing the process and working conditions, the principle of non-discrimination in its Russian understanding cannot be involved. As a result, it does not give any foundation for reasonable accommodation, as required, so that the individual characteristics and needs of each employee are considered in his conditions of labor.

At the same time, there are many rules the Russian legislation, that establishes particular working conditions for certain categories of workers. The establishment of specific rules applicable to certain special groups of subjects of labor, is the embodiment of one of the principles of the Russian labor law - the principle of unity and differentiation of legal regulation of labor. Differentiation of legal regulation of labor has specific grounds which are divided into: (1) base related to *subjective attributes of the employee* (sex, age, state of health, exercise, along with the work of other socially significant activities) and (2) base related to *the objective conditions of labor* (economic and organizational characteristics of the employer, working environment, nature of work, the geographical location of the employer and place of work).

Some of these bases (e.g., family responsibilities of the employee, educational needs) can be considered as a special case of reasonable accommodation, mediated by rules of law based on the idea of a complete and smooth implementation of the rights and freedoms of man and citizen, that is, as the third way to express this Institute.

An important feature of the Russian version of reasonable accommodation is that the legislator, usually, does not provide the employer with general indications "take the necessary measures to ensure that so-and-so". It either establishes a specific mandatory rule (e.g., reduction of working time) or obliges the employer to give the employee a specific benefit or a preference upon the latter's request.

Of course, this does not exclude the employer's possibility to establish working conditions which take into account the individual needs of his employees alone or as part of social partnership. The formal basis, to admit it, is Article 252 of the LC.

However, it should be noted that corresponding special norms are considered by participants of the labor market and jurisdictional authorities as legislative exceptions of the general rules, as kind of "kindness" of the government towards employees. Any wish of the employee is to be taken into account considering certain of his personal needs, which have no legal binding, they must be approved by the employer through negotiations between the parties. However it is often impossible to reach unanimity: there is the notorious weakness of the worker as a party to the employment relationship, and the fear of the employee to lose his job as a result of the conflict. However judicial protection in the event the employer fails to consider the wishes of the employee which are not formally based on the law, local acts of the organization, collective contracts or agreements, the employee shall not be able to receive, even when this denial makes it impossible or highly difficult to implement his rights as a human being and a citizen. In this case, the only possible way within the framework of the Russian national legal system is an appeal to the Constitutional Court of the Russian Federation to recognize the norm of the law that does not permit a situation contrary to the Constitution. However, the effectiveness of this method of protection is currently poor.

Now, considering the above-mentioned, we shall check to what extent the working conditions of the employees are adapted (and if they are adapted) to their needs and related to their individual characteristics (religion / beliefs, state of health and age) in contemporary Russian labor law.

§11.01 AN ACCOMMODATED WORKPLACE FOR RELIGION OR BELIEF

Today in Russia, according to the Ministry of Justice, there are more than 23,000 religious organizations of 60 different kinds. The largest and most influential religious organization in the Russian Federation is the Russian Orthodox Church, with more than 11,000 parishes. The second largest religious association by number goes to the

Muslim community, with about 3,500 currently registered Muslim religious organizations.

For a more complete understanding of the difficulty of taking into account the religious needs of citizens when executing their right to work, the historical context, for which Russia is very peculiar, should be taken into consideration. With the advent of Soviet power in the vast territory from Kaliningrad to Sakhalin all traditions and religious cults were purposefully destroyed and persecuted.

While religion as such was never under a total ban, and atheism was not formally proclaimed as the official part of the state ideology, the attitude of the state towards religion throughout the seventy years of Soviet rule (1917-1991) however, was generally described as ranging from "extremely undesirable with active government measures against religious education and worship" to "conditionally tolerated under strict control."

Formal texts from the Soviet Constitutions, however, contained specific reference to the rights and guarantees of citizens in the religious sphere. It should be emphasized that the Soviet Constitutions allowed religious practice, but not religious propaganda. On the contrary, atheistic propaganda is not just tolerated, but encouraged by the state.

In reality, in matters relating to citizens' religious rights, the situation was even worse, and, in some cases, it was not even possible to pose the question of how to provide citizens with some kind of special rights in labor relations in connection with their religious beliefs. There could be no granting of such rights by the employers on their own initiative due to the almost complete nationalization of the economy, i.e., in fact, believers were confronted with the state itself as their employer. Productive and rich developments that were widely used in the scientific and practical sphere before 1917 had been lost.

Echoes of the policy pursued by the Soviet Union with varying intensity, but persistent throughout the period of existence of the state, were tangible and still remain today in terms of religious "habits" of the population. It is curious that for the last two decades the number of people considering themselves believers is growing steadily and according to various estimates, it ranges from 70% to 85%. A large part of the population of Russia does not follow religious practices, visits places of worship not more than two times a year during religious events and are not fully aware of the practice of the cult of their professed religion. The fact that the population "lost" the habit of freely and fully profess their religion for almost 100 years, led to a lack in most individuals (employees) such needs as to adapt their working conditions to their religious needs. The lack of these needs mainly resulted in a large backlog of modern Russia in the study of this problem. However, present statistics give us reasons to believe that the needs of the population in this area over time, has acquired a vector of growth and, therefore, recognizes the need for at least formulating this problem.

Due to extreme subjectivity of religious interests and ambiguity of perception in the community of certain religious needs, some constitutional provisions were made to ensure the effective balance between the rights of citizens in the sphere of religion and the interests of other persons (in our case – the employer), but it is not enough.

It is necessary to state that the Russian labor law do not meet these requirements. At best they do not permit the discrimination of employees according to their religious beliefs. However, the law does not provide any positive obligations of the employer in this respect (there is no obligation to equip the production facilities with prayer rooms, modify jobs under the religious needs of employees taking into account the distribution of working hours and rest periods according to the religious wishes of the worker, etc.). These responsibilities, in fact, depend on the goodwill of the employer. Theoretically, it is possible to change this situation with the help of trade unions through collective bargaining, but in practice in the Russian context it is almost improbable.

Moreover, if based on internal regulations adopted by the employer, the workers refuse to perform on the grounds that it is contrary to their religious beliefs, it is a matter of law and will be considered a disciplinary offense.

Also, there are cases in Russian law where the state clearly and openly admits citizens' religious needs with discriminatory bias.

By virtue of the third paragraph of section 112 of the LC, Article 112, one of the public holidays January 7 – Christmas in Russia (literally specified in the law, that is, it is emphasized that this holiday is an Orthodox religious holiday).

In addition, at the request of religious organizations, relevant government authorities in Russia have the right to declare religious holidays as non-working (holiday) days in the relevant territories (Article 4 of the Federal Law "On Freedom of Conscience and Religious Associations"), but this does not solve the problem of discrimination, but rather strengthens it.

With regard to this issue, there was an appeal to the Constitutional Court of the Russian Federation, but the Court actually withdrew from its decision and refused to accept the complaint of the citizen for consideration based on the fact that:

> Paragraph three of Section 112 of the LC is a part of the legal mechanism of realization of the constitutional right to rest and cannot be considered as violating the constitutional rights of citizens, also, it contains no obstacles to the realization of the right to protection against unemployment.
>
> The disputed provision cannot be considered as a violation of the requirements of Articles 14, 28 and 29 of the Constitution as well, as it does not limit the citizen to profess, individually or jointly with others any religion or no religion at all, to freely choose religious and other beliefs and act legitimately in accordance with them (Definition of May 29, 2012 N 999-O).

Of course, life is much more diverse and complex than the text of the law, so in the practice of individual employers, operating in Russia, you can find interesting examples of religious needs of professionals being accounted for.

For example, it is known that the representative offices of several European companies in Moscow opened a special room for ablutions and prayers. Believing employees have the opportunity, by taking two to three breaks every seven to ten minutes, to fully perform their religious practice, if it is not detrimental to the working process. The elapsed time is compensated as agreed with the management at the expense of the lunch break, or otherwise.

A similar practice was common in the Muslim republics of the North Caucasus and Tatarstan, especially in cases where employees perform their duties on a rotational basis or shifts.

It is worth mentioning that the agreements in such cases are oral in nature, as to the practice in the North Caucasus, and they are all well-hidden and not made public. The only case where such an agreement was installed in a local act of the employer – open rooms for ablutions and prayers in several prisons of Moscow for persons serving a sentence (the relations connected with the implementation of this category of persons of their ability to work, subsidiarity governed by rules of labor law).

Employers often make concessions in terms of changes in modes of operation: during Ramadan (a whole month) employees comply with it, they are not sent to business trips, they are not attracted to night work and overtime work. Given that employees do not need a lunch break, they are allowed to reduce their working day by one hour. All these concessions apply only on condition that it does not create problems for the employer (does not reduce the flow of customers, production quotas, etc.).

A number of nuances as to the appearance of the employees, a practice which is extremely ambiguous. So, in the Chechen Republic Muslim women, serving in public institutions are obliged to wear a headscarf at work and clothes that cover all parts of the body. At the same time in a neighboring republic, a broadcaster of one of the local TV channels was fired for violating labor discipline. Misconduct as seen by the employer was that the presenter ignored requests of the management to get rid of his beard for several weeks, because such appearance does not match the style of the federal channel which provides regional broadcasting in multiconfessional regions of Russia. The employer's claim was met with denial, motivated by the right of workers to freely adhere to religious norms, as long as it is not illegal and does not violate the rights of others.

Not less dramatic are the conflicts in which workers were denied promotion for wearing religious attributes not compatible, according to employers, with the position, implying communication with citizens and the inadmissibility of demonstrating their religious adherence when doing so.

Thus, in some cases (usually, in certain Muslim regions of Russia) the employers account for the religious needs of the employees, which eliminates disputes between them and the workers, but in most cases this is not observed. By virtue of the above specifics of the Russian law possible conflicts that arise are not referred to the judicial authorities (due to the practical uselessness of this step).

In summary, we note that the current Russian legislation does not provide for obligations of the employer to adapt workplaces to the religious needs of employees, but does not forbid him to do so. In general, employers can adhere to any policy regarding the religious requests of employees – most importantly, this policy should not be discriminatory.

§11.02 AN ACCOMMODATED WORKPLACE FOR DISABILITY OR WORK INCAPACITY

Regarding the working conditions of employees having health problems with a persistent disorder of body functions due to illness, trauma or defect resulting in

Disability and in need for social protection (disabled), the maintenance of their employment is guaranteed by the state as defined in the Federal Law dating November 24, 1995 No. 181-FZ "On Social protection of Disabled Persons", Article 3.1. The same law establishes that discrimination is inadmissible on grounds of disability.

A substantial part of the implementation of safeguards in the employment of disabled persons is entrusted by the state to employers.

First, for employers, with employee numbers exceeding 100, the regional law establishes a quota for the employment of disabled persons at a rate of 2% to 4% of the average number of employees. For those, employing 35 to 100 people, the size of the quota should be not higher than 3%. As you can see, this is exactly the case when the size of the employer's organization is determined by the number of its staff, and affects the performance of their duties by adapting working conditions to the needs of the workers.

Second, employers in accordance with the established quota for the employment of disabled people are obliged to create or set up special workstations for such working conditions that correspond to the individual rehabilitation program of the specific disabled worker.

In addition, the burden of creating special jobs for people with disabilities fall onto the shoulders of the employer as part of labor conditions, in order to employ disabled people – workplaces that require additional measures to organization work, including the adaptation of the main and auxiliary equipment, technical and organizational equipment, additional equipment and provide technical equipment based on the individual capabilities of the people with disabilities. Special workstations are equipped by the employer, taking into account the impaired functions of the disabled people and limitations of their everyday activities in accordance with the basic requirements for such equipment. The minimum number of places is set by the authorities of the RF for each enterprise, institution or organization within the established quota for disabled people.

It is worth noting that while developing the working conditions, the employer and the disabled employee can be considered free from significant reservations. To begin with, in the individual program of rehabilitation or habilitation of the disabled person (documents are developed by a government agency for medical and social expertise and the employer is obliged to comply) contains provisions on the conditions, for which the disabled person would be able to work.

In addition, the labor legislation mandatorily sets shorter working hours, longer holidays, while working overtime, working on weekends and at night is possible only if the disabled worker and the employer come to an agreement.

However, even in the part in which the parties are free to work out the terms of the employment contract, the earlier-mentioned Federal law prohibits the establishment of working conditions in it (wages, working hours and rest periods, the duration of leave), worsening the situation of the disabled in comparison with other workers.

§11.03 AN ACCOMMODATED WORKPLACE FOR AGE

The LC contains a number of restrictions and special regulations concerning employment in relation to a certain age. In particular this applies to minors (under 18 years) employees. As a general rule, an employment contract may be signed with people who have reached the age of 16 years, except in cases established by law.

The concept of reasonable accommodation in respect to such persons is related to the prohibition of employing them at work with harmful and (or) dangerous working conditions, underground work, as well as at work, that may be harmful to their health and moral development (gambling, work in night clubs and clubs, production, transportation and trading alcohol, tobacco, drugs and other toxic substances, materials with erotic content); with the prohibition of carrying and moving heavy loads, exceeding the established limits; with the establishment of reduced working hours and extended annual leave, etc. The employer has the responsibility of conducting the preliminary and periodic medical examinations of the young employees at their own expenses.

However, reasonable accommodation, adjusted for the age of the workers, requires taking into account not only the "lower" age limit of the employees, but also concerns workers in older age groups. In Russia it is an estimated concept, however, through systematic interpretation of the law we can determine that it includes people who have reached retirement age.

It appears that the regulatory norms of labor law characterizing the concept of reasonable accommodation for workers of older age groups can be divided into two groups. Since the reasons for the difficulties of adaptation of older workers are mainly related to age, the existing labor legislation should contain general rules aimed at maintaining the health of workers in general, in order to "push" old age further (as far as possible) and to guarantee workers a long-term preservation of their health. Thus, the first group of regulations in accordance with the Guiding ILO number 162 "On older workers" should:

(1) improve the conditions and working environment that can accelerate the aging process;
(2) change the forms of work organization and regulation of working time, if they are excessive in relation to the capacity of the relevant workers leading to stress as far as rhythm is concerned, by limiting overtime;
(3) adapt the workplace and the job to the worker, using all available technical means and, in particular, the principles of ergonomics, to preserve the health and performance and prevent accidents;
(4) provide for a more systematic monitoring of the health of workers;
(5) provide workplaces with appropriate supervision to ensure the safety and health of workers.

In addition, the first group can be associated with regulatory standards and rules on social security. In particular, it is necessary that both the state pension and the additional social security (including corporate) guarantee real possibilities of implementing the principle of freedom of work to people of retirement age in their conditions and levels. That is, elderly citizens have to execute their ability to work, based on the desire to work, based on the unspent labor (including personal) potential, but not to such an extent, as they are compelled by economic insecurity, associated with the low level of public pension.

As for the second group of regulatory norms of labor law, the concept reasonable accommodation in relation with workers of older age groups, includes just those provisions which establish subjective labor rights and legitimate interests of the relevant category of workers at work.

As we know, the interest of an individual is reclassified legally to another significant interest through its legal regulation. This occurs if the specified interest is not contrary to the public interest, defining the boundaries of personal rights. After the interest goes into the category of legally significant, it can be secured and protected in various ways at the level of the rule of law. If the legitimate interests of a person oppose the legal obligation of another person, then we are talking about legitimate interests mediated by the subjective right.

In this context, it makes sense to turn to Russian legislation for the isolation and analysis of the legal rules that differentially set additional guarantees for older age groups in order to protect the workers in those groups. Thus these workers are endowed with special subjective employment rights.

Unfortunately, it should be noted that there are not enough of these rules of law. The virtual absence of differentiation in the Russian legal labor regulation for workers of older age groups cannot be considered normal, since it seems that such an approach undermines one of the essential foundations of legal recognition of our state as a social one.

However, the additional subjective rights that protect workers in older age groups are fixed in the LC. Thus, in Article 3 of the LC prohibits discrimination in employment due to circumstances unrelated to the professional qualities, which include age. Article 80 of the LC states that the employer is obliged to terminate the employment contract within the period specified in the statement of the employee (without a specific deadline set, prior warning, without explanation) in the case of retirement. Article 128 of the LC obliges the employer upon written request of a working old-age pensioner, to grant him leave of absence without pay of not less than fourteen calendar days.

It should be noted that, though not directly, but rather indirectly, the protection of labor rights of workers in older age groups is carried out together with other regulations.

In particular, Article 32 of the law "On employment" determines that citizens under the age of 60 for men and 55 years for women, who have been insured for not less than 25 and 20 years for men and women, respectively, and who have been working in the relevant types of work for the required amount of time, have the right to apply for early retirement pension due to old age, as provided in Articles 27 and 28 of the Federal Law "On labor pensions", the period of unemployment benefit surpasses the twelve months set by two calendar weeks for each year of service, exceeding the insurance period for the specified duration. The total period of unemployment benefit cannot exceed twenty-four calendar months for a total of thirty-six calendar months.

Further, the article defines the right to early retirement pension for people in older age groups, for the simultaneous meeting the following conditions:

(1) the citizen should be jobless and from among people who have been dismissed due to the liquidation or downsizing of staff or employees of the organization;
(2) lack of employment opportunities of the citizens, i.e., there is no suitable work;
(3) pension may be appointed for the period before the age of entitlement to retirement pension for old age, including early payment of employment pensions for old age, but not earlier than two years before the appropriate age;
(4) citizen shall have the insurance period of not less than 25 and 20 years for men and women, respectively, as well as the necessary experience in the relevant types of work, giving them the right to early appointment of labor retirement pension provided in Articles 27 and 28 of the Federal Law "On labor pensions";
(5) the pension is appointed upon the proposal of the employment service with the consent of the person applying for it.

Thus, without setting a specific age for the granting of appropriate facilities, the above-mentioned article restricts the number of applicants with the condition of having a relatively long insurance period. This makes the relevant provisions of Article 32 of the Law "On employment" attributable to the legal status of older age groups. Although analyzed guarantees are related to the right to payment of pensions and allowances upon losing jobs, these kinds of standards can be attributed to one of the ways to protect the labor rights of the citizens of the respective category. This position is argued, first, that the State supports older age groups by providing them in their difficult situation, saving, their ability to work as well. Second, linking reception of the relevant pensions and benefits to long years of service, the state, on the one hand, encourages citizens to realize their ability to work, on the other hand, it gives the parties an additional warranty protection in connection with work.

In these cases, the subjective right of older age groups is enshrined by the current legislation and corresponds to the legal obligation of the employer or the relevant authorities.

However, Article 21 of the LC *inter alia* establish the right of all workers to be protected not only with their subjective rights but also, their legitimate interests. In general, the legitimate interests of workers in terms of employment are aimed at the use of social benefits in the form of their additional (above the minimum established by the legislation) guarantees, taking into account, also, their individualistic characteristics. Implementation of the legal interests of the employees (in respect of such interest) linked to the discretion of the employer, which has a regulatory and policy authority, and, in the event of a dispute as to the discretion of authorities to resolve labor disputes.

Workers of older age groups, as well as all other employees, have the right to realize legitimate interests and their protection as enshrined in the LC (Article 57 – to be included in the employment contract of additional conditions; Article 111 – for the provision of weekend days in a row; Article 180 – on the termination of employment when downsizing staff without a two-month warnings, etc.). However, the current legislation directly secures the legitimate interests of the relevant category of citizens.

Thus, Part 2 of Article 59 the LC talks about the possibility of a temporary employment contract with retirees by age, but not with everyone, only those just employed. Accordingly, if an employee in labor relations, reached retirement age, he cannot renew a fixed-term contract. Furthermore, it should stipulate that the analyzed rate is not just about those who have reached retirement age but also those who are retired by age. Thus, in addition to the retirement age the employee must be appointed a national old-age pension as stipulated under the legislation of the RF. Only if these two conditions are present, then it is possible to use the provisions of Article 59 of the LC for people of older age groups. The article does not involve the employer's duty to make a fixed-term contract only with such workers. It is about the right of the employer, which, in turn, corresponds to the right of the employee.

In Part 5 of Article 25 of the Federal Law "On State Civil Service" dating July 27, 2004, the fixed legitimate interest of civil servants appointed at the position of the civil service on the basis of a service contract concluded for an indefinite period, and who has reached the age of 60 years upon the renewal of the said service contract for a term of one to five years. This norm can be considered as some sort of benefit for the workers of older age groups, since the Act restricts the post in the civil service with an age of 60. In this context, citizens older than 60 years have the possibility of extending their service for a period of one to five years (maximum 65 years).

In addition, Part 7 of Article 25 of the Federal Law "On State Civil Service" establishes a rule that after a civil servant reaches 60 years of age or the age limit for civil service and at the end of a fixed-term service contract, a fixed-term employment contract for a position of non-civil service is made with the representatives of the employer and with the consent of the citizen. Such a substitution is made with regard to the qualifications (professional level), the results of professional performance during the civil service, health and civil service position the specified citizen was appointed to. In this case, the right of workers of older age group corresponds to the employer's right to conclude a fixed-term contract.

And again, we have to state with regret that the list of the legitimate interests of workers in older age groups, enshrined in law in the Russian Federation, is actually not so great. At the same time, the ILO Recommendation No. 162 "About Older Workers" provides possible examples of fixing the legitimate interests of this category of workers in national legislation. The following are proposed in this recommendation:

(1) reduction of the normal working day or working week for older workers engaged in heavy, hazardous or harmful work;
(2) the gradual reduction of working hours for all older workers, at their request, for a specified period preceding the date of reaching the normal age for old-age benefits;

(3) an increase in the duration of annual paid leave, based on the length of service or age;
(4) permission for older workers to organize as they wish their work time and leisure, in particular by providing them with the opportunity to work part-time and on a rolling basis (flexible) schedule;
(5) facilitate the appointment of older workers, who work at a usual time of the day, after a certain number of years of exploitation on a full or partial shift work.

Of course, within the framework of the legitimate interest of one individual is opposed to the right (but not the specific duty) of another person, and there are doubts about the need for the formulation of the category of legitimate interests in the regulations. But the actual need to secure the high legal status of a person as an element of permissible type of regulation should be able to eliminate this uncertainty. Indeed, at first, the legitimate interest of the person faces resistance as it is not compulsory for each and every one to respect it. Second, a legitimate interest can be directly formulated in the legal or legitimate interest in the behavior of the media, and can be built on the basis of the entire body of law, principles, objectives, goals set by the legislator. In this regard, legal subjects receive additional legal "arguments" that contribute to the manifestation of their activity. Third, the general permissibility of a legitimate interest is established and protected by the state, which enables, where necessary, to seek its protection from the competent authorities (Dispute Settlement Body).

The legitimate interests of both the employee and the employer may be implemented by collective and individual legal regulation in the form of labor contracts, collective agreements; the parties voluntarily assume certain liabilities that meet the interests of the other side.

However, it appears that the methods of protection voluntarily not implemented by the parties of the employment relationship for the legitimate interest of the employee and employer are different. Protection the violated interests of workers can be implemented by all means not prohibited by law, including by means of appeal to the jurisdictional bodies. In this case, the labor dispute is a dispute about the application of the law, for example, an employee of the senior age group (civil servant who has reached the age of 60 years) will insist on the fact that he has a legitimate interest in the renewal of an appropriate service contract for a period of one year to five years, and the representative of the employer is able to meet the specified legally significant interest. As for the employer whose legitimate interests are also violated cannot be protected by the same method. Due to the social orientation of the labor law, legislation does not allow the employer to compel the worker "to respond" with consent to the will of the legitimate interests of the employer through jurisdictional bodies. And rightly so, because the latter by virtue of the host government has a different arsenal of methods and means to exert its influence on the employee.

§11.04 MAIN CONCLUSIONS

(1) The principle of non-discrimination in its Russian interpretation cannot be an effective engine of reasonable accommodation.
(2) In Russia, the concept of reasonable accommodation is presently at the level of statutory law, but is not called so.
(3) This concept, even at the level of statutory law is presently in a "truncated form". The corresponding legislation norms are considered as exceptions, not as a consequence of the general principle of action.
(4) Russian law usually sets the specific nature of the measures to ensure taking into account individual interests of workers.
(5) The law allows an employer to self-administer reasonable accommodation or its analogs through the adoption of local regulations or through collective bargaining with employees (collective contracts and agreements).
(6) If the requirements of the employee are taken into account when establishing his particular working conditions, not formally based on the norms of statutory law, local acts of the employer, collective agreements, then he cannot usually count on legal protection when dispute is considered in court.
(7) Reasonable accommodation is in its infancy for the religious needs of employees in Russia.
(8) Reasonable accommodation in connection with the health of workers is in line with trends in international legal regulation, since in 2012, Russia ratified the UN General Assembly on the Rights of Persons with Disabilities (2006). However, legal mechanisms for the implementation of the established legislative norms are far from perfect due to the lack of sufficient financial resources, the lack of a systematic and consistent legislator in securing the appropriate tools, and the lack of liability for non-compliance with the rules established for the most part, the negative mentality of the Russian society towards people with disabilities.
(9) Reasonable accommodation in Russia in respect of workers of older age groups can and should be achieved in different ways, both within the protective and the regulatory legal mechanism. And it's not just protecting such individuals from discrimination in employment using an appropriate mechanism. The effective legal regulation of these relations contributes to the solution of at least two social problems. Firstly, in Russia today, the demographic situation requires maximum use of accumulated human capital and, consequently, continued employment of experienced skilled workers. In this context recruitment needs to be guided, in particular, on domestic sources of organizations preferring "home-grown" candidates, thus contributing to career advancement of young professionals and hard-working experienced older workers. Second, the humane treatment of those in older age groups, provided by labor and other branches of law, shows the level of development of the society in general and this possibility of moving towards a truly civil society is the foundation of a constitutional state.

CHAPTER 12

Accommodating All? (or: 'Ask Not What You Can Do for the Labour Market; Ask What the Labour Market Can Do for You')

Guy Davidov & Guy Mundlak

§12.01 INTRODUCTION

The goal of this chapter is to consider – and justify – the expansion of the duty to accommodate in labour law. Section §12.02 explains the two basic parameters setting the breadth of the duty. One question is whether it takes the form of concrete duties in legislation (e.g., an employer must grant maternity leave after an employee gives birth) or rather includes also an open-ended general duty to do whatever can reasonably be done to accommodate. The other question is whether the duty applies to a specific group of people that are especially vulnerable or rather to many different groups of people, or even (ultimately) every employee. Otherwise put, do employers have to accommodate every special need, or just specific needs such as those of workers with disabilities? Section §12.03 argues that there is a gradual change (as a descriptive matter) towards expansion on both fronts: more open-ended duties and more reasons for accommodation (or: more groups of people possessing a right to enjoy accommodation). We draw on Israeli developments for the purpose of stylizing this process of change, but also give some examples from other countries. Section §12.04 justifies this development and calls for further expansion towards a universal duty to accommodate. We argue that such a change goes beyond the context of equality and reaches into the fundamental structure of the employment contract, deeply affecting the primacy of the managerial prerogative. Section §12.05 addresses some possible critiques.

§12.02 DEVELOPING THE DUTY TO ACCOMMODATE: THE INTERPLAY OF LEGAL TECHNIQUE AND SCOPE

Drawing on Christine Jolls's definition, the term 'mandates' refers to the requirement that employers provide specified benefits to all employees (sometimes subject to exceptions).[1] Accommodation mandates are a more tailored technique, where employers are mandated to extend positive measures to particular groups of workers with distinct needs. These mandates can be further delineated into two paradigmatic forms of accommodation. Traditionally, accommodation was associated with women, on the basis of the assumption that women are 'different' and require particular 'protections.'[2] As gender values changed over time, the accommodation of women, often associated with pregnancy and childcare, was partially replaced by the accommodation of parents. Other groups (e.g., religious and cultural minorities) have sometimes enjoyed accommodation mandates as well.[3] A common feature of these mandates has been their taking the form of specified rights secured in legislation. A second and more recent form in many countries is that of a general open-ended duty to accommodate people with disabilities. Such a duty extends what has already become a well-developed body of antidiscrimination law, requiring employers not only to refrain from discriminating, but also to abolish components in the physical or organizational structure of the workplace that disadvantage workers with disabilities, albeit only within 'reasonable' limits.

[A] The Duty to Accommodate in Israeli Law

We consider Israeli law as an example, although similar developments have been common throughout the world. At the outset, employment standards established rights for all workers. Accommodation of women was introduced at the same time, extending special protections to women generally (e.g., the right to receive a warm drink in night-shifts), and to pregnant women in particular (notably the right to maternity leave). Over the years, numerous amendments to the law added various duties of accommodation that gradually abandoned some of the particular 'women's protection' rules in favour of 'parental accommodation.'[4]

1. Christine Jolls, 'Antidiscrimination and Accommodation' (2001) 115 Harv. L. Rev. 642.
2. The critique of the sameness/difference distinction is voiced most aptly by Catherine MacKinnon, *Toward a Feminist Theory of the State* (1989).
3. Kevin Banks, Roberta Nunin & Adriana Topo, 'The Lasting Influence of Legal Origins: Workplace Discrimination, Social Inclusion and the Law in Canada, the United States and the European Union' in Matthew Finkin & Guy Mundlak (eds.), *Comparative Labor Law* (2015) 220-267.
4. In the framework of the duties associated with parenthood and care, employers cannot refrain from accepting an applicant for a position because of pregnancy, despite the potential inconvenience that is expected when a new employee leaves for maternity leave; they cannot dismiss a pregnant employee (even for reasons unrelated to the pregnancy) without a special permit from a government official; they must grant mothers a maternity leave of at least fourteen weeks, and a longer unpaid leave if the mother so chooses (the maximum length depends on the employee's tenure with the employer); and for a period of four months after the maternity leave, an employee can work an hour less, for the same salary. There are also some (similar, although not equal)

In 1998 the Israeli legislature enacted the Equal Rights for People with Disabilities Act (ERPDA), which followed the model of the Equal Employment Opportunities Act of 1988 (EEO) by prohibiting discrimination, both direct and indirect. However, the ERPDA also stipulates that discrimination includes the failure to implement reasonable adjustments in the workplace to accommodate the employment of a disabled person. In practice, it took several years for workers to start suing based on this law, but recently this is becoming more common, with some important successes.[5]

All instances of accommodation duties impose costs on the employer, but these are deemed to be important for advancing the social good.[6] The legislation limits the employers' costs, for example by prescribing a fixed number of weeks for parental leave, or by requiring only 'reasonable' accommodation. Moreover, the State is actively implicated in all accommodation arrangements, further alleviating the employers' costs. For some parental benefits, the National Insurance scheme substitutes for the direct costs to employers whose workers go on leave, serving as a social insurance plan. For people with disabilities, the State extends funding for accommodations, with the level of funding taken into consideration when assessing the reasonableness of the employers' accommodation efforts.[7]

[B] Conceptualizing Change in the Nature of Accommodation Duties

The different kinds of mandates in Israeli law reflect practices that are largely universal in nature, although their sequence may vary between legal systems. First, particular well-defined employment benefits were granted to all workers (sometimes universalizing benefits that were previously accorded to specific groups); second, and sometimes concurrently, particular and well defined accommodation rights and benefits were granted to a specific category of workers; and third, we see a move to a general

rights for fathers, and additional rights for more specific situations. See the Women's Work Act 1951 (as amended) and the Equal Employment Opportunities Act 1988, s. 2.

5. Some landmarks in the Labour Court's development of the law include: Jerusalem Labour Court 2968/01 *Balilti v. Jerusalem Post Publications Ltd.* (2 December 2001); Tel-Aviv Labour Court 5712/03 *Steinberg v. Israel Electric Corporation Ltd.* (30 December 2003); Tel-Aviv Labour Court 49588-11-11 *Afek v. Karnei Shomron Regional Council* (16 July 2013). Most decisions thus far have been made by the regional labour courts, and the first guiding case was written by the Supreme Court - HCJ 6069/10 *Machmali v. Israel Prison Service* (5 May 2014).

   Despite these important decisions of Israeli courts, criticism remains that their impact on equality is currently insufficient, and that they have failed to change the political-economic structure of the Israeli labour market. See Einat Albin and Sagit Mor, 'Adequate Representation of Persons with Disabilities in Employment in Israel' 15 Labor, Society and Law (forthcoming 2016, Hebrew).

6. There is also a business case to be made for diversity in the workplace, and as a derivative – for accommodating a diverse workplace. This argument holds that short-term costs are offset by long-term gains, including a more loyal and committed workforce, a broader perspective on a diverse clientele that is of particular importance in service-oriented firms, but also in research and development, an instrument for building teamwork and organizational culture, avoiding discrimination lawsuits by establishing an appearance of 'beyond compliance' with the law, and drawing on diversity as a form of social reputation with an economic value.

7. Equal Rights for People with Disabilities Regulations (The State's Participation in Funding Accommodation) 2006.

duty of accommodation toward a category of workers. In the following sections we will argue that a fourth wave is already underway – the extension of the general duty toward a growing number of categories, culminating in what we claim should be considered the ultimate step – a general duty of reasonable accommodation toward all workers.

Hence, the two factors that aid in understanding the duty to accommodate are:

(a) *Whether accommodation is extended by particular rules and benefits, or by an open-ended standard of accommodation.* Generally, the objective of both is the same and the difference is only in the legal technique. Someone in a wheelchair cannot be employed in a workplace that has a non-accessible stairway, just as parents cannot remain employed without parental leave rights. Concrete rules may seem better for the employees enjoying them, because they are much easier to enforce – the right is clear and not subject to the discretion of the employer. However, an open-ended standard that supplements particular rules can aid workers with regard to issues that are not sufficiently addressed by the particular norms.[8]

(b) *Whether the norm is extended to a particular group or to all workers.* Norms that target particular groups can be used to level the playing field in the labour market. The difficulties of the recognized group (parenthood, disability or religious restrictions) are compensated for by norms of accommodation. However, accommodating a particular group may also have negative effects on the group, either in the form of employers' attempts to prevent their hiring, or in lower wages, inferior working conditions, lack of promotion opportunities, or denial of other quantitative and qualitative benefits that offset the costs of accommodation.[9]

In the next section we argue that there is a gradual development towards a universal duty to accommodate, which is both open-ended (above and beyond specific rules) and extended to all workers (rather than only specific vulnerable groups).
To summarize:

Stage	*Legal Technique*	*Scope of Application*
(a)[1] general employment norms	Particular rules and benefits	All employees
(b)[1] accommodation mandates in the form of maternal/ parental rights	Particular rules and benefits	Particular groups [extension from women to parents; also in some countries to religious groups]

8. On the advantages of *standards* v. *rules*, see Guy Davidov, *A Purposive Approach to Labour Law* (forthcoming OUP) Ch. 7.
9. Michael Ashley Stein, Anita Silvers, Bradley A. Areheart & Leslie Pickering Francis, 'Accommodating Every Body' (2014) 81 U. Chic. L. Rev. 689.

Stage	*Legal Technique*	*Scope of Application*
(c) accommodation for an especially vulnerable group	General standard (open-ended duty)	Particular groups, mostly workers with disabilities [extension to other particular groups, such as religious]
(d) the next step? – towards the universalization of accommodation	General standard (open-ended duty)	All employees

1. Stages (a) and (b) do not necessarily appear in this order; in some countries they appear at the same time or even in reverse order.

§12.03 CURRENT DEVELOPMENTS TOWARDS EXPANSION

The concept of accommodation was at first rather synonymous with employment law's mission to foster greater equality in the labour market. It reflected the idea of compensating for difference and disadvantage (women's maternity benefits), and was later considered part of a robust conception of *constructed equality*. Initially it appeared in the form of clear rules, and is currently growing into an overarching standard that is nested in the context of antidiscrimination and equal opportunities law.

Constructed equality, as framed by John Donohue,[10] refers to a concept of equality that casts the greatest doubt on the market's ability to undo the effects of discrimination. Unlike contingent equality, which draws on the market to identify differences, and intrinsic equality, which assumes that markets can be effectively perfected to secure equality between equals (e.g., by removing market barriers and correcting market failures), constructed equality requires that we amend the operations of the market rather than rely on it. It is claimed that the market drives unequal outcomes because it maintains a situation that is ill-adapted to the integration of some individuals and groups.

Constructed equality is not wholly distinct from intrinsic equality, and some doctrines that were developed to pursue intrinsic equality link the two precepts. It can therefore be viewed as an extension of developments in antidiscrimination law. Indeed, a growing number of commentators are rejecting the distinction between antidiscrimination laws and accommodation mandates, arguing that the former sometimes impose positive and/or costly duties as well.[11] And even commentators who

10. John J. Donohue III, 'Employment Discrimination Law in Perspective: Three Concepts of Equality' (1994) 92 Mich. L. Rev. 2583.
11. Christine Jolls, 'Antidiscrimination and Accommodation' *supra* n.1; Samuel R. Bagenstos, ''Rational Discrimination', Accommodation, and the Politics of (Disability) Civil Rights' (2003) 89 Virginia L. Rev. 825; Michael Ashley Stein, 'Same Struggle, Different Difference: ADA Accommodations as Antidiscrimination' (2004) 153 U. Penn. L. Rev. 579; Noah Zatz, 'Managing the Macaw: Third-Party Harassers, Accommodation, and the Disaggregation of Discriminatory Intent' (2009) 109 Columbia L. Rev. 1357.

insist that as a matter of current law there is a sharp difference between the two kinds of regulations expect the right of accommodation to expand as well.[12]

It is not difficult to see the connection between antidiscrimination and accommodation. The Israeli EEO Act, for example, lists fifteen prohibited grounds for discrimination, then stipulates that the setting of irrelevant conditions shall be regarded as discrimination as well;[13] it further adds that differential treatment necessitated by the character or nature of the position (i.e., a bona fide occupational requirement) shall not be regarded as discrimination.[14] Although in most cases this might not lead to any positive requirement, in some cases it will. Consider, for example, an Israeli gender discrimination case, in which the employer sought a male for the job of marketing photocopying machine supplies, claiming in court that the requirement is a bone fide occupational distinction because the job requires heavy lifting of machines (or supplies), and men are physically stronger, as a group, than women.[15] The employer was therefore making a claim of economically driven statistical discrimination – to reduce screening costs by statistically limiting the pool of applicants. The National Labour Court rejected the claim, but would have approved a gender-neutral requirement that the applicants must demonstrate adequate physical stamina. Hence, the employer's screening costs were discounted in favour of enhancing more equality. However, the expected outcome of this ruling is that weight-lifting capability would be considered a requirement that is tailored to the job, but the difference between men and women regarding the likelihood of getting the job would be maintained. An accommodation mandate would introduce an additional question – can the employer purchase, at reasonable cost, a small hydraulic lift that would minimize the need to lift and carry heavy photocopying machines/supplies? Technology could thereby fully eliminate disadvantage.

Hence, doctrines of constructed equality build upon and extend the prevailing doctrines of equal opportunities. Such doctrines display a greater scepticism about the market's performance, and include measures such as comparable worth (establishing worth and value that is independent and distinct from market value) or affirmative action (determining desert on grounds other than market-based preferences, such as affiliation to a group that has been systematically denied opportunity by market and non-market players alike). Accommodation of people with disabilities is the epitome of constructive equality. It does not merely assume that removing barriers that are embedded in realized and latent biases will be enough to integrate people with disabilities into the marketplace. The marketplace itself has to change.

While the same idea theoretically can apply to other categories of workers, in practice the duty to accommodate has thus far not been generalized beyond the category of disability. A Supreme Court judgment from 2000 aptly demonstrates the

12. Stewart J. Schwab & Steven L. Willborn, 'Reasonable Accommodation of Workplace Disabilities' (2003) 44 William & Mary L. Rev. 1197.
13. Equal Employment Opportunities Act 1988, s. 2(b). On the Act generally, see: Guy Mundlak, 'The Law of Equal Opportunities in Employment: Between Equality and Polarization' (2009) 30 Comp. Lab. L. & Policy J. 213.
14. *Ibid*, s. 2(c).
15. National Labour Court 3-8/1991 *State of Israel v. Gestetner Israel* (22 January 1992).

traditional rejection of the expansive view of accommodation. A police officer who was required to attend a fourteen-week training camp in dormitory conditions refused to attend, because she did not want to leave her one-year old child for such an extended period of time. She was subsequently dismissed because of her refusal to attend the training. In her petition to the Supreme Court, she argued that the training could have been organized in a way that accommodates parents. The case was dismissed outright, without the Court even considering her innovative claim.[16]

Nonetheless, more recently there are several signs suggesting that this restrictive approach could be in the process of changing in Israel:

[A] Extending Doctrines of Anti-discrimination Law

Growing recognition of accommodation can be traced in two types of cases. First, in the context of religion – in a couple of cases before regional labour courts, a duty to accommodate was imposed as part of the interpretation of the EEO Act. For example, a maintenance worker at a municipality, who had refused to work on Saturdays for religious reasons and had been dismissed, was reinstated by the court and also awarded significant damages, based on explicit statements that the municipality should have accommodated him.[17] A second context is age – in a number of cases Israeli courts ruled that employers must perform individual checks and cannot assume that an employee is less productive (or in insufficient physical shape) after a certain age.[18] Although the main objective of such decisions is to prevent discrimination based on generalizations and stereotypes, in the future this may lead to accommodation requirements for those who do not conform to the statistical assumptions with regard to the group.

On top of expanding accommodation to new groups by means of requiring individualized attention, the court also hinted at the need to adopt the logic of accommodation in the choice of remedies. In a recent case the Supreme Court chastised the Israel Prison Service for refusing to promote an employee working part-time (six hours a day) due to health issues.[19] The evidence suggested that the employee was highly qualified and the employer was satisfied with his work; however, when he applied for promotion he was repeatedly rejected because of the perception that the higher-level jobs require a full-time commitment. The Court noted that the Prison

16. Supreme Court – HCJ 5235/01 *Tenenbaum V. The Chief of Israeli Police* (10 February 2002). The case was discussed and thoroughly criticized in Dafna Hacker & Michal Frenkel, 'Active Parenting and Equal Employment Opportunities: The Need to Change the Labour Market', 11 Lab. Soc. & L. 275 (2006).
17. Tel Aviv Labour Court 4785/02 *Yigal Kashani v. The Municiplaity of Ra'anana* (15 July 2002). The Hours of Work and Rest Act 1951 grants employees a right not to work on their Sabbath. However, this Act does not include a right to damages, which is why the court turned also to the EEO Act. See also Tel Aviv Labour Court 41794-02-12 *Sivan Koren v. Kenyon Hazahav Management* (30 August 2014). For further discussion of these cases, see: Revital Turner, 'Using Soft Law to Encourage the Participation of Working Parents in the Labour Market' 15 Work, Society and Law (forthcoming 2016, Hebrew).
18. Supreme Court HCJ 4191/97 *Rekant v. El-Al* (10 December 2000).
19. Machmali, *supra* n.5.

Service should have made a much greater effort to accommodate the employee. Although the case was decided on the basis of the explicit provision in the ERPDA, its reasoning arguably has broader implications. In requiring the employer not only to allow the worker to have a part-time job (which in itself is an accommodation) but also to be eligible for promotion just like fulltime employees, the court's remedy can be applied to other groups as well, most notably – women and parents.

[B] 'Spill Over' from Litigation on Unemployment Insurance and Income Assurance

We see growing engagement with questions of accommodation outside the framework of employment discrimination *stricto sensu*. An important context is in the labour courts' review of administrative decisions regarding the duty of people receiving unemployment benefits and welfare to accept suitable work. Although some cases emphasize that 'suitable work' offered to an unemployed person must simply be within her range of experience and status (unemployment benefits), or that she must be able to physically perform the job (welfare benefits), other cases point at the need to consider accommodation. Notably, there are some cases that recognize the special needs of single mothers for work schedules that are aligned with day-care schedules.[20]

[C] 'Spill Over' from Debates about General Employment Regulations

Growing attention is being devoted to problems of accommodation that are rooted in existing employment rights and not in the traditional domain of antidiscrimination law. Most notably, this is apparent in the context of time-regulation. In debates over reforming general employment standards,[21] there is a growing concern that the law must reconsider the extent of overtime permitted, given that time requirements are gendered, and that equality must be adjusted to accommodate women's situation, or parents' needs, at the seam between care-work and work in the labour market. Such debates reflect a growing interest in reconsidering the basic regulatory infrastructure of the market, instead of taking it for granted and simply 'correcting' it with a prohibition on discrimination.

[D] Expanding Duty of Accommodation in Other Countries

While the expansion of accommodation in Israel is tentative and embryonic, and sometimes still encounters a contradictory insistence on preserving a confined and narrower sense of antidiscrimination law, other legal systems have committed to it

20. See, e.g., National Labour Court 91-3/1995 *Israeli Employment Service v. Gaon* (20 May 1996).
21. See, e.g., Yifat Metzner Cheruti, Dad Goes to Work, Ma'asei Mishpat (2014) [Hebrew]; Forum for Workers Rights, Report to the committee on Work Hours and Rest Law (2012), available at http://www.acri.org.il/he/wp-content/uploads/2012/10/forum-workers-rights-poistion-oct-2012.pdf [Hebrew].

much more decidedly. Canada is the leading example of a general duty to accommodate; Federal as well as provincial human rights acts, which prohibit workplace discrimination, explicitly add such a duty. The Federal Act, for example, lists 11 prohibited grounds for discrimination,[22] then stipulates that employers' actions/decisions are not discriminatory if based on a bona fide occupational requirement,[23] and finally qualifies this exception by adding that 'for any practice... to be considered to be based on a *bona fide* occupational requirement... it must be established that accommodation of the needs of an individual or a class of individuals affected would impose undue hardship on the person who would have to accommodate those needs, considering health, safety and cost.'[24] The duty to accommodate thus becomes an inseparable part of the principle of equality; any failure to accommodate could lead to a conclusion of discrimination.

Further evidence of expansion comes from 'flexible work' regulations adopted in several European countries over the last fifteen years. In the UK, legislative amendments to the Employment Rights Act since 2002 give employees who have been with the same employer for at least six months a right to request flexible work - in effect, accommodation in terms of moving to part-time employment, or changing the time they start or finish work, or working from home, etc. - and the employer can only refuse for reasonable business reasons, detailed in the legislation. Originally this right was granted only to parents caring for children under 6 years of age; it was later extended to employees with children up to 18 years old and also those caring for older relatives; and recently, in 2014, the same right was extended to all employees, who can now request flexible work arrangements for any reason whatsoever.[25] The UK arrangement is now quite similar in structure to the one extant in the Netherlands since the adoption of the Dutch Working-Time Adjustment Act 2000. This Act gives all workers employed for more than a year the right to request a decrease (or increase) in the number of working hours. Employers are required to accommodate such requests unless they have a substantive business reason to refuse. Moreover, the law requires employers to take into consideration personal circumstances of workers when establishing individual working patterns, to the extent reasonable. Germany's Part-Time and Fixed Term Employment Act 2000 offers a somewhat similar trajectory. The law allows most employees (with at least six months of service, in companies with fifteen workers or more) to ask for a part-time schedule, including temporary work-reductions, flex-time and a compressed workweek.[26]

International trends are particularly important, as Israeli courts are receptive to changes in other systems, particularly when they interact with those emerging ideas that are developed by the Israeli legal system itself. It is noteworthy that the European arrangements engage mostly in the regulation of time-related accommodation, and in

22. Canadian Human Rights Act, R.S.C., 1985, c. H-6, s. 3.
23. Section 15(1)(a).
24. Section 15(2).
25. See Employment Rights Act 2002, s. 80F (inserted 2002), as amended most recently by the Children and Families Act 2014.
26. Antoine Jacobs & Marlene Schmidt, 'The Right to Part-time Work: The Netherlands and Germany Compared' (2001) 17 Int'l J. Comp. Lab. L. & Indus. Rel. 371.

this they present a considerably thinner perception of general accommodation in comparison to the Canadian jurisprudence and the idea proposed here – favouring a general right to be accommodated at work.

Consequently, we argue that these developments, taken together, amount to more than mere speculation about the law's trajectory. Rather, they extend the idea of accommodation in several complementary ways. First, there is the gradual expansion of accommodation beyond the category of people with disability. Second, there is a particular emphasis on questions of employability, i.e., whether the absence of accommodation measures may exclude some people from having a job. Third, accommodation potentially can be taken from the realm of addressing victimization in the labour market, and applied to the acceptance of personal preferences, or at least to choices made under social constraints.

§12.04 IMAGINING A UNIVERSAL DUTY TO ACCOMMODATE

Should we expand the duty in the direction of a universal open-ended duty, requiring employers to make reasonable efforts to accommodate the needs of all workers (rather than a specific vulnerable group)? As noted above, the duty to accommodate has traditionally been justified on equality grounds: to ensure substantive (rather than formal) equality. To some degree, an expanded duty to accommodate can be justified as necessary for the achievement of substantive equality, even more so if one sees the goal of equality laws as not only promising recognition of disadvantaged groups, but also as counteracting systemic patterns of group-based stigma and subordination,[27] addressing the previous allocation of resources, and promoting redistribution.[28] We believe that a duty to accommodate can be revolutionary in advancing the goal of equality, especially in the context of gender. It has the potential to confront the myth of the 'ideal worker'[29] and to push employers into changing the structure of work (especially work hours and time off work).[30] This proposal builds on other recent contributions along the same line, taking them a step further.[31]

27. Samuel R. Bagenstos, '"Rational Discrimination", Accommodation, and the Politics of (Disability) Civil Rights' (2003) 89 Virginia L. Rev. 825.
28. Claire Mummé, 'The Ontario Human Rights Code's Distributive and Recognitional Functions in the Workplace' (2014) 18 Canadian Lab. & Emp. L.J. 145.
29. Joan Williams, *Unbending Gender: Why Family and Work Conflict and What To Do About It?* (2000).
30. Peggie R. Smith, 'Accommodating Routine Parental Obligations in an Era of Work-Family Conflict: Lessons from Religious Accommodations' (2001) Wisconsin L. Rev. 1443.
31. Particularly noteworthy is a recent important contribution by Michael Ashley Stein and his colleagues, who argue that the duty to accommodate workers with disabilities should be extended by adopting a functional test – requiring accommodation whenever it is shown to be necessary to give people meaningful access to the workplace (Michael Ashley Stein, Anita Silvers, Bradley A. Areheart & Leslie Pickering Francis, 'Accommodating Every Body' (2014) 81 U. Chic. L. Rev. 689). They propose a duty to accommodate every 'body,' defined to include physical as well as psychological characteristics (*ibid.* at fn 18). Our proposal takes the same idea a step further, requiring accommodation for reasons unrelated to personal characteristics as well.

But to justify a truly universal duty to accommodate, we have to extract it from the context of employment discrimination and relocate it in the context of the employment contract's basic structure. In this, the duty to accommodate significantly impacts the centrality of the managerial prerogative and reshapes the basic structure of individual employment bargaining.[32]

Back to the basics: The employment contract fundamentally constitutes a relationship of subordination, in which one party (the employer) is assigned the property right and a managerial prerogative, while the other party (the employee) can draw on her freedom of contract to restrict the use of the managerial prerogative. The concept of the managerial prerogative was originally developed to confer unilateral powers on employers, while maintaining the contractual structure (some would say illusion) of the employment relationship. Where there is a worry about the adequacy, efficiency or justness of market mechanisms (the freedom of contract), restrictions are imposed on the managerial prerogative. Moreover, the public promotes and facilitates collective bargaining as a solution to correct, counter-balance or improve the market. However, when there are no such interventions or nothing beyond the minima defined by statute or in collective agreements, the basic structure remains – the employer determines and the employee (or candidate) must either comply, negotiate or opt out. In other words, as is commonly known – the former is the contract-maker, and the latter is the contract-taker.

For example, the employer can require the employee to work night-shifts, work over-time or stand near noisy machines (albeit within the legal range). The statutes and agreements seek to create minimal (and higher) standards that are adapted to what the public generally wants, or the people within the bargaining domain prefer (or succeed in bargaining). However, Sally, a single mother, may not be able to commit to excessive overtime (even if within the range of the 'permissible'); Eric, who values his participation in the local community theatre, may not be able to work night-shifts; and Stephan, who is gradually losing his hearing, is extremely sensitive to excessive background noise. According to the basic structure, none of them has any legal claim vis-à-vis the employer. Individual needs and preferences may be individually negotiated, but most often they are not.

Now consider the impact of a general duty to accommodate. If the employer must accommodate, then particular rules and norms become mere demonstrations of the basic duty to accommodate. They do not exhaust the duty. The employer must accommodate Sally's preference to work fewer hours, Eric's interest in developing his hobby, and Stephan's sensitivity, even if objectively exaggerated, to noise. This would be the true significance of a universal duty to accommodate.

While such a duty may seem at first to be obscure, it is no more obscure than the common structure in which employers may, within the confines of statutory or

32. On the importance of improving the legal infrastructure to accommodate meaningful individualized bargaining (as opposed to the more familiar terms that structure collective bargaining), see Matthew Finkin, 'Employee Self-Representation and the Law in the United States' 50 Osgoode Hall L. J. 937 (2013). It is important to underscore that the proposed expansion of the right and duty to accommodate does not substitute for or undermine rights and duties of collective bargaining.

collective interventions, demand that their workers work only every alternate hour, or alternate shifts on short notice in a way that prevents any kind of regularity in life habits, or require workers to work, unnecessarily, in conditions of continuous noise. Just as society does not deem the managerial prerogative to be insulated from restrictions, there is no assumption that accommodation enjoys supremacy over and above other public (regulatory) and collective attempts to organize the workplace. However, as a starting point, *the duty to accommodate mirrors the managerial prerogative.* Instead of asking workers to fit into a job for which the employer has determined a host of requirements (of course within limits), we may ask: how can the employer comply with a host of requirements made by the employees (or job candidates), again of course within public and collectively negotiated limits? For the same reason we do not think that an employee would be willing to submit her labour power, working time and sense of being to the *absolute* control of the managerial prerogative, we should not assume that owners of capital would be willing to enter a contract in which they are at the mercy of the workers' whims concerning accommodation demands. But with regard to the point of departure for designing the construct of the employment contract, both are equally reasonable, just as they are equally obscure.

Assuming we recognize a general duty to accommodate, it must be qualified and constrained, just as there are constraints on the managerial prerogative. Constraints can be made by statute, or by collective agreement; by particular rules or general standards. Take, for example, the existing regulation of time, days off, annual vacations and the like – these are all particular appearances of a general claim for fairness at work (or 'decent work'). Instead of simply stating that the employment contract permits the employer to determine work schedules, but 'within reason,' where reason reflects public morals and public interests, particular statutes provide a more concrete specification of the content attributed to 'within reason.' Over and above such particular rules, there are three interrelated standards that are currently used to tame the managerial prerogative, and which may be equally useful to guide the right to be accommodated: reasonableness, proportionality, and good faith.

As we change the default situation, the duty to accommodate maintains the current common sense and jurisprudence whereby accommodation is only required to the extent that it is *reasonable*. This test of reasonableness therefore designates the residual limitation on the right to be accommodated. Once the default structure changes, it is possible to determine particular limitations as rules in legislation. These can refer to the rights of particular groups (e.g., people with disabilities), or to limits on specific demands to accommodate (e.g., an employee can ask to reduce her working hours, as long as she works no less than a certain minimum of hours). Beyond such specific rules, the test of reasonableness defines the limits of accommodation.

The thorny question is to what extent the employer should be required to assume costs imposed by the requested accommodation. Is it justified to impose such costs on the employer for any reason, as opposed to a system imposing such costs only in favour of groups suffering from inherent or historical vulnerability/discrimination?

It is not necessary to give a clear-cut answer to this question. The law allows flexibility in deciding whether it is justified to impose some costs on the employer on a case-by-case basis, while at the same time maintaining a degree of certainty and predictability. This is achieved through the principle of *proportionality*. In recent years the idea of proportionality has been increasingly referenced in labour law, in several legal systems. Moreover, the proportionality tests are arguably being used in many other contexts as well, even absent explicit reference to this concept.[33]

The idea of proportionality is that the means chosen to achieve some goal have to be 'proportional' to the goal, in the sense that (a) they can rationally advance this goal; (b) they are only what is necessary, i.e., they impair the rights of others only to the extent needed to achieve the goal, and no more ('minimal impairment'); and (c) the advantage gained by the act/decision is not outweighed by the harm caused by the infringement of rights ('proportionality *stricto sensu*'). Although these tests are nested in the domain of public law, limiting the use of power by governments and legislatures, they are increasingly being used to limit the use of power by private-sector employers as well.[34] Similarly, they can be used to construct the limits of reasonable accommodation (or otherwise put: to examine whether an employer's decision to reject an accommodation demand is justified - in the sense of standing up to the proportionality tests - or not).

Finally, consider the duty of *good faith*. The duty of good faith can be understood as an overarching principle, from which duties such as reasonableness and proportionality are derived. A duty to accommodate can similarly be derived from this general principle and justified by it.[35] In practice, good faith has been increasingly used in different countries as an anchor for deriving new duties on employers, including positive duties, so adding a duty to accommodate in similar fashion may be less revolutionary than it appears on first sight.[36] Moreover, the fact that a duty of good faith applies equally to both employers and employees aptly demonstrates the idea of 'compromising from both ends' - the managerial prerogative and the duty to accommodate.

33. See Guy Davidov, 'The Principle of Proportionality in Labor Law and Its Impact on Precarious Workers' (2012) 34 Comp. Lab. L. & Policy J. 63; Pnina Alon-Shenker and Guy Davidov, 'Applying the Principle of Proportionality in Employment and Labour Law Contexts', 59 McGill L. J. 375 (2013).
34. For example, when employers infringe their employees' privacy rights, courts in many legal systems ask whether this infringement conformed to the three proportionality tests. If it did, then it was justified. If not, it cannot be justified and it is not legally allowed. See also Guy Mundlak, 'Workplace - Democracy: Reclaiming the Effort to Foster Public and Private Isomorphism' 15 Theoretical Inquiries in L. 159 (2014).
35. For this view, see also Lisa Waddington & Aart Hendriks, 'The Expanding Concept of Employment Discrimination in Europe: From Direct and Indirect Discrimination to Reasonable Accommodation Discrimination' (2002) 18 Int. J. Comp. Lab. L. & Ind. Rel. 403, 417.
36. For example, in Germany employers have been required to disclose information (Bernd Waas, 'Good Faith in the Law of the Employment Relationship: Germany' (2011) 32 Comp. Lab. L. & Policy J. 603, 619-620), in New Zealand they must hold a hearing before dismissals (see Gordon Anderson, 'Good Faith in the Individual Employment Relationship in New Zealand' (2011) 32 Comp. Lab. L. & Policy J. 685), and in the UK they have to give notice before certain decisions (Alan Bogg, 'Good Faith in the Contract of Employment: A Case of the English Reserve?' (2011) 32 Comp. Lab. L. & Policy J. 729, 759-763). To such positive duties we can add a duty to accommodate.

If good faith eventually mediates the opposite sides, is there really a need to recognize a universal duty to accommodate? There are several responses to this question. First, the legal construct of the employment relationship has an expressive value. Recognizing the duty to accommodate, even within well-defined limits, designates the employment relationship as one that serves the workers, thereby reimagining the social position of the human labourer. Second, even if a duty to accommodate is derived from the good faith duty, there is much to be gained from making this explicit and known to the parties in advance. Finally, Coase's theorem suggests that under conditions of zero transaction costs, the choice of default rules does not really matter. However, the labour market, ridden with market failures, can hardly be said to conform to the assumption of 'zero transaction costs.' Hence, shifting the default rule may fundamentally change bargaining outcomes.

[A] Operationalizing the General Duty to Accommodate

It is possible to imagine a market in which the worker's right to be accommodated would fully replace the managerial prerogative. This would be akin to flipping over the property bases of the corporation, from the traditional capital-owned entity to a workers' cooperative. Instead of financial capital enjoying the fundamental right of property, it would be the workers-members who contract with financial capital. Such a worker-owned economy is not inconceivable; there are several examples that illustrate it.[37] Under such conditions, we may want to assume that workers are contract-makers, capital owners contract-takers, and that restrictions of reasonableness and proportionality that are often placed on employers should be switched wholesale to constrain workers. Such a shifting of property rights, and the associated rights and responsibilities, is obviously far removed from current developments in the law. Moreover, even in the daily management of worker-owned enterprises there is an important role for the right to be accommodated, because management may tend to move operational goals to the forefront, at the expense of workers' needs, regardless of the stakeholders and the assignment of property rights. However, it is useful to mention this alternative before moving to a more 'moderate' solution that fosters a shared notion of rights and duties.

Leaving aside the worker-owned corporation, then, we focus on the developments described in the previous section as pointing towards a model in which the managerial prerogative remains, but workers are equipped with a general and far-reaching right at their disposal, which can significantly affect power relations. Otherwise stated, rather than being a matter of flipping over property rights, the duty of accommodation can be considered as a method to facilitate a joint project of sorts, in which management is entrusted with the prerogative to manage, but is at the same time generally required to serve the actual needs of the workforce. How should such a view be operationalized?

37. The clearest example was the former Yugoslav model of a worker-owned economy. For the implications of flipping over property rights altogether, see David Ellerman, *Property and Contract in Economics: The Case for Economic Democracy* (1992).

Imagine, for example, an employee who is also a student at a university. Before the exam period, the employee requests a two-week unpaid leave. Can he legally require the employer to oblige? Assume that such a leave would impose some costs on the employer – the need to reorganize the work schedule accordingly or perhaps to hire a replacement through a temporary employment agency. Should the law impose on the employer the duty to accommodate the employee's request? Using the principle of good faith and proportionality, the proposed analysis would proceed as follows:

- *Procedural good faith*: The employer must consider the employee's request and respond on the merits with a justification of its decision. Of course, this may settle the question at stake. However, assuming it does not, then:
- *The goal must be justified*: Rejecting the worker's request requires a justification that is in the interest of the corporation. Merely rejecting it for the reason that management is the sole agent to decide on work schedules (or the choice of technology and equipment, or a reference to any other type of accommodation) will not suffice. Moreover, the purpose of management is directly linked to the national law on the purpose of the corporation. In countries where the sole responsibility is to maximize the shareholders' benefits, the type of justification that can be accepted may be different from that which will be considered in countries with more extensive stakeholders' legislation. Finally, managerial denial of the request because of costs must consider not only expenditures for accommodation, but also the often more latent *benefits* of accommodation (commitment, responsibility, organizational culture and the like). Merely stating that a request to accommodate entails costs may too easily empty the right of content.
- *Minimal impairment*: The employer would have to show that it is not possible to achieve its legitimate business needs while also accommodating the employee. Otherwise put, the employer can only infringe the employee's right to be accommodated if this is necessary for its legitimate interests. At the same time, if there are alternative methods of accommodation that can address the employee's special needs, the employer could be justified in preferring such alternatives.
- *Proportionality stricto sensu*: This test is the most instructive, and would require assessing such factors as the size of the employer, the type of work provided by the worker (whether there are others who can 'cover up' or the worker holds unique firm-specific knowledge), prior understandings between the parties, and the like. An important factor – albeit, with the move towards universal accommodation, not the sole factor – is the distinction between category-needs and individual needs. For example, more weight may be given to needs that characterize a category (parenting needs) than to needs that are wholly individual (e.g., a personal event such as a friend's marriage).

In a system where management is responsible to different stakeholders, there is more leeway for considering a broader range of questions already at the outset (e.g., was the managerial decision's objective valid?). In a system that adheres to a stricter commitment to shareholders' short-term profits, there is a greater likelihood that the earlier stages will reaffirm the managerial refusal of the accommodation request, and so greater weight will be placed on the final stage. These differences indicate that our proposal does not, in itself, transform the division of property rights, power and responsibilities in the corporation. National differences will persist, reflecting the web of norms, a puzzle of which the duty to accommodate is only one piece.

§12.05 POSSIBLE CRITIQUES

There are several possible arguments *against* expanding the duty to accommodate that must be considered. The first is the cost to employers. If the cost is excessive, it is inefficient, and could lead to loss of jobs. The purpose of the right to be accommodated as a means of increasing employability and inclusion would therefore be undermined. However, the limitation of reasonableness and the principle of proportionality would ensure that the costs are limited. In practice, experience with the duty in the context of disabilities, and also with the more general duty where it exists (notably Canada and the UK), shows that it works well, without placing unreasonable burdens on employers.[38]

Second, there is a risk of moving towards the lowest common denominator, or losing focus on what's more important. By analogy, extending the duty of affirmative action to many may undermine the efficacy of measures targeted at those who are most vulnerable.[39] The same can be argued against universalizing the duty to accommodate. Harking back to our previous example, if we help Alex who simply wants a balance between work and hobbies, we may undermine the claims of parents, such as Sally, whose needs may be greater. Arguably, we should focus on those whose need is greater. Moreover, accommodation can no longer 'level the playing field' if it is extended to everyone. As such, it is likely to replicate existing structural and systemic inequalities.

This is a serious concern, but we can offer several responses. First, accommodation does not have to be a zero sum game, unlike affirmative action that necessarily advances some at the expense of others. Second, as noted earlier, the application of the proportionality tests can and should take social context into consideration. Thus, a group that historically has been discriminated against would entail more efforts on the part of the employer, i.e., a more costly accommodation might be required, compared to other groups.[40] At the same time, this should not prevent people who are not part of a vulnerable group from demanding accommodation from the employer as well. Sometimes, this can be done without cost; at other times, the cost may be minimal and therefore still justified, and when individualized needs are exceptional, costs can be

38. It is noteworthy that the duty has been expanded (in the UK) and maintained (in Canada) even by centre-right governments, more sympathetic to employers.
39. For a critique along these lines, see Jessica Clarke, 'Beyond Equality? Against the Universal Turn in Workplace Protections' (2011) 86 Indiana L. J. 1219.
40. Clarke, *ibid.*, adopts a similar solution, arguing (albeit not specifically in the context of accommodation) in favour of 'inclusive' protections rather than 'universal' ones applied equally to all workers.

considered accordingly. A third reason to reject the claim that benefits are diffused draws on the advantage of universal benefits. The larger the political basis of people who enjoy a benefit, the stronger is the political support for it. It will not be considered as a form of aid to the poor and the oppressed, but rather as a benefit to the welfare of all workers. Hence, it legitimizes special needs, denies stigma, does better in insulating the norm from political pressures at times of austerity, and eliminates social constructs of victimization. People who demand accommodation do so because everyone is entitled to it, not because they were granted a special privilege.

Two additional critiques against a duty to accommodate specific groups can actually be alleviated by the expansion towards a *universal* duty. One is the fear of backfire – the more we grant special rights to a specific group of workers, the higher the concern that this will harm their chances of getting employment in the first place. Although employers are not allowed, of course, to discriminate against people on this ground – the fact that they wish to avoid special rights is not a legitimate reason not to hire someone – in practice this is very difficult to prove. So the concern is real. But it disappears if the rights are granted to everyone rather than a specific group.

It has been noted that accommodation mandates, like other mandates, have cross-employee distributional impacts.[41] When awarding preference to specific groups on the back of other employees is problematic, this can be alleviated by expanding the right to accommodation to others, who can then enjoy similar rights. The distributional impact would then be concentrated vis-à-vis employers rather than other employees. In contrast, when awarding preference to a specific group of employees over others is justified – for example, in favour of a historically disadvantaged group – this can be achieved through the proportionality analysis, as noted above.

The other argument that has been advanced is that a duty to accommodate reinforces and perpetuates a distinction between 'normal' employees and those who need special help (such as people with disabilities, or women). An analysis focusing on accommodation in favour of a specific vulnerable group serves to legitimize the basic structures created by the hegemonic group. These structures in themselves are not questioned, even though they may be discriminatory in the sense of being created by the powerful, majority groups in their mould.[42] Once again, this drawback is avoided when the right to be accommodated is expanded in the way proposed here. Once we understand the duty to accommodate as an inseparable part of the employment relationship – grounded in the duties of good faith and proportionality and limiting the managerial prerogative – it becomes clear that an employer is required to take into consideration the needs and constraints of different employees, at the stage of setting the structures as well. This approach was adopted by the Supreme Court of Canada, which stressed 'the need to develop standards that accommodate the potential contributions of all employees in so far as this can be done without undue hardship to

41. Sharon Rabin-Margalioth, 'Anti-Discrimination, Accommodation and Universal Mandates – Aren't They All the Same?' (2003) 24 Berkeley J. of Emp. & Lab. L. 111.
42. Shelagh Day & Gwen Brodsky, 'The Duty to Accommodate: Who Will Benefit?' (1996) 75 *Can. Bar Rev.* 433, 462; *British Columbia (Public Service Employee Relations Commission) v. BCGSEU*, [1999] 3 S.C.R. 3, at paras 39-42 (the Meiorin judgment).

the employer ... Employers designing workplace standards owe an obligation to be aware of both the differences between individuals, and differences that characterize groups of individuals.'[43] These ideas can be taken further to justify a universal duty to accommodate, with potentially revolutionary implications.

A final critique that should be considered concerns the reliance on open-ended standards, which requires a degree of confidence in the ability of the judicial system to enforce these standards. Such confidence is obviously more realistic in legal systems that have independent labour courts, with judges that have an understanding of the unique characteristics of employment relations. In general, however, as noted above, we are not suggesting that the duty to accommodate should be adopted *instead* of specific accommodating rules, but rather on top of them. The risk is therefore minimal, but the potential gain significant.

43. Meiorin judgment, *ibid.*, at para. 55 and para. 68.

BCLR - BULLETIN OF COMPARATIVE LABOUR RELATIONS

Vol. Author/Title/Year/ISBN

1. Roger Blanpain, *Individual Employment Contracts: Collective Agreements*, 1970.
2. Roger Blanpain, *Social Planning*, 1971 (ISBN 90-312-0018-2).
3. Roger Blanpain, *Guaranteed Income Funds*, 1972 (ISBN 90-312-0019-0).
4. Roger Blanpain, *Employee Participation at the Level of the Enterprise*, 1973 (ISBN 90-312-0020-4).
5. Roger Blanpain, *Vastheid van Betrekking: Staking en Bezetting*, 1974.
6. Roger Blanpain, *Labour Law and Industrial Relations (International Bibliography)*, 1975 (ISBN 90-312-0023-9).
7. Roger Blanpain, *Multinational Enterprises*, 1976 (ISBN 90-312-0024-7).
8. Roger Blanpain, *Worker's Participation in the European Company*, 1977 (ISBN 90-312-0044-1).
9. Roger Blanpain, *Women and Labour*, 1978 (ISBN 90-312-0077-8).
10. Roger Blanpain, *European Conference on Labour Law and Industrial Relations: Multinational Enterprises*, 1979 (ISBN 90-312-0091-3).
11. Roger Blanpain, *Job Security and Industrial Relations*, 1980 (ISBN 90-312-0147-2).
12. Roger Blanpain, Greg Bamber & Russell Lansbury, *Technological Change and Industrial Relations: An International Symposium*, 1983 (ISBN 90-312-0205-3).
13. Roger Blanpain, James Janssen van Raay & A. Moulty, *Worker's Participation in the European Community: The Fifth Directive*, 1984 (ISBN 90-654-4187-5).
14. Roger Blanpain, *Equality and Prohibition of Discrimination in Employment*, 1985 (ISBN 90-654-4215-4).
15. Roger Blanpain, *Restructuring Labour in the Enterprise: Law and Practice in France, F.R. of Germany, Italy, Sweden and the United Kingdom*, 1986 (ISBN 90-654-4283-9).
16. Roger Blanpain & E. Kassalow, *Unions and Industrial Relations: Recent Trends and Prospect: A Comparative Treatment*, 1987 (ISBN 90-654-4294-4).
17. Roger Blanpain & Marco Biagi, *Trade Union Democracy and Industrial Relations*, 1988 (ISBN 90-654-4394-0).
18. Roger Blanpain & Jelle Visser, *In Search of Inclusive Unionism*, 1990 (ISBN 90-654-4439-4).
19. Roger Blanpain, *Flexibility and Wages: A Comparative Treatment*, 1990 (ISBN 90-654-4461-0).

20. Roger Blanpain, Stephen Frenkel & Oliver Clarke, *Economic Restructuring and Industrial Relations in Industrialised Countries,* 1990 (ISBN 90-654-4488-2).
21. Roger Blanpain & Friedrich Fürstenberg, *Structure and Strategy in Industrial Relations,* 1991 (ISBN 90-654-4559-5).
22. Roger Blanpain, Amira Galin & Ozer Carmi, *Flexible Work Patterns and Their Impact on Industrial Relations,* 1991 (ISBN 90-654-4572-2).
23. Roger Blanpain, *Workers' Participation: Influence on Management Decision-Making by Labour in the Private Sector,* 1992 (ISBN 90-654-4600-1).
24. Roger Blanpain, Brian Brooks & Chris Engels, *Employed or Self-Employed,* 1992 (ISBN 90-654-4613-3).
25. Roger Blanpain & Tiziano Treu, *Industrial Relations Developments in the Telecommunications Industry,* 1993 (ISBN 90-654-4642-7).
26. Roger Blanpain & Marco Biagi, *Industrial Relations in Small and Medium Sized Enterprises,* 1993 (ISBN 90-654-4696-6).
27. Roger Blanpain & Marco Biagi, *Participative Management and Industrial Relations in a Worldwide Perspective,* 1993 (ISBN 90-654-4769-5).
28. Roger Blanpain, Jacques Rojot & Hoyt N. Wheeler, *Employee Rights and Industrial Justice,* 1994 (ISBN 90-654-4804-7).
29. Roger Blanpain & Ruth Ben-Israel, *Strikes and Lock-Outs in Industrialized Market Economies,* 1994 (ISBN 90-654-4841-1).
30. Roger Blanpain, Kazuo Sugeno & Yasuo Suwa, *The Harmonization of Working Life and Family Life,* 1995 (ISBN 90-411-0064-4).
31. Roger Blanpain & Laszio Nagy, *Labour Law and Industrial Relations in Central and Eastern Europe,* 1996 (ISBN 90-411-0298-1).
32. Roger Blanpain, *Labour Law and Industrial Relations in the European Union,* 1997 (ISBN 90-411-0527-1).
33. Taco Van Peijpe, *Employment Protection under Strain,* 1998 (ISBN 90-411-0528-8).
34. Roger Blanpain, Takashi Araki & Ryuichi Yamakawa, *The Process of Industrialization and the Role of Labour Law in Asia,* 1999 (ISBN 9-041-1104-7-X).
35. Roger Blanpain & Marco Biagi, *Non-standard Work and Industrial Relations,* 1999 (ISBN 90-411-1117-4).
36. Roger Blanpain, *Private Employment Agencies: The Impact of ILO Convention 181 (1997) and the Judgment of the European Court of Justice of 11 December 1997,* 1999 (ISBN 90-411-1118-2).
37. Roger Blanpain, *Multinational Enterprises and the Social Challenges of the XXIst Century: The ILO Declaration on Fundamental* Principles *at Work, Public and Private Corporate Codes of Conduct,* 2000 (ISBN 90-411-1280-4).
38. Roger Blanpain, Ryuichi Yamakawa & Takashi Araki, *Deregulation and Labour Law: In Search of a Labour Concept for the 21st Century,* 2000 (ISBN 90-411-1370-3).
39. Roger Blanpain, *The Council of Europe and the Social Challenges of the XXIst Century,* 2001 (ISBN 90-411-1543-9).

40. Roger Blanpain, *On-Line Rights for Employees in the Information Society, Use & Monitoring of E-Mail & Internet at Work,* 2002 (ISBN 90-411-1626-5).
41. Roger Blanpain, *The Evolving Employment Relationship and the New Economy: The Role of Labour Law & Industrial Relations,* 2001 (ISBN 90-411-1691-5).
42. Roger Blanpain, *Involvement of Employees in the European Union, Works Councils, Company Statute, Information and Consultation Rights,* 2002 (ISBN 90-411-1760-1).
43. Michele Colucci, *The Impact of the Internet and New Technologies on the Workplace: A Legal Analysis from a Comparative Point of View,* 2002 (ISBN 90-411-1824-1).
44. Roger Blanpain, *White Paper on the Labour Market in Italy: The Quality of European Industrial Relations and Changing Industrial Relations,* 2002 (ISBN 90-411-1841-1).
45. Roger Blanpain, Russell D. Lansbury & Young-Bum Park, *Impact of Globalisation on Employment Relations: A Comparison of the Automobile and Banking Industries in Australia and Korea,* 2002 (ISBN 90-411-1850-0).
46. Roger Blanpain & Antoine Jacobs, *Employee Rights in Bankruptcy: A Comparative-Law Assessment,* 2002 (ISBN 90-411-1942-6).
47. Roger Blanpain, Takashi Araki & Shinya Ouchi, *Corporate Restructuring and the Role of Labour Law,* 2003 (ISBN 90-411-1949-3).
48. Roger Blanpain, *Collective Bargaining, Discrimination, Social Security and European Integration,* 2003 (ISBN 90-411-2010-6).
49. Roger Blanpain & Luis Aparicio-Valdez, *Labour Relations in the Asia- Pacific Countries,* 2004 (ISBN 90-411-2239-7).
50. Roger Blanpain & Ronnie Graham, *Temporary Agency Work and the Information Society,* 2004 (ISBN 90-411-2252-4).
51. Roger Blanpain, *The Actors of Collective Bargaining: A World Report,* 2004 (ISBN 90-411-2253-2).
52. Roger Blanpain & Michele Colucci, *The Globalisation of Labour Standards: The Soft Law Track,* 2004 (ISBN 90-411-2303-2).
53. Roger Blanpain, Takashi Araki & Shinya Ouchi, *Labour Law in Motion: Diversification of the Labour Force & Terms and Conditions of Employment,* 2005 (ISBN 90-411-2315-6).
54. Roger Blanpain, *Smoking and the Workplace,* 2005 (ISBN 90-411-2325-3).
55. Roger Blanpain, *Confronting Globalization: The Quest for a Social Agenda,* 2005 (ISBN 90-411-2381-4).
56. Roger Blanpain, Thomas Blanke & Edgar Rose, *Collective Bargaining Wages in Comparative Perspective: Germany, France, the Netherlands, Sweden and the United Kingdom,* 2005 (ISBN 90-411-2388-1).
57. Roger Blanpain & Anne Numhauser-Henning, *Women in Academia & Equality Law: Aiming High - Falling Short?,* 2006 (ISBN 978-90-411-2427-6).
58. Roger Blanpain, *Freedom of Services in the European Union: Labour and Social Security Law: The Bolkestein Initiative,* 2006 (ISBN 978-90-411-2453-5).
59. Roger Blanpain, Frans Pennings & Nurhan Sural, *Flexibilisation and Modernisation of the Turkish Labour Market,* 2006 (ISBN 978-90-411-2490-X).

60. Roger Blanpain & Boel Flodgren, *Corporate and Employment Perspectives in a Global Business Environment*, 2006 (ISBN 978-90-411-2537-X).
61. Roger Blanpain, Shinya Ouchi & Takashi Araki, *Decentralizing Industrial Relations and The Role of Labor Unions and Employee Representatives*, 2007 (ISBN 978-90-411-2583-3).
62. Roger Blanpain, *European Framework Agreements and Telework: Law and Practice: A European and Comparative Study*, 2007 (ISBN 978-90-411-2560-4).
63. Roger Blanpain, Jim Kitay, Leanne Cutcher & Nick Wailes, *Globalization and Employment Relations in Retail Banking*, 2007 (ISBN 978-90-411-2620-1).
64. Roger Blanpain, Russell Lansbury, Jim Kitay, Nick Wailes & Anja Kirsch, *Globalization and Employment Relations in the Auto Assembly Industry: A Study of Seven Countries*, 2008 (ISBN 978-90-411-2698-6).
65. Roger Blanpain & Michele Tiraboschi, *The Global Labour Market: From Globalization to Flexicurity*, 2008 (ISBN 978-90-411-2722-8).
66. Roger Blanpain, Michele Colucci & Frank Hendrickx, *The Future of Sport in the European Union: Beyond the EU Reform Treaty and the White Paper*, 2008 (ISBN 978-90-411-2761-7).
67. Roger Blanpain, Linda Dickens, *Challenges in European Employment Relations: Employment Regulation, Trade Union Organization, Equality, Flexicurity, Training and New Approaches to Pay*, 2008 (ISBN 978-90-411-2771-6).
68. Roger Blanpain, Hiroya Nakakubo & Takashi Araki, *New Developments in Employment Discrimination Law, 2008* (ISBN 978-90-411-2782-2).
69. Roger Blanpain, Andrzej Marian Świątkowski, *The Laval and Viking Cases: Freedom of Services and Establishment v. Industrial Conflict in the European Economic Area and Russia*, 2009 (ISBN 978-90-411-2850-8).
70. Roger Blanpain, William Bromwich, Olga Rymkevich, Silvia Spattini, *The Modernization of Labour Law and Industrial Relations in a Comparative Perspective*, 2009 (ISBN 978-90-411-2865-2).
71. Roger Blanpain, Juan Pablo Landa & Brian Langille, *Employment Policies and Multilevel Governance*, 2009 (ISBN 978-90-411-2866-9).
72. Roger Blanpain, European Works Councils; *The European Directive 2009/ 38/EC of 6 May 2009, 2009* (ISBN 978-90-411-3208-6).
73. Roger Blanpain, William Bromwich, Olga Rymkevich & Silvia Spattini, *Labour Productivity, Investment in Human Capital and Youth Employment: Comparative Developments and Global Responses*, 2010 (ISBN 978-90-411-3249-9).
74. Greg J. Bamber & Philippe Pochet, *Regulating Employment Relations, Work and Labour Laws: International Comparisons between Key Countries*, 2010 (ISBN 978-90-411-3199-7). General Editor: Roger Blanpain.
75. Roger Blanpain, Desislava Nikolaeva Dimitrova, *Seafarers' Rights in the Globalized Maritime Industry*, 2010 (ISBN 978-90-411-3349-6).
76. Roger Blanpain, Hiroya Nakakubo & Takashi Araki, *Regulation of Fixed- Term Employment Contracts*, 2010 (ISBN 978-90-411-3356-4).
77. Roger Blanpain, William Bromwich, Olga Rymkevich & Iacopo Senatori, *Rethinking Corporate Governance*, 2011 (ISBN 978-90-411-3450-9).

78. Roger Blanpain & Frank Hendrickx, *Labour Law between Change and Tradition: Liber Amicorum Antoine Jacobs,* 2011 (ISBN 978-90-411-3424-0).
79. Roger Blanpain, Thomas Klebe, Marlene Schmidt & Bernd Waas, *Trade Union Rights at the Workplace,* 2012 (ISBN 978-90-411-3460-8).
80. Roger Blanpain, William Bromwich, Olga Rymkevich & Iacopo Senatori, *Labour Markets, Industrial Relations and Human Resources Management: From Recession to Recovery,* 2012 (ISBN 978-90-411-4004-3).
81. Roger Blanpain, Hiroya Nakakubo & Takashi Araki, *Systems of Employee Representation at the Enterprise: A Comparative Study*, 2012 (ISBN 978-90-411-4080-7).
82. Roger Blanpain & Frank Hendrickx, *Temporary Agency Work in the European Union and the United States*, 2013 (ISBN 978-90-411-4769-1).
83. Roger Blanpain, Toker Dereli, Y. Pınar Soykut-Sarıca & Aslı en-Tabaı, *Emerging Patterns of Work and Turkish Labour Market Challenges under Globalization: Readings on Labour and Employment Relations,* 2014 (ISBN 978-90-411-4983-1).
84. Roger Blanpain, Pablo Arellano Ortiz, Marius Olivier & Gijsbert Vonk, *Social Security and Migrant Workers: Selected Studies of Cross-border Social Security Mechanisms*, 2014 (ISBN 978-90-411-4770-7).
85. Roger Blanpain & Nikita Lyutov, *Workers' Representation in Central and Eastern Europe: Challenges and Opportunities for the Works Councils' System*, 2014 (ISBN 978-90-411-4746-2).
86. Roger Blanpain, Ulla Liukkunen & Chen Yifeng, *China and ILO Fundamental Principles and Rights at Works*, 2014 (ISBN 978-90-411-4984-8).
87. Roger Blanpain, *The Use of Languages and Employment Relations*, 2014 (ISBN 978-90-411-5606-8).
88. Roger Blanpain, Hiroya Nakakubo & Takashi Araki, *Protection of Employees' Personal Information and Privacy*, 2014 (ISBN 978-90-411-5608-2).
89. Roger Blanpain, Jan Wouters, Glenn Rayp, Laura Beke & Axel Marx, *Protecting Labour Rights in a Multi-polar Supply Chain and Mobile Global Economy*, 2015 (ISBN 978-90-411-5662-4).
90. Roger Blanpain & Stefania Marassi, *Globalization and Transnational Collective Labour Relations: International and European Framework Agreements at Company Level,* 2015 (ISBN 978-90-411-4748-6).
91. Roger Blanpain, Frank Hendrickx & Petra Herzfeld Olsson, *National Effects of the Implementation of EU Directives on Labour Migration from Third Countries*, 2016 (ISBN 978-90-411-6257-1).
92. Roger Blanpain, Frank Hendrickx & D'Arcy du Toit, *Labour Law and Social Progress: Holding the Line or Shifting the Boundaries?* 2016 (ISBN 978-90-411-6747-7).
93. Roger Blanpain & Frank Hendrickx, *Reasonable Accommodation in the Modern Workplace: Potential and Limits of the Integrative Logics of Labour Law*, 2016 (ISBN 978-90-411-6258-8).

www.ingramcontent.com/pod-product-compliance
Lightning Source LLC
Chambersburg PA
CBHW071441230926
51846CB00001B/301
9789041162588